JN073225

髙木秀太事務所白書

The White Paper
by TAKAGI SHUTA OFFICE

2016–2022

誠文堂
新光社

はじめに
INTRODUCTION

——— 最高の便利屋になる。

髙木秀太事務所は「デジタル技術で建築設計業界最高の便利屋になる」ことを目標に2016年に創業しました。以来、様々な建築・都市計画で、あらゆるデジタル技術を駆使し、クライアントやパートナーをサポートしてきました。

本書は髙木秀太事務所の作品集ではありません。我々には「作品」はありません。すべての「作品」は我々を信頼し迎え入れてくれたデザイナーやアーティスト、あるいはチームに帰属します。髙木秀太事務所はその中でほんのささやかな（しかし、決して小さくはない）問題を解決し、プロジェクトの成功に僅かながら寄与したに過ぎません。だからこそ、髙木秀太事務所の誇りは「何を行ったか」だけではなく、「誰とどのように行ったか」にあります。

本書はそのような素晴らしいパートナーたちとのプロジェクトの紹介、報告をコンセプトとしています（=白書)。すべてのプロジェクトにおいて関係者の相関図、そして、そのなかで採用されてきたデジタルメソッドを余すところなく記録しました。

我々は最高の便利屋だからこそ、最高のパートナーを選びます。これからまだ見ぬ新たなパートナーに本書が届き、そして、新しい未来が開かれることを期待します。

Becoming the best handyman.

Takagi Shuta Office was established in 2016 with the aim of "becoming the best handyman with digital technology in the field of architectural design". We have been supporting clients and partners with every possible means of digital technologies in architectural and urban planning ever since.

This White Paper is not an anthology of works by Takagi Shuta Office. We do not own so-called "work". All "works" belong to designers, artists, or teams who have invited and entrusted us. Takagi Shuta Office solves intricate, yet not insignificant, issues within each project to lead to its eventual success. Thus, Takagi Shuta Office takes pride not only in "what was done" but also "how it was done with whom".

The concept of this book is to introduce and report the projects with such wonderful partners (= white paper). In all projects, correlation diagrams of related parties and the digital methods adopted have been recorded exhaustively.

As the best handyman, we select the best partners. We look forward to our potential future partners to receive this book and a new future to be discovered.

目次

CONTENTS

プロジェクトマップ
PROJECT MAP

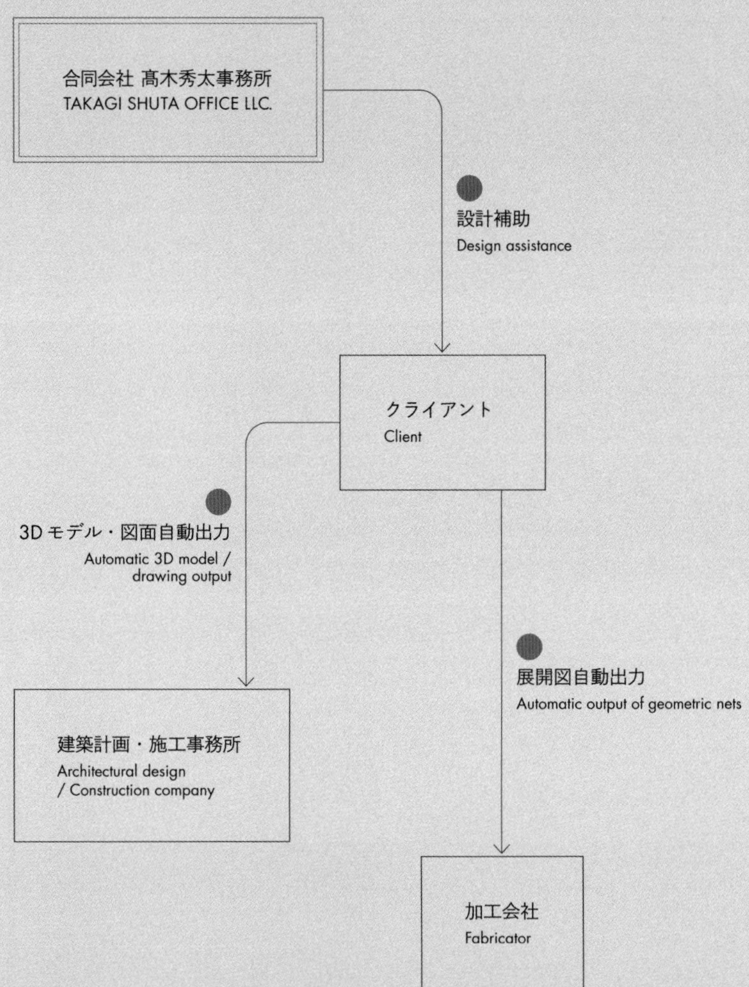

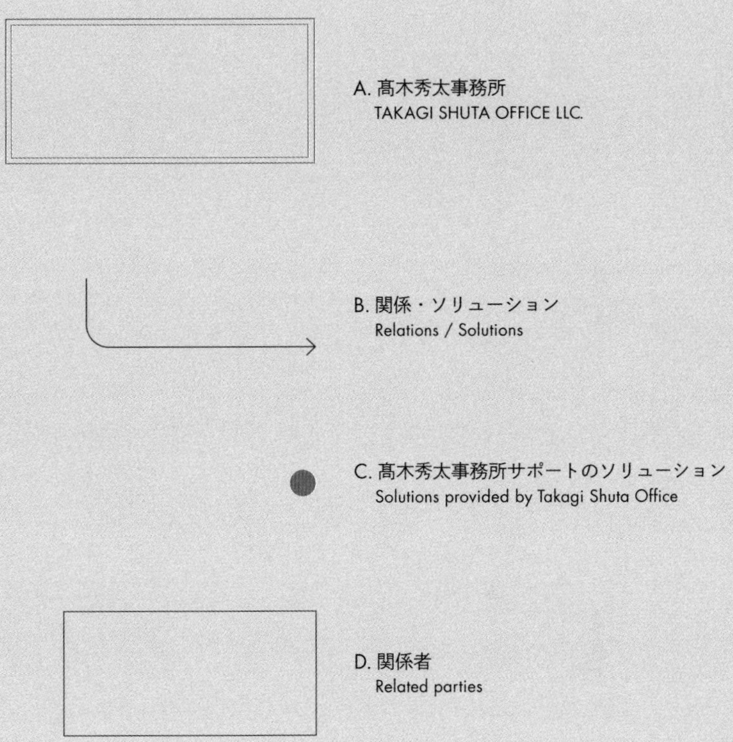

　各プロジェクトの末頁にプロジェクトマップを用意した。高木秀太事務所がどのような関係性の中で、どのようなソリューションを提供したのかが一覧できるようになっている。コンセプト立案からソフトウェア開発、造形処理など、その役割は多岐にわたるのでプロジェクト毎に参照されたい。

At the end of every project introduction is a project map, which is an overview of what kind of relationships were formed with Takagi Shuta Office as well as what kind of solutions were provided. From concept generation, software development, to modeling and processing, our role covers a broad range for each project.

スタッフリスト
STAFF LIST

STAFF

髙木 秀太　Shuta TAKAGI
代表
2016.04-

髙塚 悟　Satoru TAKATSUKA
マネージャー
2017.05-

竹中 美穂　Miho TAKENAKA
プログラマー / デザイナー
2018.04-2020.03

布井 翔一郎　Shoichiro NUNOI
プログラマー
2020.05- (PART TIMER : 2017.09-)

竹内 瑠奈　Runa TAKEUCHI
デザイナー
2021.01-

田野口 貴成　Atsuhiro TANOKUCHI
プログラマー
2021.04- (PART TIMER : 2020.08-)

槇山 武蔵　Musashi MAKIYAMA
アーキテクト / プログラマー
2021.08- (PART TIMER : 2021.02-)

多田 星矢　Sayer TADA
プログラマー
2022.04-

宮國 俊介　Shunsuke MIYAKUNI
プログラマー
2022.08- (PART TIMER : 2019.08-)

永井 宏　Hiroshi NAGAI
プログラマー
2022.09- (PART TIMER : 2018.04-)

PARTNER

飛田 剛太　Gota HIDA
プログラマー
2017.09-2022.03

南 佑樹　Yuki MINAMI
プログラマー
2018.01-

竹中 虎太郎　Kotaro TAKENAKA
プログラマー
2021.02-

PART TIMER

太田 周作 Shusaku OTA
2016.12-2017.03

菊池 毅 Tsuyoshi KIKUCHI
2017.07-2018.03

三原 義弘 Yoshihiro MIHARA
2018.01-2018.06

澤田 幸希 Kouki SAWADA
2018.04-2019.09

井上 絵里加 Erika INOUE
2018.05-2019.03

瀬戸 滉平 Kohei SETO
2018.06-2019.08

川上 朔 Hajime KAWAKAMI
2018.07-2022.03

小河原 佑莉 Yuri OGAHARA
2018.08-2019.07

大河内 隼 Shun OKOCHI
2018.09-2018.12

岡本 陸 Riku OKAMOTO
2018.12-2020.04

熊 一楽 Ichiraku YU
2018.12-2019.05

下田 悠太 Yuta SHIMODA
2019.04-2019.07

芝村 朋宏 Tomohiro SHIBAMURA
2019.04-2019.10

伊藤 世玲奈 Serena ITO
2019.08-

金子 竜太郎 Ryutaro KANEKO
2019.09-2019.10

江藤 遥奈 Haruna ETO
2019.10-

森 大樹 Daiki MORI
2019.11-2021.03

野末 誠斗 Makoto NOZUE
2020.07-2022.03

曽根 巽 Tatsumi SONE
2020.07-

川西 愛子 Aiko KAWANISHI
2020.07-

建道 佳一郎 Keiichiro KONDO
2020.08-

石橋 湧太 Yuta ISHIBASHI
2020.09-

早川 遥菜 Haruna HAYAKAWA
2020.09-2022.03

橋口 真緒 Mao HASHIGUCHI
2020.11-

高見澤 勇太 Yuta TAKAMIZAWA
2020.12-

林 飛良 Hira HAYASHI
2021.02-

田川 直樹 Naoki TAGAWA
2021.02-

成瀬 将司 Masashi NARUSE
2021.04-2022.03

山口 丈太郎 Jotaro YAMAGUCHI
2021.07-

八木 このみ Konomi YAGI
2021.11-2021.12

林 彩葉 Iroha HAYASHI
2022.01-

浦中 美里 Misato URANAKA
2022.01-

木村 さくら Sakura KIMURA
2022.05-

松井 美歩 Miho MATSUI
2022.08-

高山 真 Shin TAKAYAMA
2022.10-

東京タワー トップデッキ

TOKYO TOWER TOP DECK

Licensed by TOKYO TOWER

クライアント　株式会社 TOKYO TOWER
Client　TOKYO TOWER Co., Ltd.

アーティスト　KAZ SHIRANE
Artist

東京タワー展望台の内装計画プロジェクトである。アーティスト KAZ SHIRANE 氏とのコラボレーション。

三角形分割されたミラーを密充填させた空間は東京の景色を映し出し、ドラマチックな空間体験を提供する。髙木秀太事務所では、3D モデラー上でのミラーパネルの自動配置プログラムと、展開図の自動出力プログラムを作成。幾何処理の知見と技術からプロジェクトをサポートした。

An interior renovation project of the Tokyo Tower Observation Deck in collaboration with the artist Kaz Shirane.

Close-packed triangulated mirrors reflect Tokyo's cityscape for a dramatic spatial experience. Takagi Shuta Office created programming for automatic placement of the mirror panels in 3D modeling software, in addition to programming for automatic output of the geometric nets. Our knowledge and technical skills in geometry processing helped support the project.

鏡面反射で東京の街並みが映し出される。特に夜間は無数の照明と夜景があらゆる角度で拡散し、万華鏡のような表情を見せる。KAZ SHIRANE 氏のアート作品である。

Reflections from the mirrors project the cityscape of Tokyo. Particularly at night, countless lights and night scenes are dispersed at every angle like a kaleidoscope. It is an art installation by Kaz Shirane.

01_TOKYO TOWER TOP DECK

天井 [A]、壁・ブレース [B][C]、ありとあらゆる内装部材が三角形ミラーパネルに置き換えられた。すべてのパネル形状を全体で幾何制御しなければ部分で破綻する。

Every possible interior element, including the ceiling [A], walls and braces [B][C], were covered by triangulated mirror panels. Unless all panel shapes are geometrically controlled as a whole, certain parts would disintegrate.

B

C

A

01_TOKYO TOWER TOP DECK

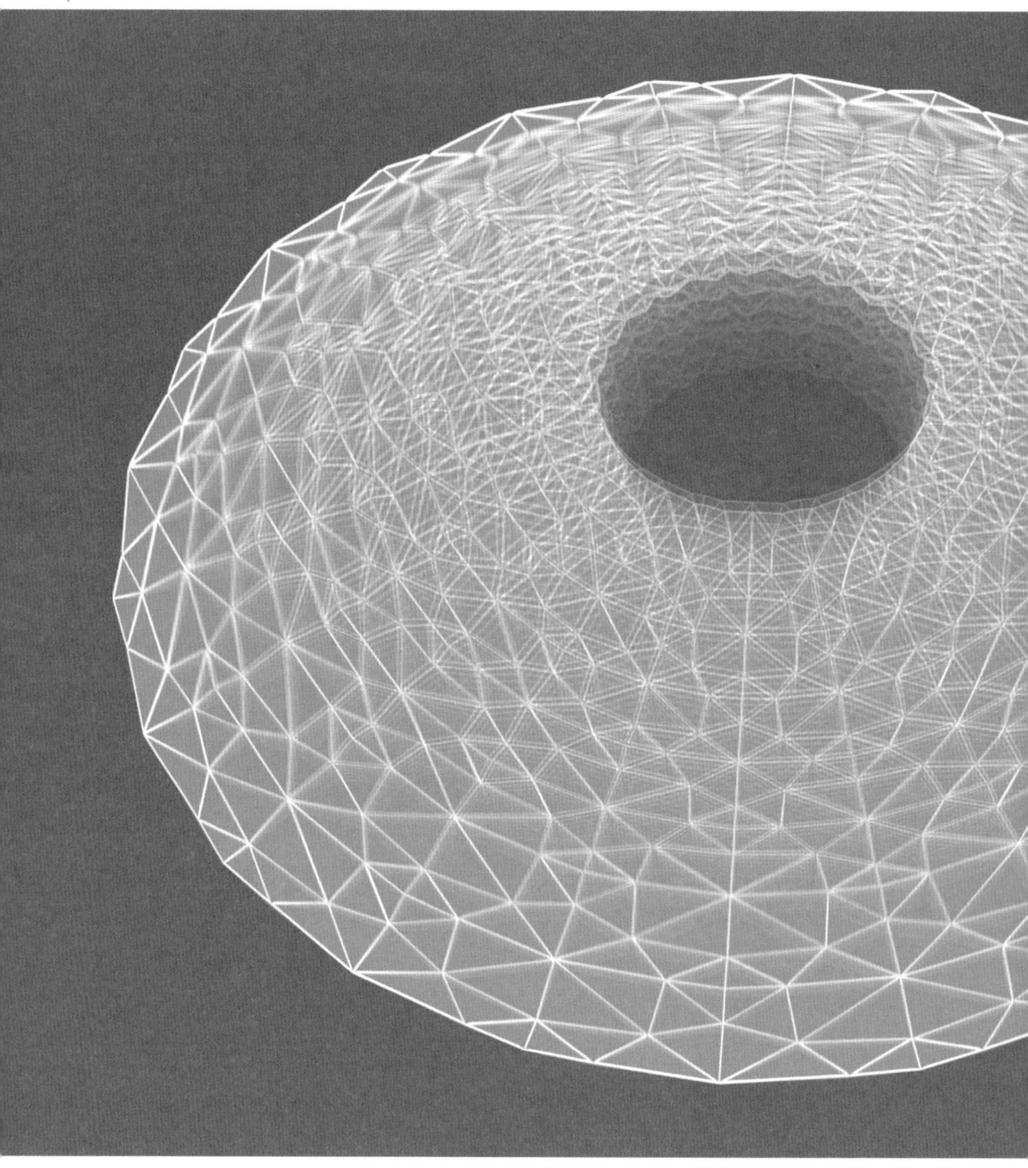

パラメトリックモデルプログラム
Parametric model program

3Dモデラー上にミラーパネルを自動配置するプログラム。写真は天井部に同心円状に配置した例。各種入力パラメーターで形状を微調整することができる。天井の傾斜に沿ってすべてのミラーパネルが干渉することなく密充填することができる。

The program allows automatic placement of mirror panels on 3D modeling software. The image is an example of concentric circle arrangement on the ceiling. The shapes could be fine-tuned with various input parameters, and all mirror panels could be closely packed along the ceiling slope without interference.

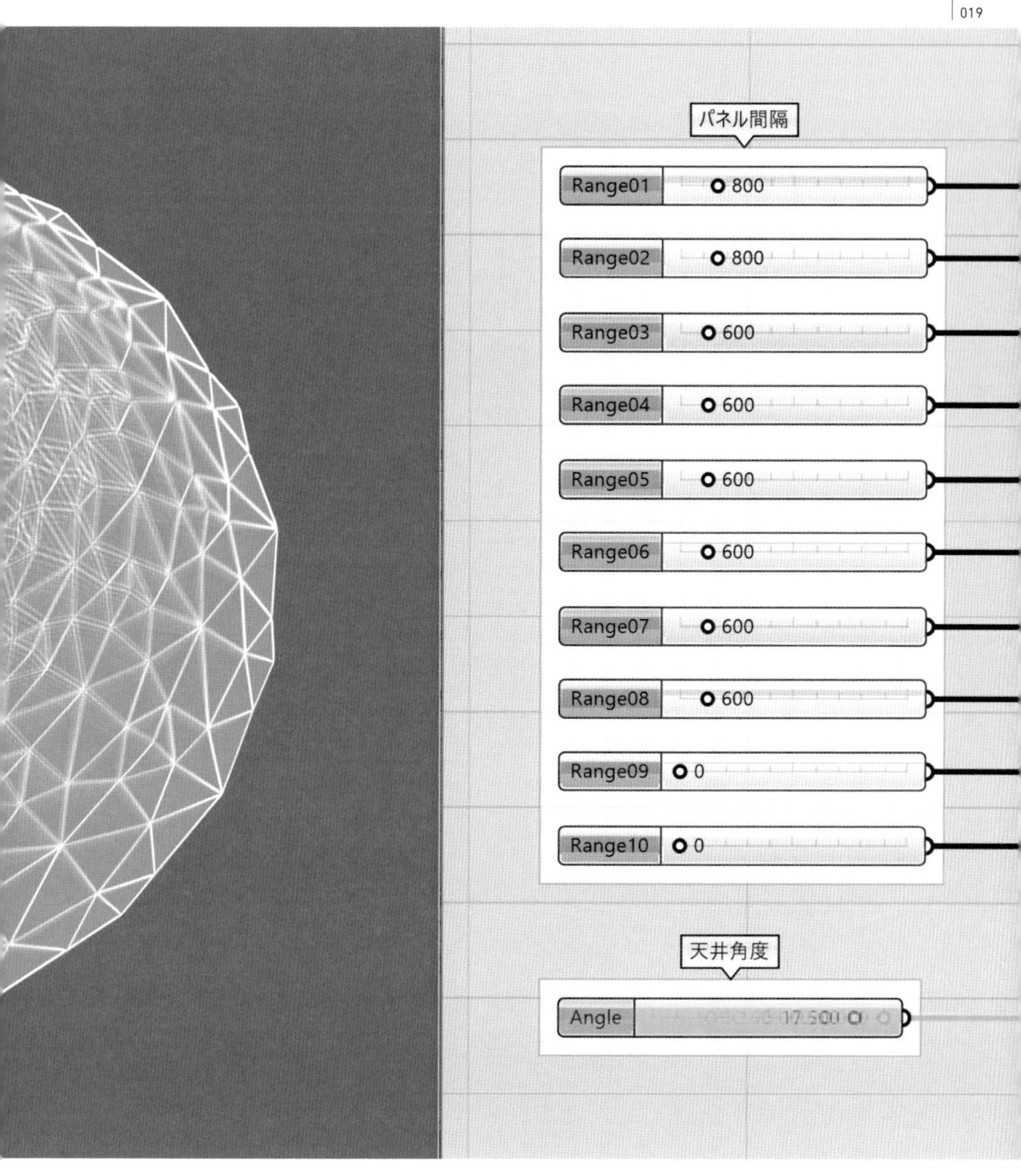
パネル間隔
Range01
800
Range02
800
Range03
600
Range04
600
Range05
600
Range06
600
Range07
600
Range08
600
Range09
0
Range10
0
天井角度
Angle
17.500

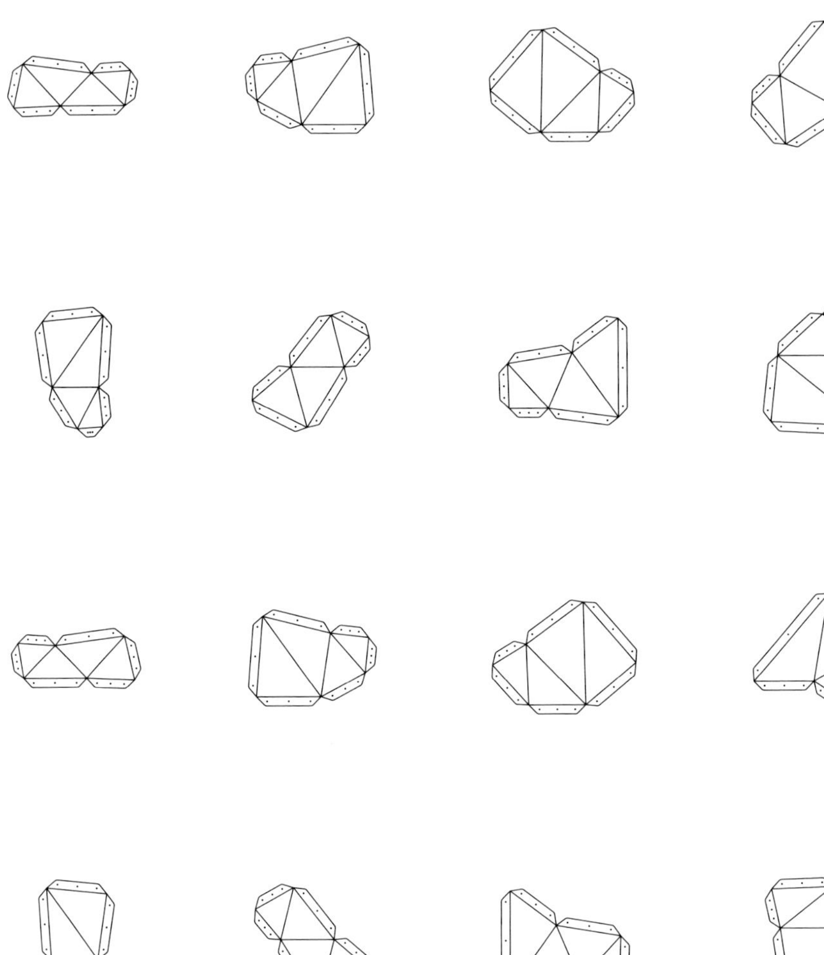

ミラーパネル展開図
Geometric nets of mirror panels

ミラーパネルの制作工場に加工指示を出すには１枚１枚のパネルの展開図を出力しなければならない。形状がそれぞれ異なるので手動による作図は困難である。3Dモデルから展開図への自動作図システムを開発し、サポートした。

To provide processing instructions to the fabricator of mirror panels, geometric net for each panel had to be output. Since each shape is distinct, drawing them manually would be arduous. We developed an automatic drawing system to produce the geometric nets from 3D models.

1/60 scale

A	B
C	D

ミラーパネルは金属板を折り曲げて制作された[A][B]。パネル同士を接合するリブは折り曲げ角度や接合穴の位置など、幾何学的に厳密な指定がなされる[C][D]。

The mirror panels were fabricated by bending metal plates [A][B]. Ribs where the panels would be joined required geometric precision in their specifications, including bending angles and positioning of the holes for joints [C][D].

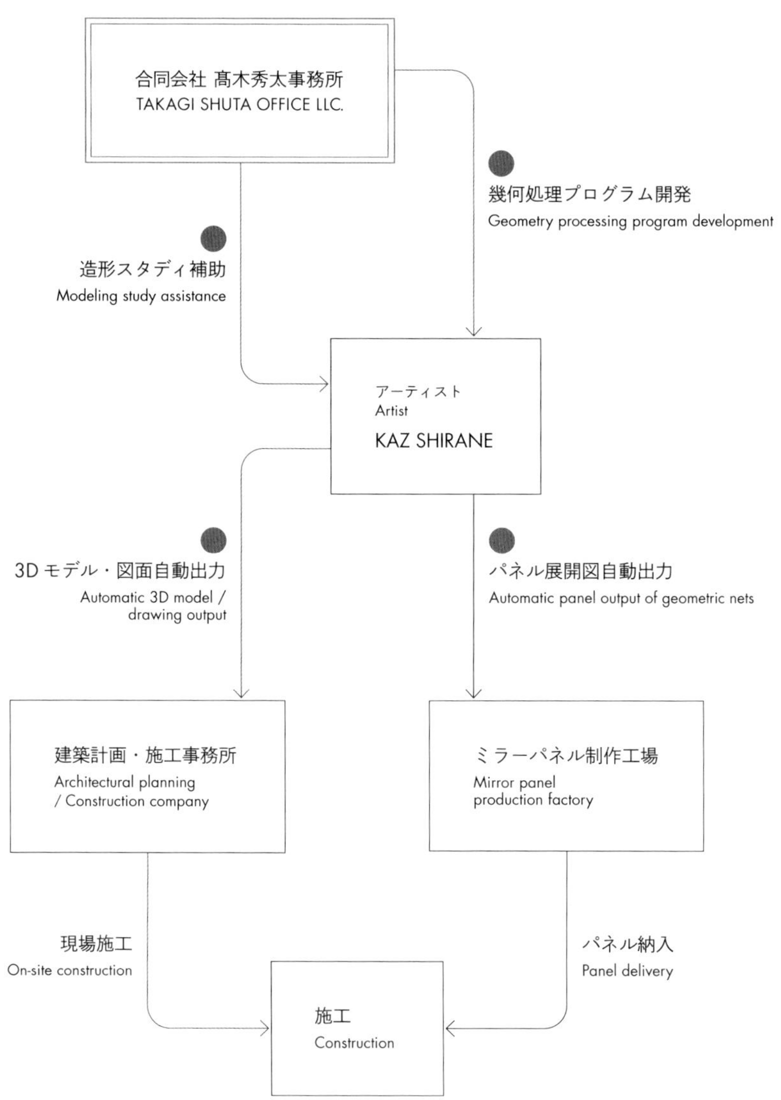

髙木秀太事務所はKAZ SHIRANE氏を幾何処理の技術でバックアップ。造形処理の提案から図面出力の補助まで幅広いサポートを行った。加えて、高精度の出力で施工会社や制作工場との円滑なコミュニケーションを促した。

Takagi Shuta Office assisted Kaz Shirane through geometric processing techniques, which ranged widely from proposal of modeling processing methods to assisting in drawing productions. Additionally, high-precision output were instrumental in smooth communication with the construction companies and fabricators.

プロジェクト ID プロジェクト期間	160027 2016.10–2017.12
クライアント	株式会社 TOKYO TOWER
アーティスト	KAZ SHIRANE
プロジェクトマネージメント メインプログラマー	髙木 秀太 髙木 秀太
ソフトウェア / 開発環境 プログラミング言語 キーワード	Rhinoceros Grasshopper, Python 内装設計、幾何計算、図面自動出力

Project ID Project term	160027 2016.10–2017.12
Client	TOKYO TOWER Co.,Ltd.
Artist	KAZ SHIRANE
Project management Main programmer	Shuta TAKAGI Shuta TAKAGI
Software / SDE Programming language Keywords	Rhinoceros Grasshopper, Python Interior design, Geometry calculation, Automatic drawing output

キーワードは「幾何計算」。手順は複雑ではあるが、個々に使用されている理論は高校数学の域を出ないシンプルなものである。ベクトル、三角関数などの組み合わせでプログラムは構成される。

"Geometry calculation" was the keyword. While the procedure was complicated, each of the theories applied was as simple as high school mathematics, with the program consisting of a combination of vectors and trigonometric functions.

NTT DATA INFORIUM 豊洲イノベーションセンター

NTT DATA INFORIUM TOYOSU INNOVATION CENTER

02

クライアント　株式会社ＮＴＴデータ
Client　NTT DATA Corporation

ディレクター　コクヨ株式会社
Director　KOKUYO Co., Ltd.

株式会社ＮＴＴデータのイノベーションセンターの内装計画である。プロジェクトディレクションはコクヨ株式会社。髙木秀太事務所は壁面・ガラス面の計２ヶ所をデザイン、ファブリケーションでデジタルサポートした。ＮＴＴデータのビジュアルアイデンティティのひとつ「イノベーションカーブ」を共通のモチーフとし、「木材」「ガラスフィルム」という異なる素材でデジタル処理されたそれぞれのデザインは、「情報技術で新しい『価値』を創造する」というクライアントの理念を表象した。

An interior design for NTT DATA Corporation showroom, with project direction by KOKUYO Co., Ltd. Takagi Shuta Office designed the wall and glass surfaces and provided support for digital fabrication. Employing the common motif "innovation curve" from NTT DATA's design code, each wall was digitally processed with distinct materials of "wood" and "glass films" to showcase our client's philosophy of "creating a new 'value' with information technology."

「壁面アート」の面。施設のエントランスに位置する。最小単位の「ピース」と、それらの構成による「ユニット」の入れ子構成であり、凹凸による陰影がその形状の多様さをより引き立てる。

"Wall art" surface located at the floor's entrance. The smallest unit of "pieces" that compose the "units" create a nested composition, with shadows from lighting fixtures accentuating the variety of forms.

data

より豊かな表情を演出するために、隣り合う「ピース」同士の奥行が微細にずらされている。プログラムによるデジタルモデリングで、様々な組み合わせが繰り返し検討された [A]-[C]。

In order to achieve a more expressive appearance, the depths of adjacent "pieces" were subtly adjusted. Utilizing digital modeling through programming, numerous combinations were explored iteratively [A]-[C].

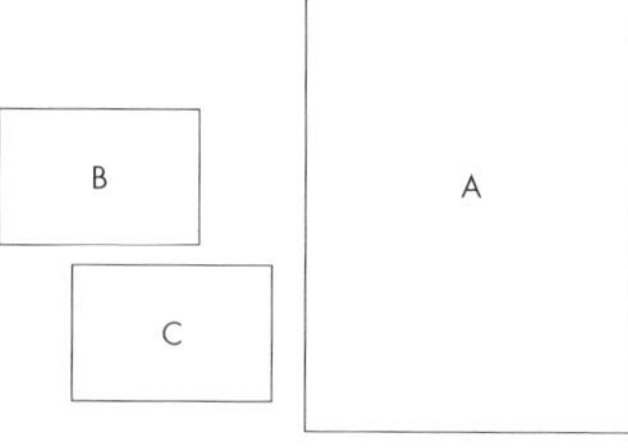

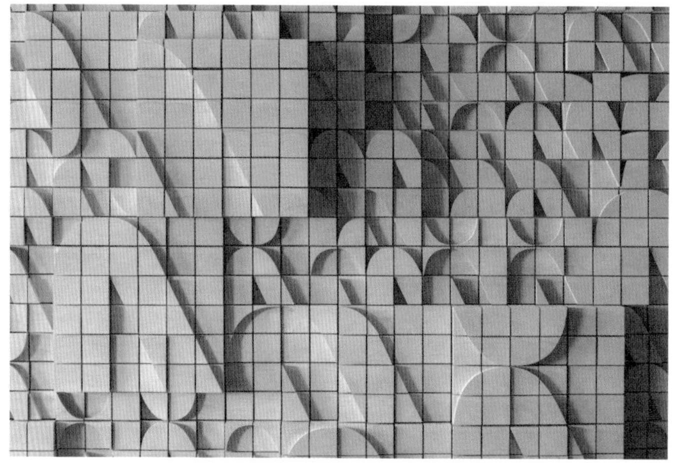

02_NTT DATA INFORIUM TOYOSU INNOVATION CENTER

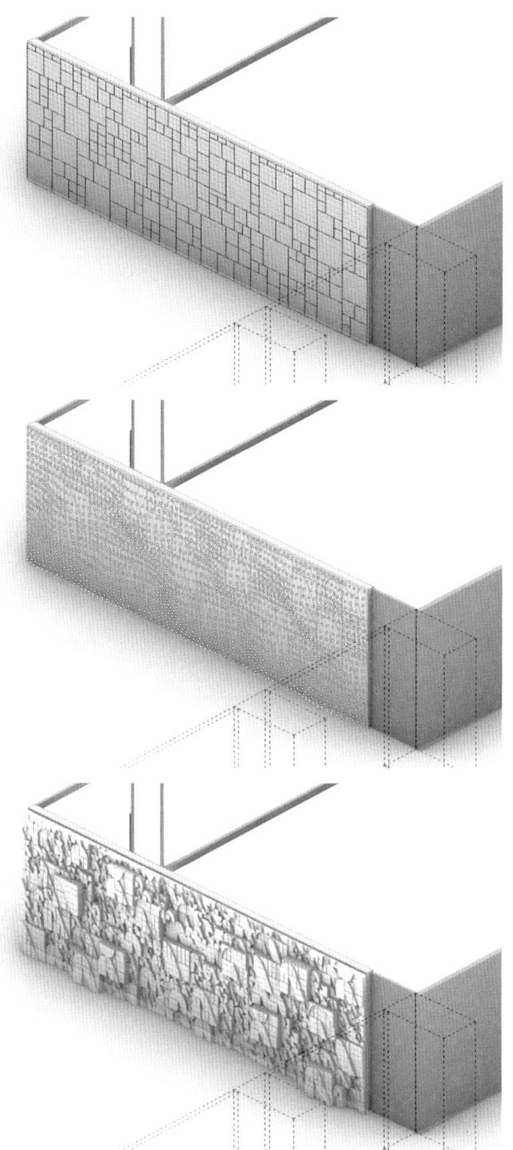

壁面アート構成
Wall art composition

計画初期段階からパラメトリックモデルが用いられ、流動的に追加・変更される意匠条件を柔軟に取り込むことに成功した。決定案では全体で緩やかな曲面を描くように配置が制御されている。

A parametric model was employed from the early phase of planning, which allowed for flexible additions and changes in design requirements throughout the fluid process. In the final version, the arrangement was controlled to create a gentle curvature.

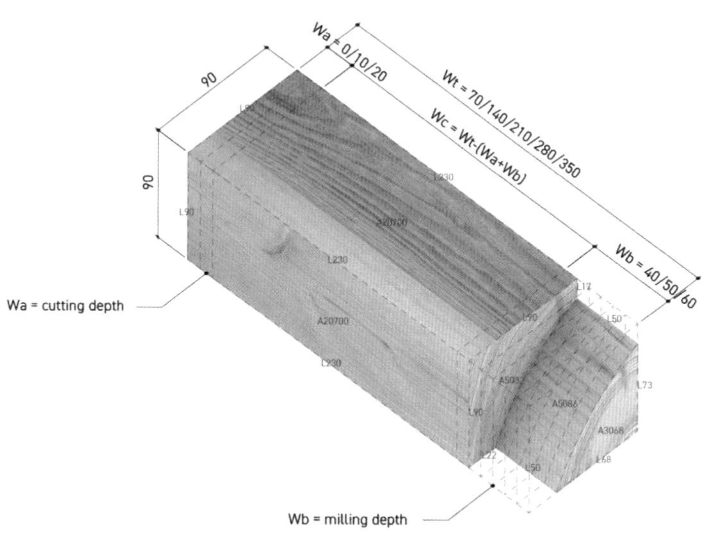

木材（＝ピース）の加工には3軸CNC加工機ShopBotが用いられた。加工可能範囲内で、最大限多様な凹凸が演出できるような制御プログラムが開発された。

A CNC router was used for the fabrication of the wooden components. A program was developed to maximize and control the varying depths within the router's fabrication capability.

図柄 - 凸パターン
Protruding design patterns

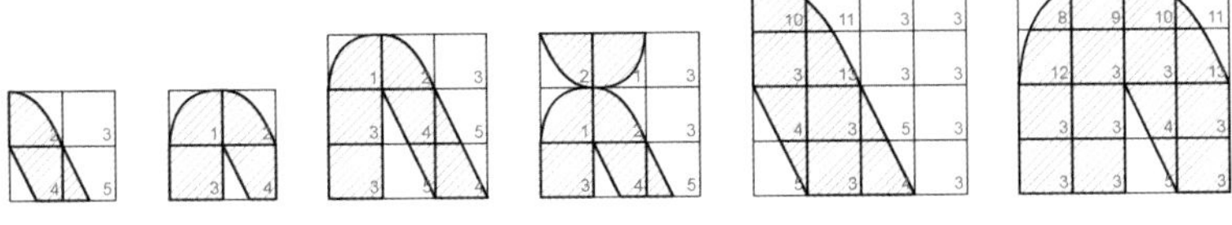

図柄 - 凹パターン
Indented design patterns

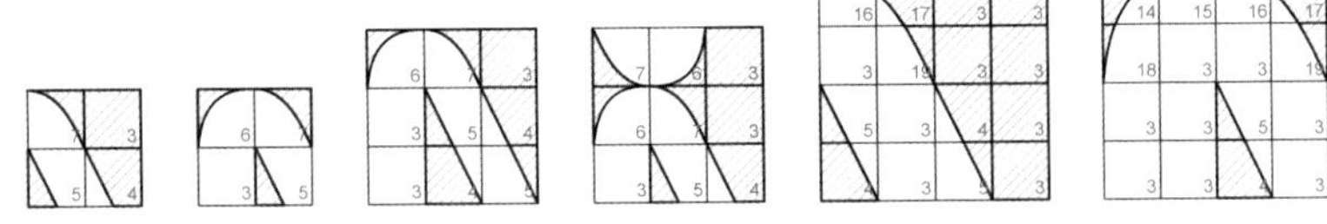

壁面アート立面図
Wall art elevation drawing

立面の配置構成 [A]。「ピース」は 90mm 角材の加工による製造。「ユニット」は 4 種の図柄、3 種のサイズ、凹凸の違いで無数の組み合わせからなる [B]。

Elevation configuration [A]. "Pieces" are made by processing 90mm square lumber. "Units" are comprised of 4 patterns, 3 sizes, and variable unevenness, resulting in countless combinations [B].

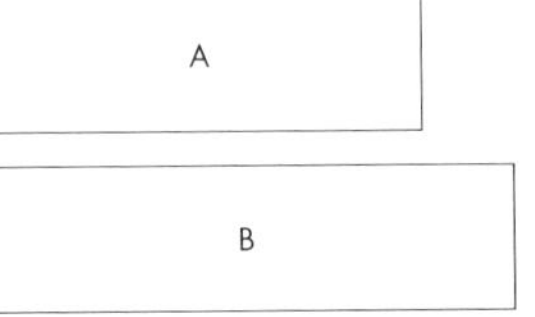

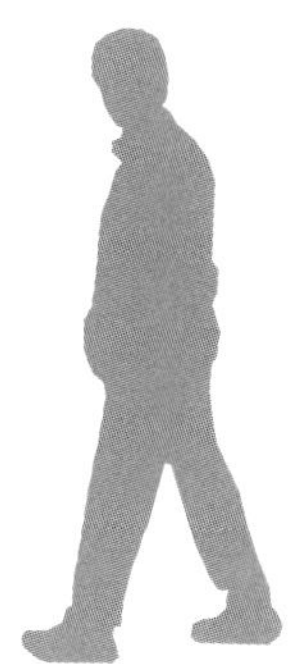

1/40 scale

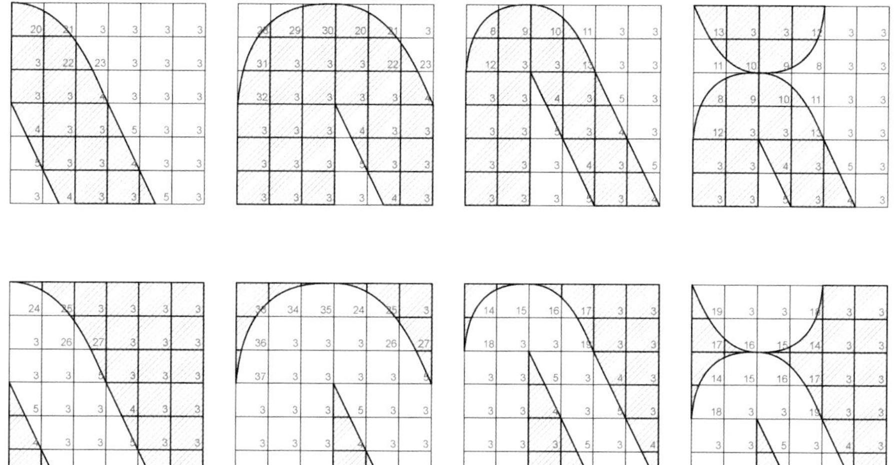

「ガラスフィルム」の面。NTT DATA INFORIUM 豊洲イノベーションセンター内を仕切る可動のガラス壁面である。連続性を持たせつつプライバシーを確保するため、パターンの多層構成が可能なガラスフィルムによって視覚操作を行った。

The surface of "glass film" on a glass wall that separates the showroom from the administrative space. To maintain spatial continuity while ensuring privacy, we adopted a glass film material that creates a multiple layering effect.

フィルム表面に立体的な凹凸を生むクリアインクは、視線の動きや光の変化によって対象の見え方を変化させ、時間やモノ、ヒトなど様々な情報の変化を機敏に映し出す [A]-[C]。

Clear ink, which creates three-dimensional unevenness on the film surface, alters the appearance of objects according to the movement of one's gaze or fluctuations in light. Informational changes in time, object, and people are promptly reflected [A]-[C].

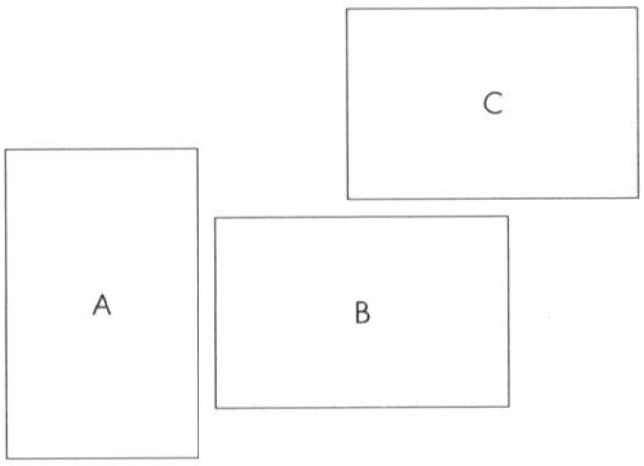

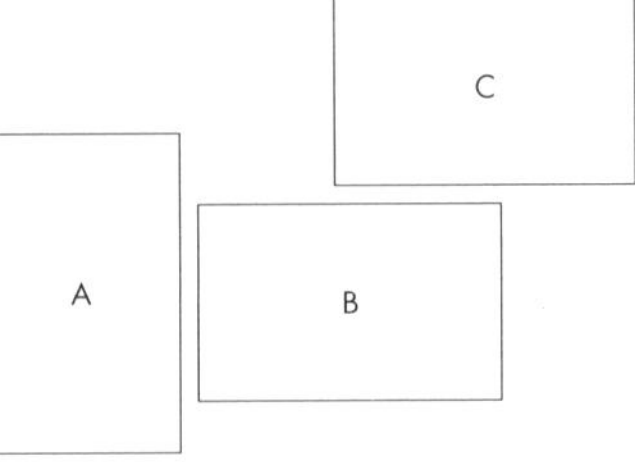

ガラスフィルムの積層構造

Structure of laminated glass film

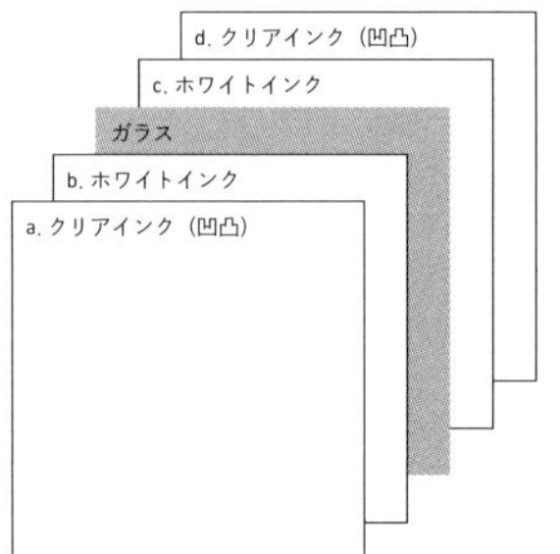

ガラスフィルムの組み合わせ一覧

List of glass film combinations

	00	01	02	03	04	05	06	07	08	09	10	11	12	13	14	15
a		●				●	●	●				●	●	●		●
b			●			●			●	●		●		●	●	●
c				●			●			●	●	●	●		●	●
d					●			●	●		●		●	●	●	●

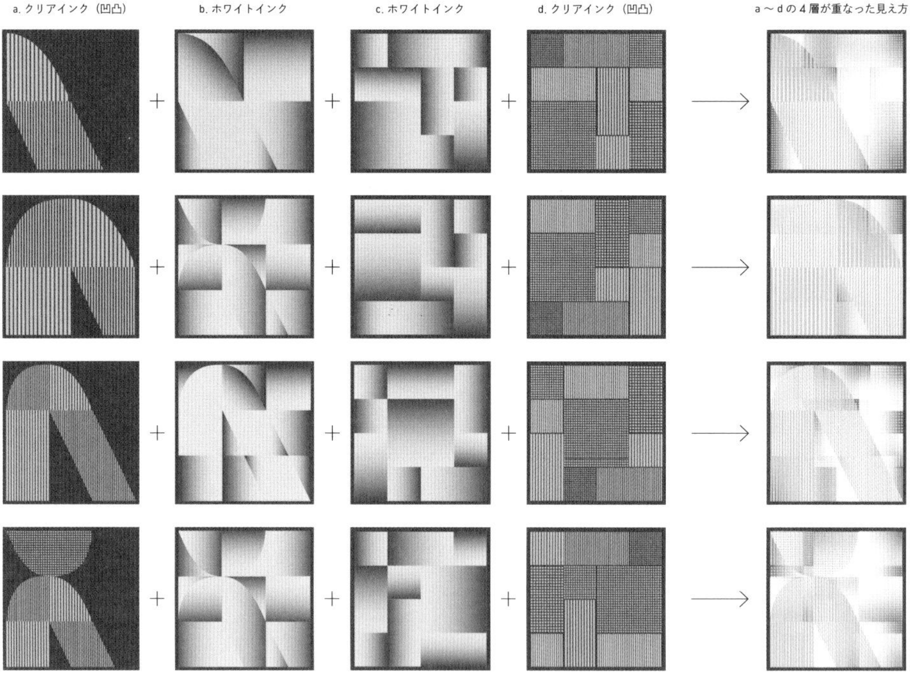

a. クリアインク（凹凸）　b. ホワイトインク　c. ホワイトインク　d. クリアインク（凹凸）　a～dの4層が重なった見え方

ガラスフィルムの構造とパターン

Structure and patterns of glass film

1枚のガラスフィルムにクリアインク（凹凸表現）とホワイトインクを印刷して2層構造をつくる。さらにそれらをガラスの表面と裏面に貼ることでトータル4層の奥行きを生み出した [A]。各インク印刷の有無による組み合わせは全16通りとなる [B]。

The two-layer structure was composed by printing clear ink to express a dented texture, and white ink onto one sheet of glass film. Fixing them on the front and back of the glass, four layers of depths were achieved [A]. There was a total of 16 combinations depending on whether or not each ink is printed [B].

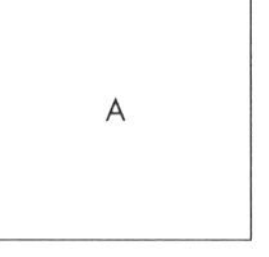

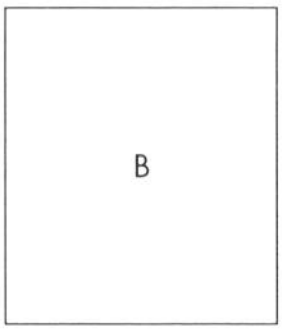

B

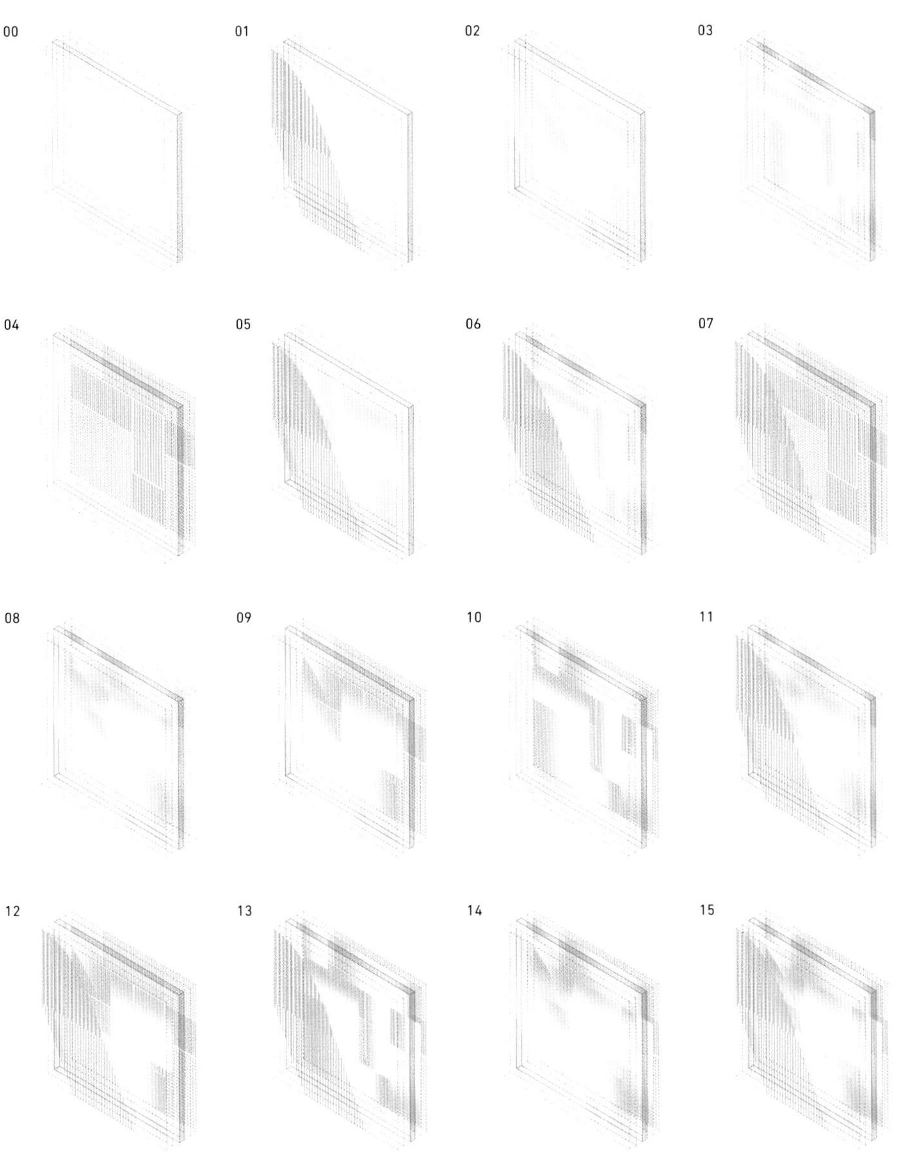
00
01
02
03
04
05
06
07
08
09
10
11
12
13
14
15

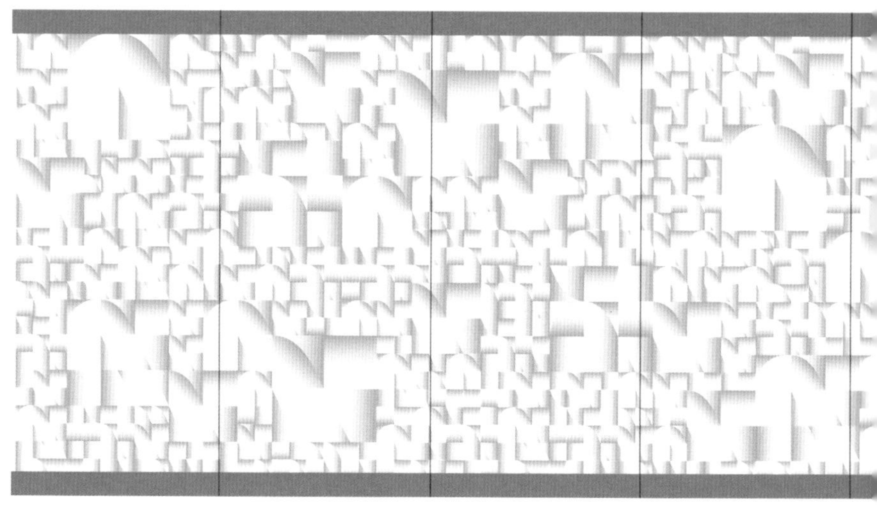

ガラスフィルム立面図

Glass film elevation drawing

表面にはロゴをモチーフとしたグラフィックを「壁面アート」と同じモジュールで配し、裏面にはモンドリアングリッドのパターンを配置した。パターン構成はプログラムによって半自動的に制御され、多角的な検討がなされた。

On the front is a logo-based graphic arranged in the same module as the "Wall art", while the back surface is designed with a Mondrian-grid pattern. Pattern compositions were semi-automatically controlled by a program through numerous studies.

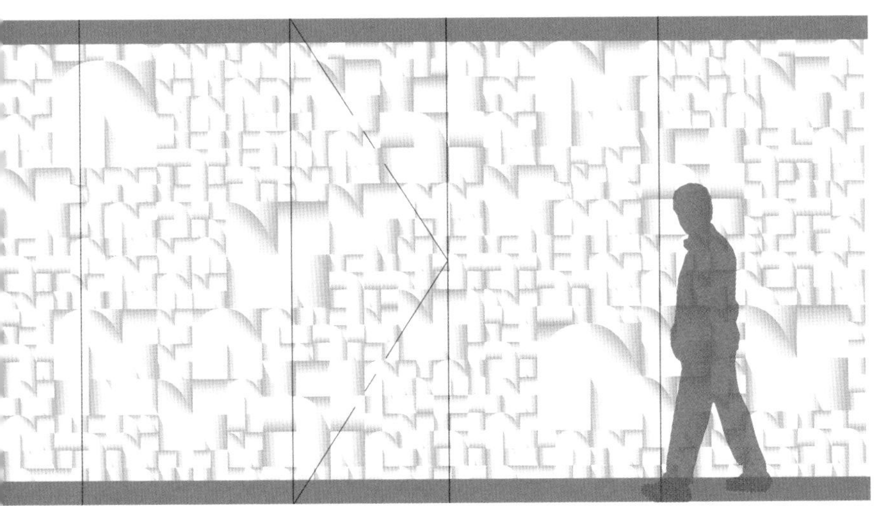

1/40 scale

1/40 scale

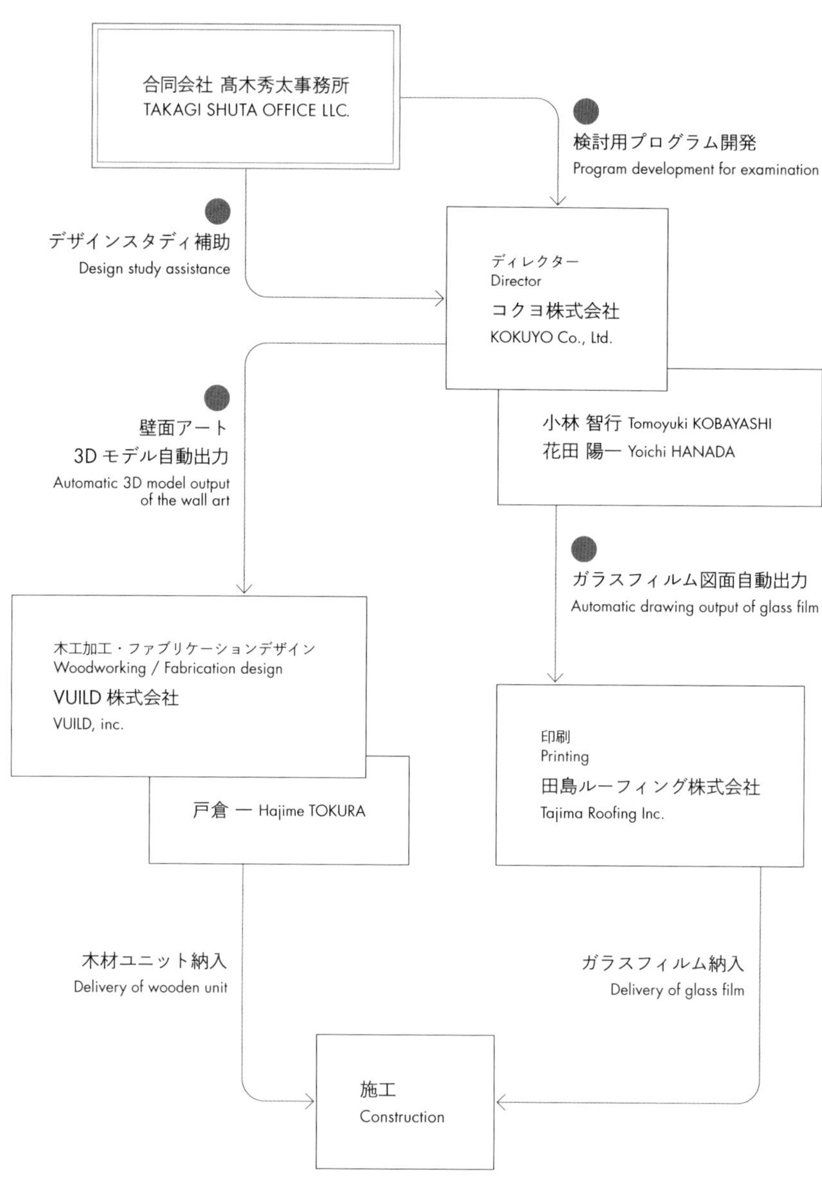

髙木秀太事務所は計画から製造加工での過程で、制作会社への円滑なデータ納品が期待された。木工加工は VUILD 株式会社、ガラスフィルム制作は田島ルーフィング株式会社によるもの。

Takagi Shuta Office was expected to deliver the data smoothly to the manufacturer over the process of planning to fabrication. Wood pieces were fabricated by VUILD, Inc., and glass films were produced by Tajima Roofing Inc.

プロジェクトID プロジェクト期間	210063 2021.12–2022.06
クライアント	株式会社ＮＴＴデータ
ディレクター 担当	コクヨ株式会社 小林 智行、花田 陽一
プロジェクトマネージメント メインプログラマー デザイナー	髙木 秀太、槙山 武蔵 髙木 秀太、槙山 武蔵 竹内 瑠奈
ソフトウェア / 開発環境 プログラミング言語 キーワード	Rhinoceros, Adobe Illustrator Grasshopper, Python 内装設計、幾何計算、図面自動出力、デジタルファブリケーション

Project ID Project term	210063 2021.12–2022.06
Client	NTT DATA Corporation
Director Project team	KOKUYO Co., Ltd. Tomoyuki KOBAYASHI, Yoichi HANADA
Project management Main programmer Designer	Shuta TAKAGI, Musashi MAKIYAMA Shuta TAKAGI, Musashi MAKIYAMA Runa TAKEUCHI
Software / SDE Programming language Keywords	Rhinoceros, Adobe Illustrator Grasshopper, Python Interior design, Geometry calculation, Automatic drawing output, Digital fabrication

壁面アートのプログラム構築はGrasshopperで行った。意匠スタディに加えて、3軸CNC加工機ShopBotで使用するCAMデータへの変換を見据えたアウトプットデータの出力、検算までを一貫したプログラム上で行った。

Grasshopper was used in the programming for the wood pieces. In addition to design studies, production of output data in anticipation of conversion to CAM data for the CNC router and verifications were conducted within one consistent program.

PRISM TV STUDIO

クライアント　YOUテレビ株式会社
Client　YOU Communications Corporation

設計　クマタイチ
Design　Taichi KUMA

横浜、川崎エリアをカバーするケーブルテレビ会社のサテライトスタジオの外装／内装デザインプロジェクトである。建築家クマタイチ氏とのコラボレーション。

杉の板材を用いたデザインの条件がクライアントから提示され、クマタイチ氏のデザインのもと、アイコニックな流れ・動きのある造形を実現した。髙木秀太事務所では3Dモデルのコンピューテーショナルスタディや杉板加工のデジタル処理、さらには現場管理も担当し、プロジェクトを多角的にサポートした。

An exterior / interior design project for a satellite studio of a cable TV company that broadcasts in the Kawasaki area in Yokohama, in collaboration with architect Taichi Kuma.

The client had proposed the use of cedar boards as a design precondition, and we realized an iconically fluid and motional form based on the design by Taichi Kuma. Takagi Shuta Office also oversaw the computational studies in 3D models, digital processing of cedar board fabrication, and construction administration, supporting the project in various ways.

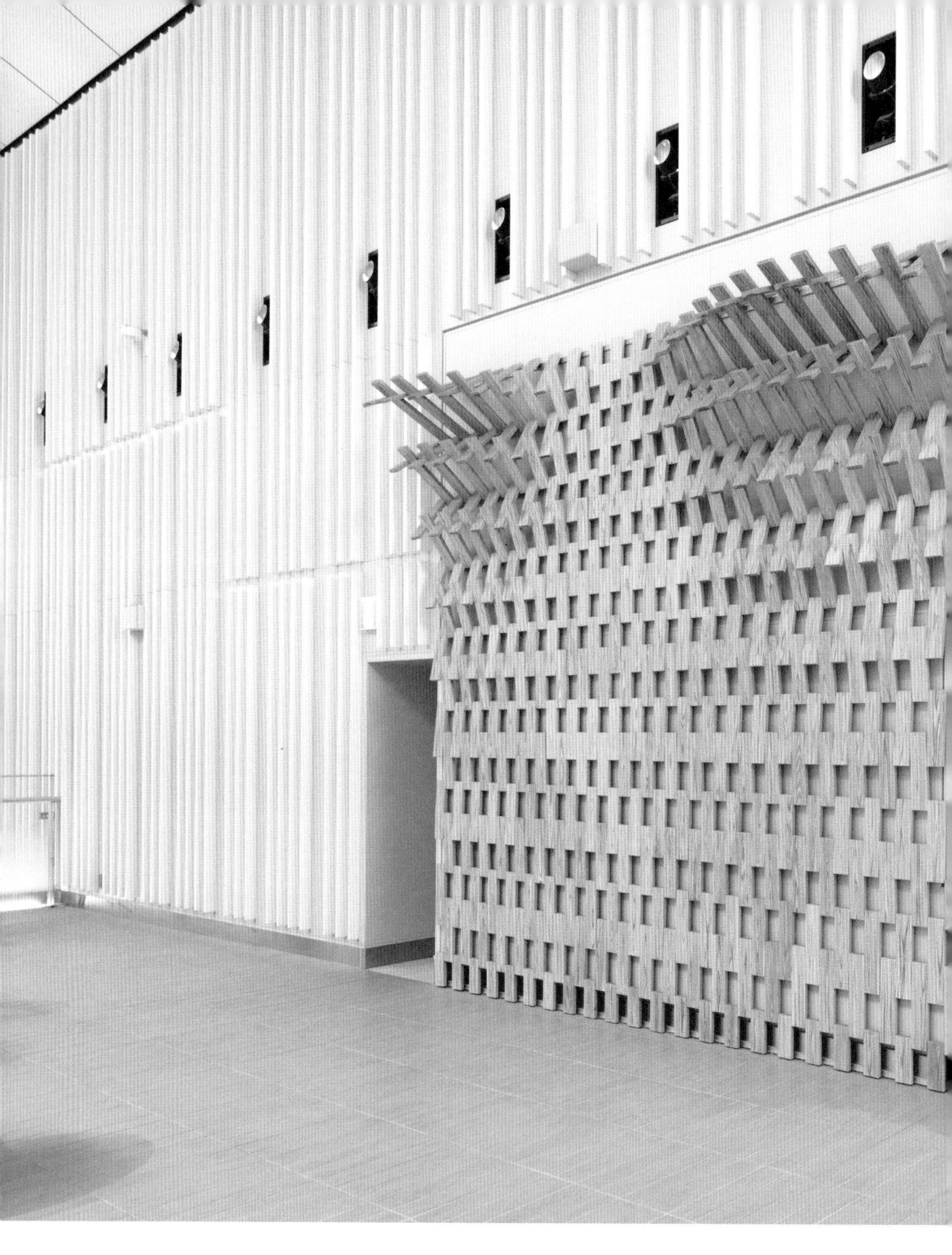

JR川崎駅の構内に位置する収録スタジオ。街のシンボルになるような外装になることを目標とし計画された。杉板を立体的に組むオリジナルの工法が開発された。

The recording studio is located within JR Kawasaki Station. A symbolic exterior for the city was sought after, and an original construction method was developed to assemble the cedar boards three-dimensionally.

PRISM TV
STUDIO

外装 [A] で採用された工法が構成向きを 90 度回転されて内装 [B][C] にも適用されている。内装と同様の工法ではあるが内外では異なる印象を与えるように計画された。

The construction method adopted for the exterior [A] has been rotated 90 degrees to be applied to the interior [B][C]. While the construction methods are analogous, impressions of the exterior and interior are intentionally distinct.

B

C

A

03_PRISM TV STUDIO

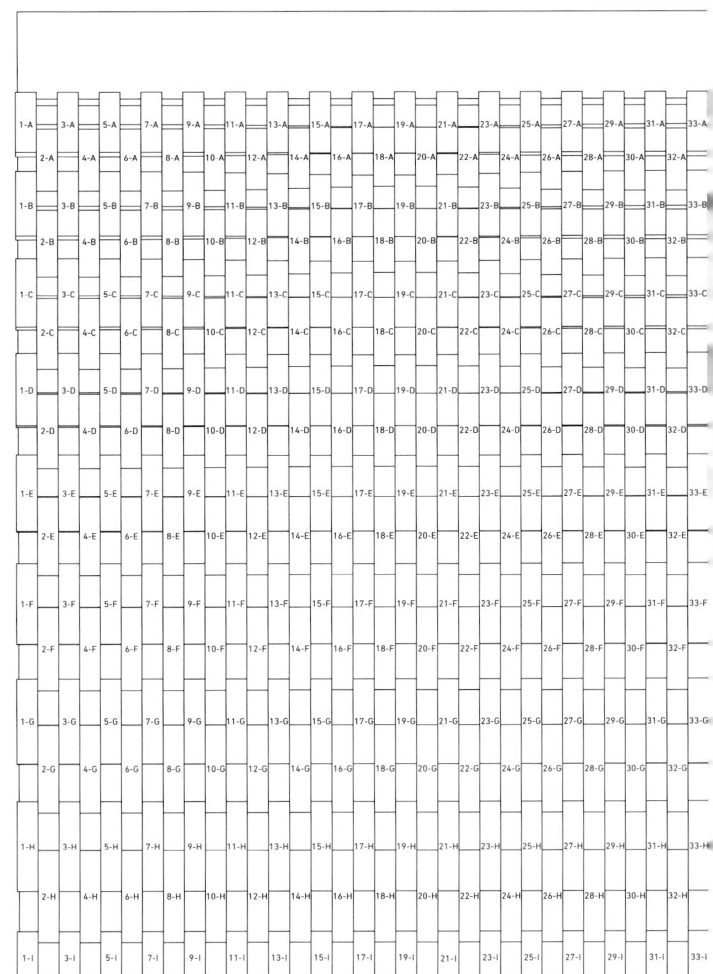

ファサード立面図
Facade elevation

本プロジェクトでは手作業で各種図面を作図することはコストがかかり過ぎるため、プログラムでの自動作図に置き換えられた。この立面図もコンピューターによる自動作図である。

Since it would have been too costly to manually draw each necessary plans in this project, an automatic drawing program was used. This elevation is also a result of automatic drawing by the computer.

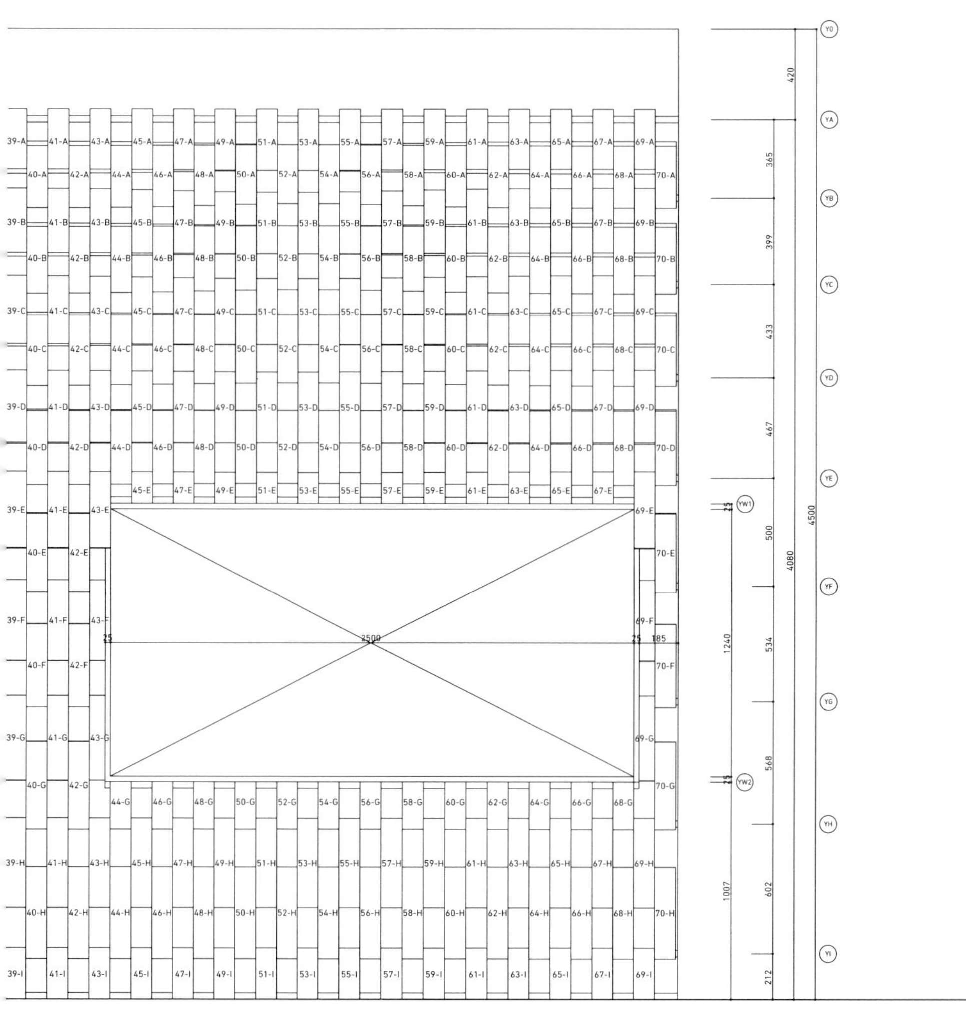

scale : 1/35

木板加工図

Wood board shop drawings

木工工場に杉板1枚1枚の製材を指示するため、数百枚単位のオーダーで加工図を作図する必要があった。各種図面と同様に加工図の作図もすべてプログラムが行っている。

To give instructions to the wood fabricator for each of the several hundred cedar boards, shop drawings were required for every piece of timber. As with other drawings, all shop drawings were also produced within the program.

scale : 1/35

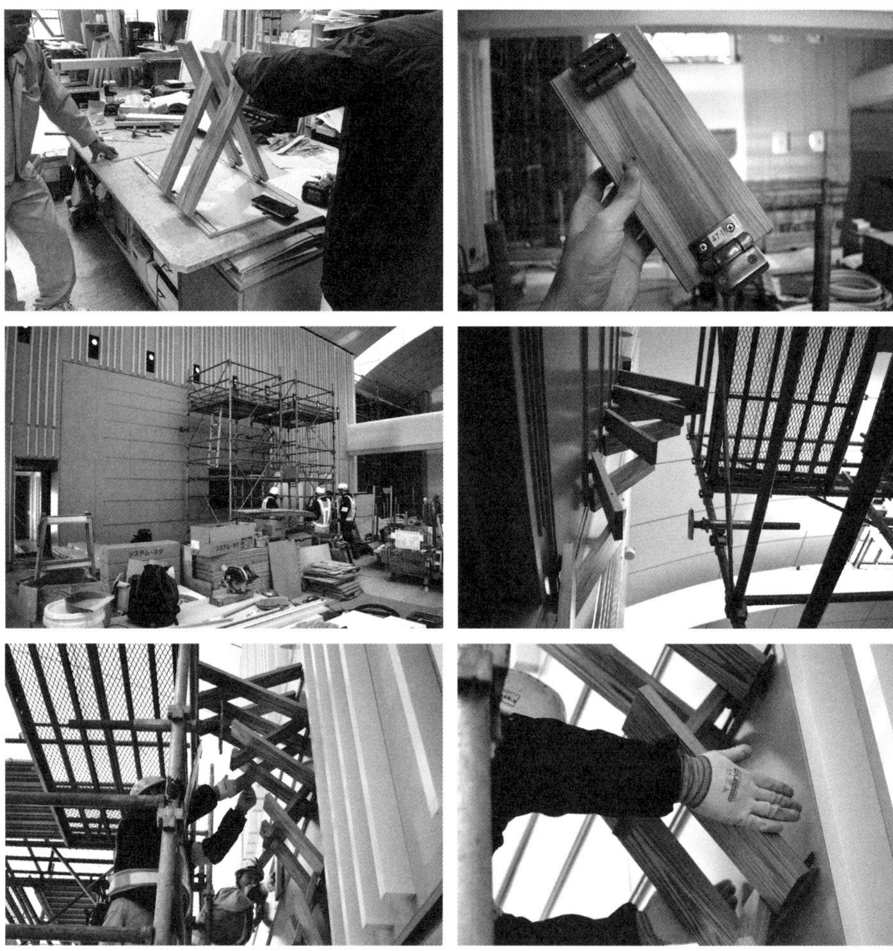

木工工場における杉板の加工・処理スタディ [A][B] から、施工現場での管理 [C]-[L] までのプロセス。現場に計画がインストールされるまでのマネージメントを一括して髙木秀太事務所が担当した。

From studies related to processing and handling of cedar boards at the wood fabricator [A][B] to construction management on site [C]-[L], Takagi Shuta Office was in charge of the comprehensive management of the project up to its installation.

A	B	G	H
C	D	I	J
E	F	K	L

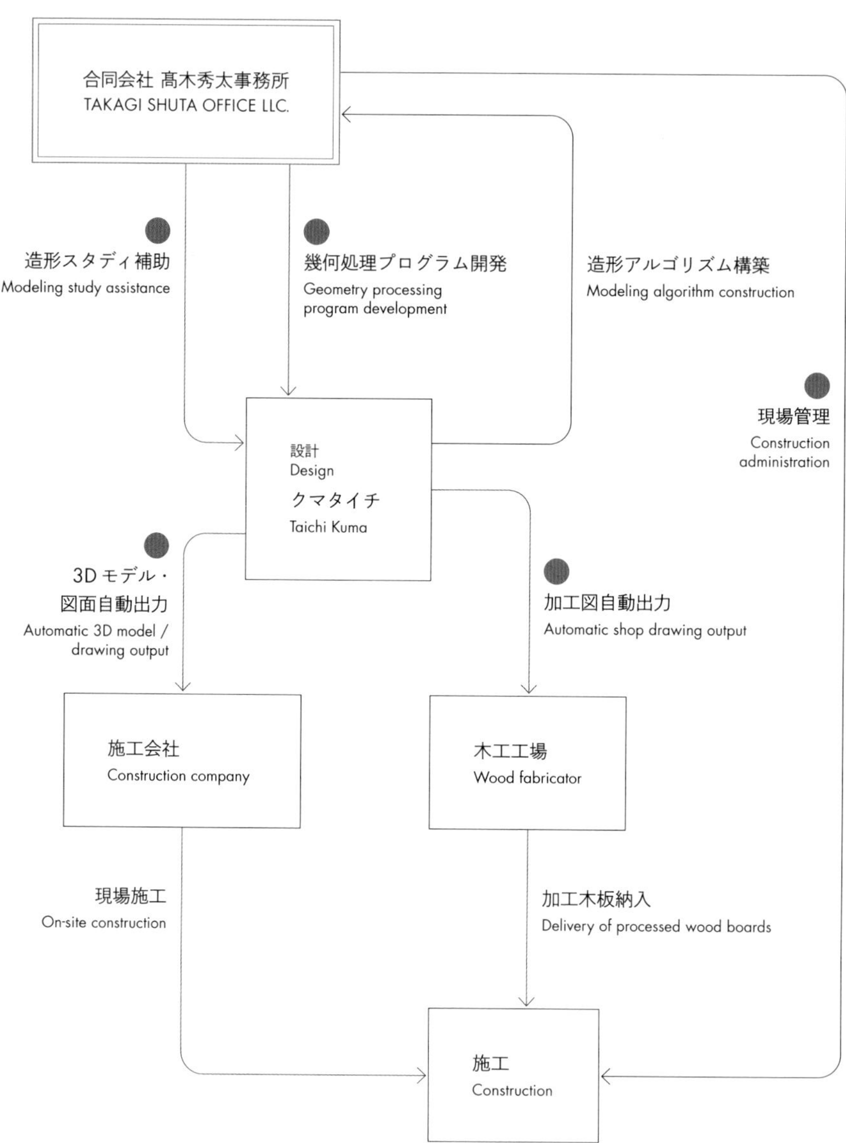

クマタイチ氏との造形スタディはGrasshopperプログラムを介して行われた。同氏もデジタルスキルに優れ、積極的にプログラム開発を行う。造形アルゴリズムをお互いにチェックし合うというプロセスで進行した。

Design studies with Taichi Kuma took place via Grasshopper software, as he was also highly skilled in digital design and program development. The process advanced with each party checking the design model algorithm.

プロジェクト ID プロジェクト期間	170019 2017.08–2018.09
クライアント	YOUテレビ株式会社
設計	クマタイチ
プロジェクトマネージメント メインプログラマー アシスタントプログラマー	髙木 秀太、髙塚 悟 髙木 秀太 布井 翔一郎、竹中 美穂
ソフトウェア / 開発環境 プログラミング言語 キーワード	Rhinoceros Grasshopper, Python 外装設計、内装設計、幾何計算、図面自動出力、現場管理

Project ID Project term	170019 2017.08–2018.09
Client	YOU Communications Corporation
Design	Taichi KUMA
Project management Main programmer Assistant programmer	Shuta TAKAGI, Satoru TAKATSUKA Shuta TAKAGI Shoichiro NUNOI, Miho TAKENAKA
Software / SDE Programming language Keywords	Rhinoceros Grasshopper, Python Exterior design, Interior design, Geometry calculation, Automatic drawing output, Construction administration

幾何処理のプログラムはビジュアルプログラミング言語Grasshopperで開発がなされた。プログラム構築のミス（＝バグ）を避けるために、数々の検算プログラムも用意された。

The geometry processing program was developed in the visual language Grasshopper. To avoid mistakes (= bugs) in the programming, many other verification programs were also prepared.

FUJIHIMURO ギャラリーエントランス

FUJIHIMURO GALLERY ENTRANCE

設計
Design

Taku Sakaushi + Hirofumi Nakagawa O.F.D.A.

山梨県富士吉田市の複合施設「FUJIHIMURO」における、アートギャラリーのエントランス造形。設計計画は建築家・坂牛 卓氏が率いる設計事務所 O.F.D.A.。

FRP（繊維強化プラスチック）シートによる極薄の自立構造で、光の透過による幻想的な空間演出が印象的である。髙木秀太事務所では、物理シミュレーションの技術から最適なドーム形状の決定や施工時の型枠生成をサポートした。

Art gallery entrance design for FUJIHIMURO, a multi-use facility in Fujiyoshida City, Yamanashi Prefecture. Architectural design by O.F.D.A., led by architect Taku Sakaushi.

The ultrathin self-standing structure made of FRP (fiber-reinforced plastic) sheets created a semi-transparent, illusionary spatial atmosphere. Takagi Shuta Office provided support in determining optimal dome shapes through physical simulation technologies and forming of the mold during construction.

製氷工場で製造された氷を貯蔵する「氷室」をコンバートして計画されたギャラリー。新たに計画された造形からは、かつて貯蔵された氷や、富士山麓から流れいでる伏流水を想起させる。

The gallery was a renovation of "himuro," a storage space for ice produced at an ice plant. The newly designed forms were reminiscent of the ice previously stored and the underground water flowing from the foothills of Mt. Fuji.

04_FUJIHIMURO GALLERY ENTRANCE

B

A　C

各種ギャラリースペースへとつながるエントランスの造形[A][B]。ペンダントライトによる光の演出が素材と形状の透過性を強調している[C]。

Entrances leading into different gallery spaces [A][B]. The effects from pendant light fixtures emphasize the permeability of both material and form [C].

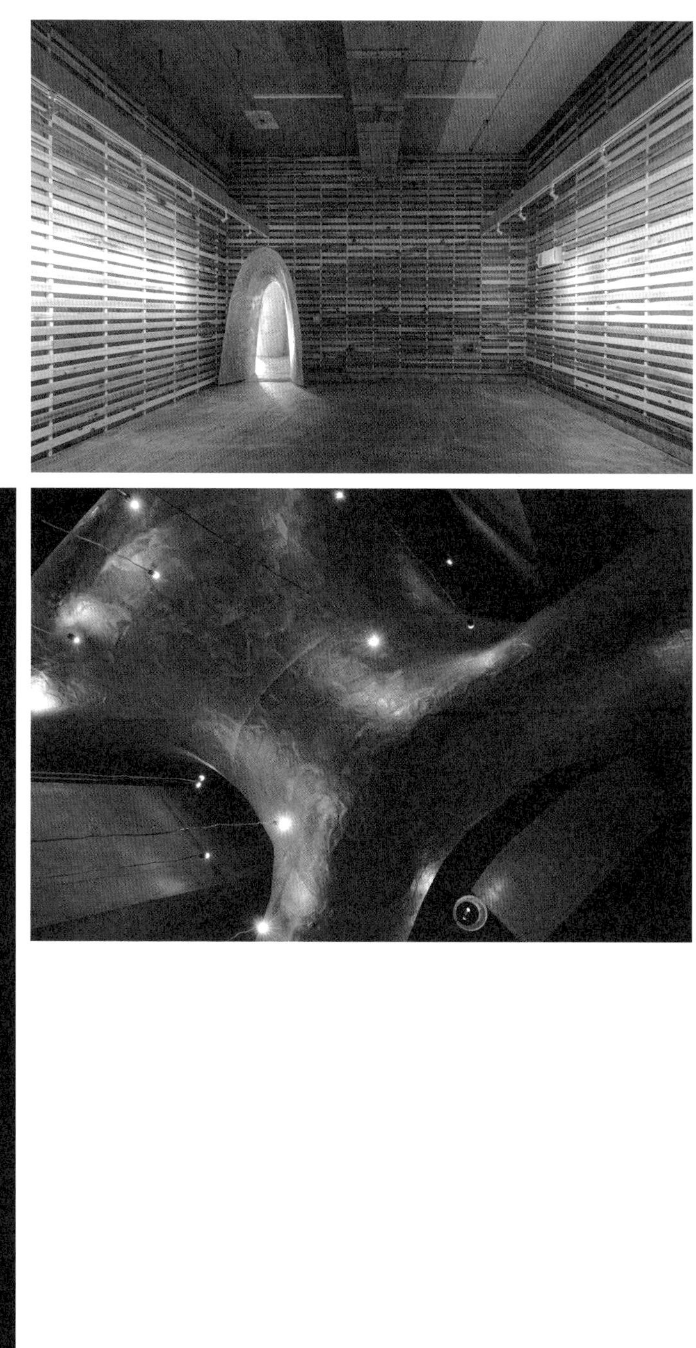

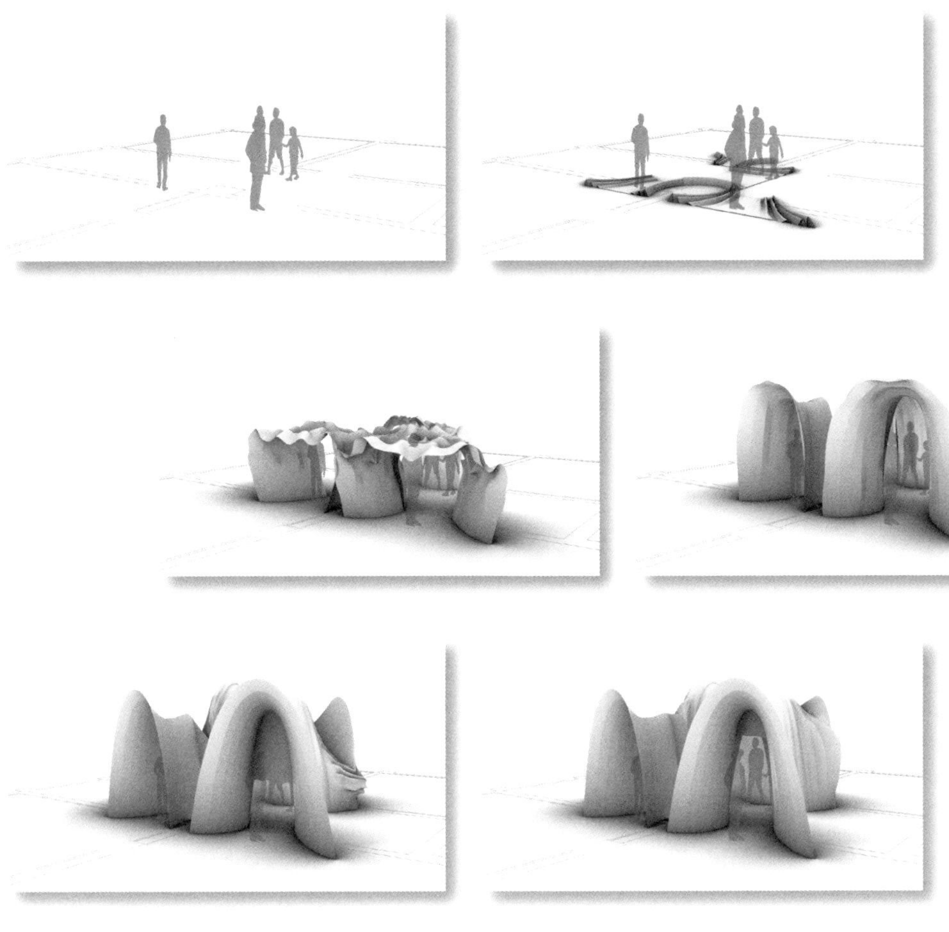

物理シミュレーション
Physical simulations

FRP（繊維強化プラスチック）シートは、自重をスムーズに受け流す形状を計画しなければ崩壊してしまう。「カテナリー」と呼ばれる自然な形状を物理シミュレーションで算出した。

If the dead weight of the structure is not properly directed in the designed form, FRP (fiber-reinforced plastic) sheets would collapse. Physical simulations were used to determine the logical "catenary" form.

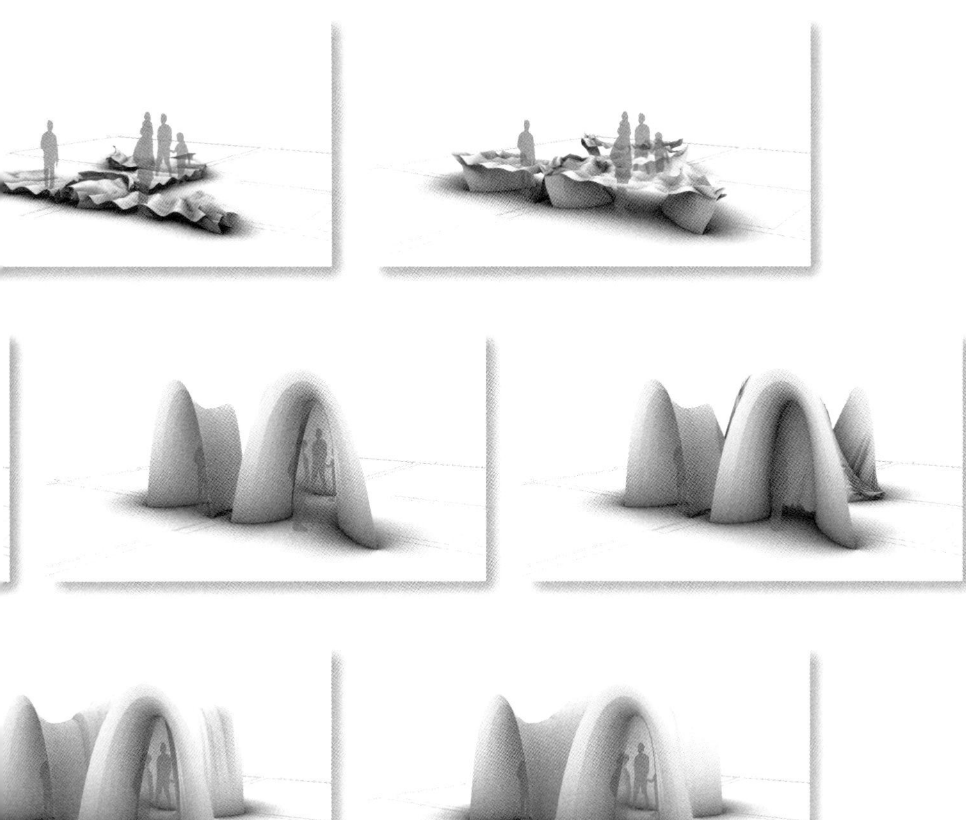

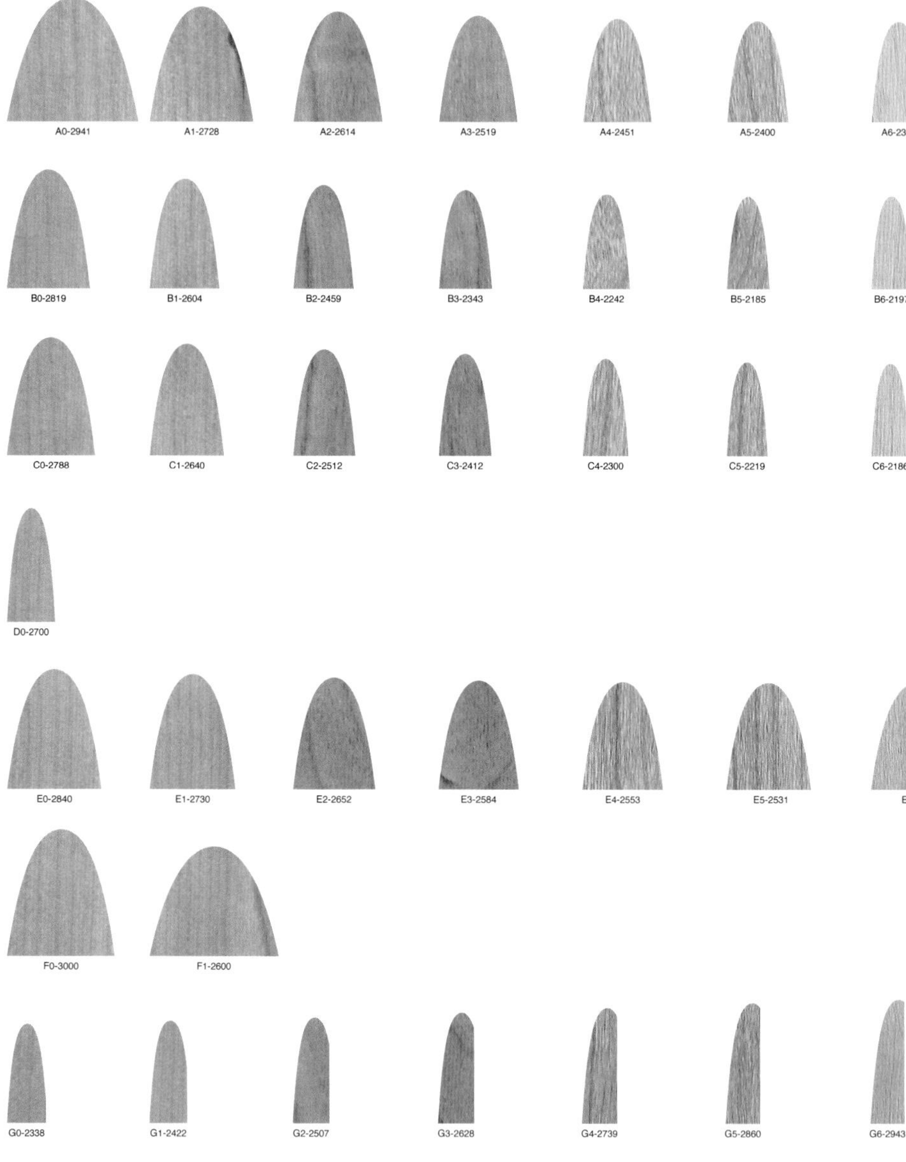

型枠図
Formwork drawings

ドームの制作は自主施工で行われた。ドームの断面を輪切りにした施工用型枠の自動作図・出力を髙木秀太事務所でサポート。型枠はベニア板で作成された。

The domes were self-built. Takagi Shuta Office supported automatic drawing and output for the domes' cross sections to facilitate the making of formwork, which were made of plywood.

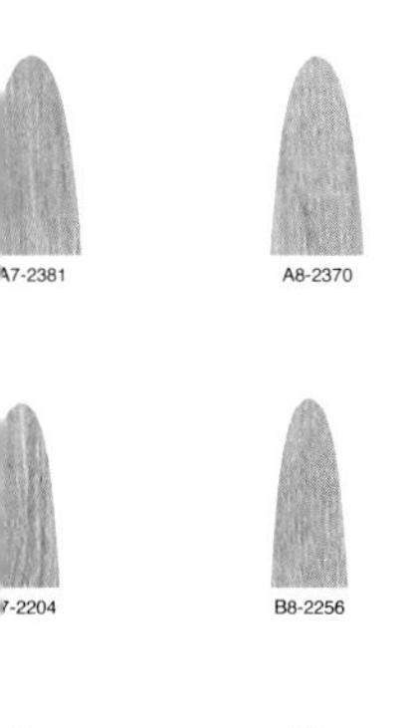

A7-2381 A8-2370

7-2204 B8-2256 B9-2302

7-2214 C8-2274 C9-2358

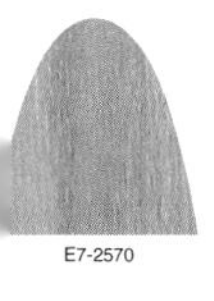

E7-2570

-2993 G8-3018 G9-3007 G10-2969 G11-2899 G12-2798 G13-2705

not to scale

A	B	C		
		D	E	F

自主施工の様子。ベニア板の型枠をスタイロフォームで埋めて曲面を造形していく [A]-[C]。その後、FRP シートを重ね合わせて、プラスチック樹脂で固める [D]。最後に型枠を外して完成である [E][F]。

Construction process. Gaps between plywood formwork were filled with styrofoam to create a smooth curvature [A]-[C], after which the FRP sheets were layered and solidified with plastic resin [D]. Lastly, formwork was removed to reveal the completed dome [E][F].

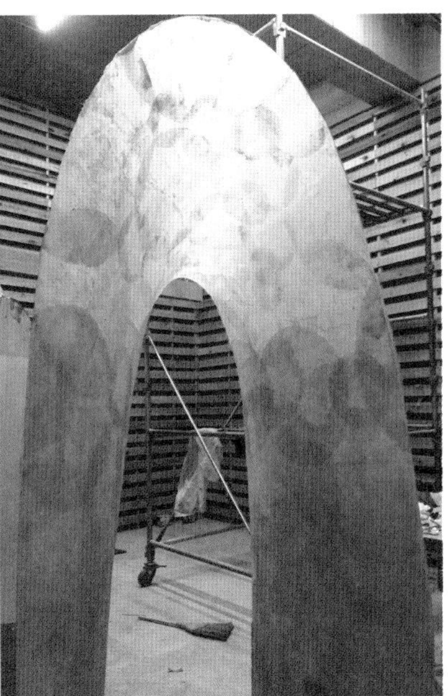

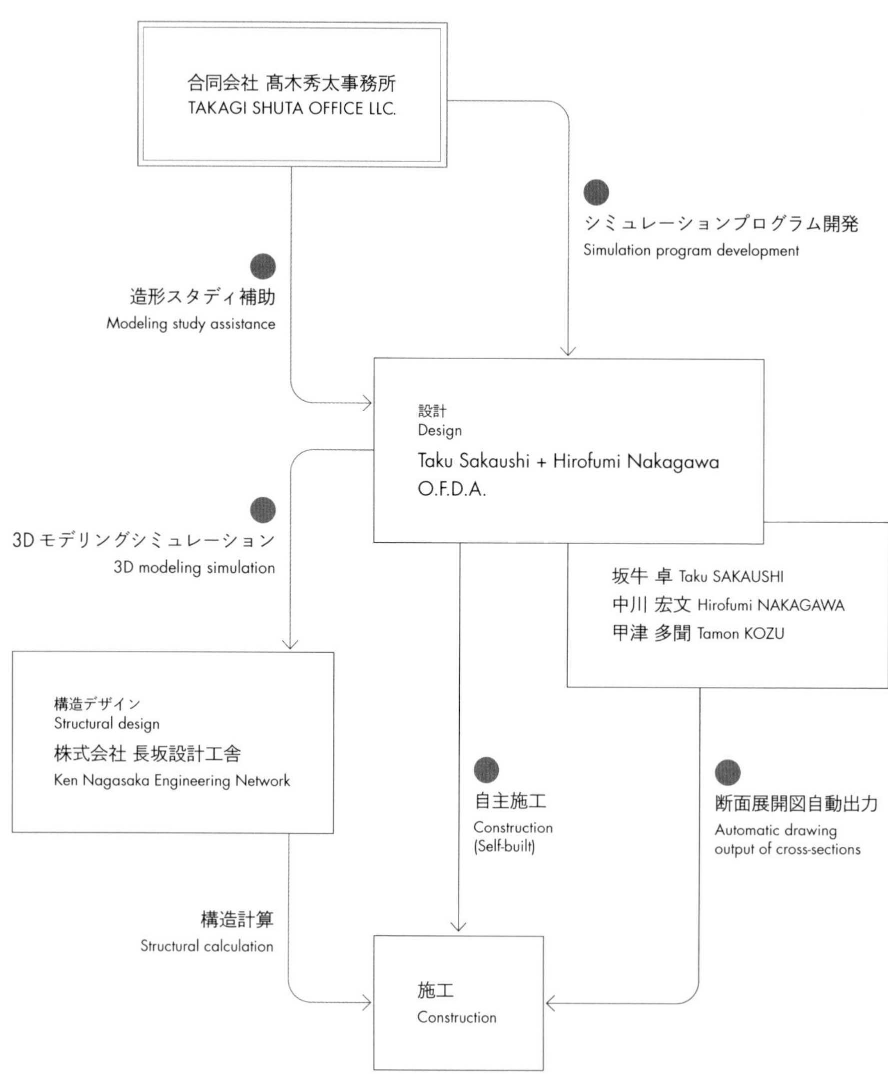

髙木秀太事務所のミッションは物理シミュレーターの構築であった。ガウディのサグラダファミリアでも採用された理論をコンピューター上に構築し、最適な形状を構造計算の確認に引き渡した。

Takagi Shuta Office's mission was to generate a physical simulator. The theory applied in Antoni Gaudi's Sagrada Familia was recreated on the computer and handed over for structural calculations to confirm the optimal form.

プロジェクトID	180045
プロジェクト期間	2018.12–2019.01
設計	Taku Sakaushi + Hirofumi Nakagawa O.F.D.A.
担当	坂牛 卓、中川 宏文、甲津 多聞
プロジェクトマネージメント	髙木 秀太
メインプログラマー	髙木 秀太
アシスタントスタッフ	瀬戸 滉平
ソフトウェア / 開発環境	Rhinoceros, Kangaroo
プログラミング言語	Grasshopper, Python
キーワード	内装設計、物理シミュレーション、構造最適化計算、図面自動出力

Project ID	180045
Project term	2018.12–2019.01
Design	Taku Sakaushi + Hirofumi Nakagawa O.F.D.A.
Project Team	Taku SAKAUSHI, Hirofumi NAKAGAWA, Tamon KOZU
Project management	Shuta TAKAGI
Main programmer	Shuta TAKAGI
Assistant staff	Kohei SETO
Software / SDE	Rhinoceros, Kangaroo
Programming language	Grasshopper, Python
Keywords	Interior design, Physical simulation, Structural optimization calculation, Automatic drawing output

物理シミュレーションはGrasshopperの物理演算プラグインKangarooで開発。重力による自然な形のドーム造形をプログラムで実現した。

Physical simulation was developed with Grasshopper's physical operation plug-in, Kangaroo. A logical form for the dome guided by gravity was realized in the program.

沖電気 OKI 本庄工場 H1 棟 ファサード

OKI ELECTRIC INDUSTRY FACADE

クライアント 沖電気工業株式会社
Client Oki Electric Industry Co., Ltd.

設計 大成建設株式会社一級建築士事務所
Design TAISEI DESIGN Planners Architects & Engineers

沖電気工業株式会社 新工場の設計計画である。大成建設株式会社とのコラボレーション。新工場の顔となるCLT木パネルによるルーバーをパラメトリックに制御した。ルーバーパターンの作成には日照、視線などの多目的最適化が施され、さらに最終モデルの決定には機械学習を用いた。髙木秀太事務所では、ルーバーの幾何学制御から評価アルゴリズムの構築に至るまで、3Dモデリングとプログラミングで幅広くプロジェクトをサポートした。

Architectural design for a new factory of Oki Electric Industry in collaboration with TAISEI DESIGN. The CLT wood louvers, as the face of the new factory, were parametrically controlled. Louver patterns were adjusted for multi-purpose optimizations, including sunlight and views, and the final pattern was determined through machine learning. Takagi Shuta Office supported the project extensively, from geometric control of the louvers to creation of evaluation algorithm through 3D modeling and programming.

国内初の『ZEB（Net Zero Energy Building）』認定工場。環境を考慮した様々な計画がなされた中で木質部材の積極活用もそのうちのひとつに挙げられる。髙木秀太事務所では木質ファサードデザインをデジタルサポートした。

As the first ZEB (Net Zero Energy Building) certified factory in Japan, one of the many environmental considerations made during its planning was the enthusiastic use of wood as a material. Takagi Shuta Office provided digital support for the wood facade design.

OKI
OKI ITSテストコース

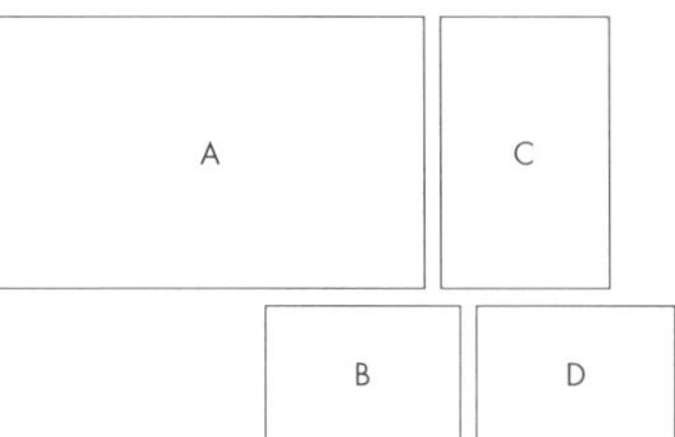

夜間は照明がCLTパネルに反射し、外観に淡い光の揺らぎが生まれる[A][B]。この揺らぎが、現地の環境にマッチするようなCLTパネルの配置検討が求められた。内観においては木の質感に溢れるような空間の計画となった[C][D]。

The CLT panels reflect lighting at night, prompting muted light fluctuations on the exterior [A][B]. Since it was imperative that these fluctuations harmonize with the surrounding environment, arrangement of the CLT panels was carefully considered. For the interior, materiality of the wood is prominent [C][D].

OKI

北面ファサード：ガラス裏の CLT パネル
North Facade: CLT panels behind glass

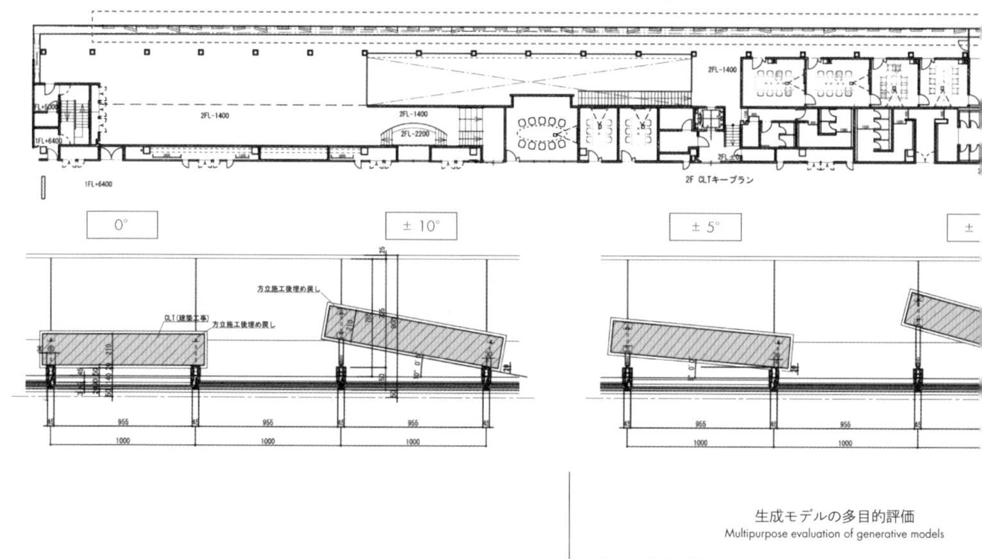

生成モデルの多目的評価
Multipurpose evaluation of generative models

CLT パネル配置の多目的最適化シミュレーション

Multipurpose optimization simulations for CLT panel layout

CLT パネルの配置について、そのサイズや回転角をパラメーターとし、日照、視線、照明の項目で評価。遺伝的アルゴリズムによる多目的最適化が行われ、半自動的に「優れた個体群」を抽出した。

For the arrangement of CLT panels, their sizes and rotation angles were used as parameters, and solar radiation, views, and lighting were evaluated. Multipurpose optimization by genetic algorithm was conducted in order to semi-automatically extract the "superior genotype".

評価 A

日照時間：少なく

評価 B

視線の抜け：多く

評価 C

電車から見た照明に
照らされたルーバー面：広く

Ladybug

視線
シミュレーション

光シミュレーション

Octopus

多目的最適化ソルバー

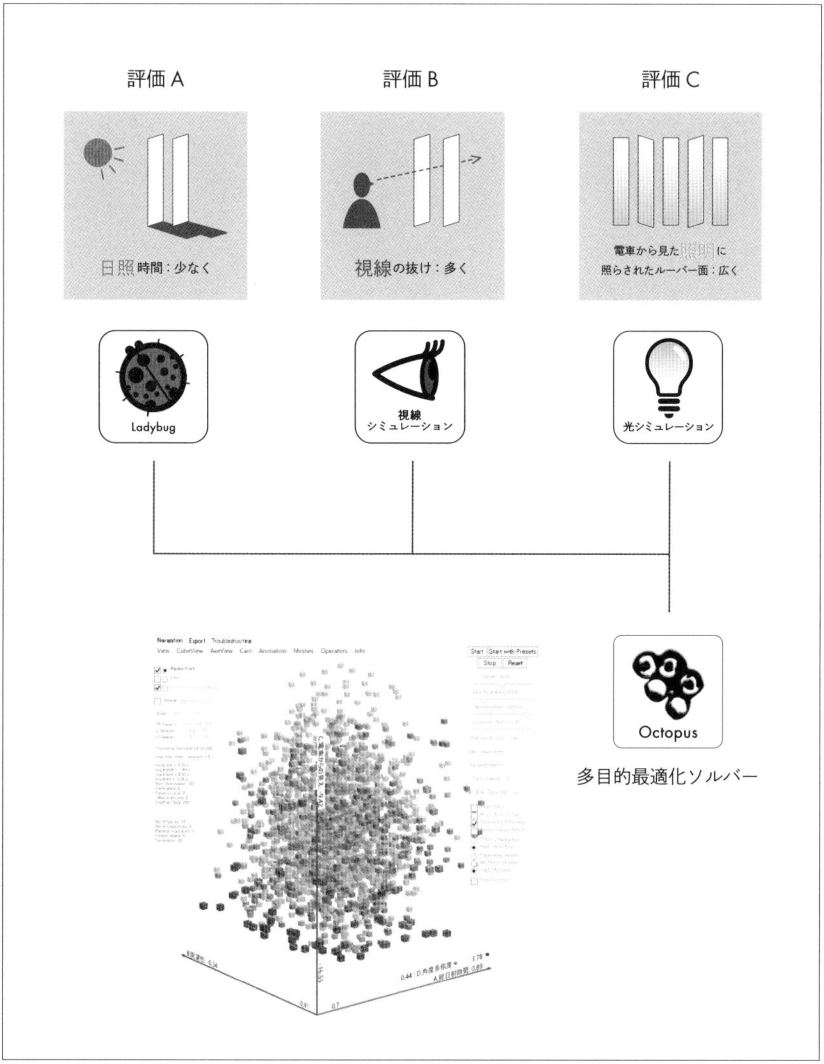

優れた個体群の出力

Output of superior genotypes

多目的最適化シミュレーションにより作成された「優れた個体群」の一部。この中から「照明の揺らぎが現地の環境に最もマッチする」1案を機械学習のサポートによって決定するプロセスが採用された。

Part of the "superior genotypes" created by multipurpose optimization simulation. From this group, one with "light fluctuations that most harmonize with the surrounding environment" was then selected with the support of machine learning.

05_OKI ELECTRIC INDUSTRY FACADE

学習フェーズ
Learning phase

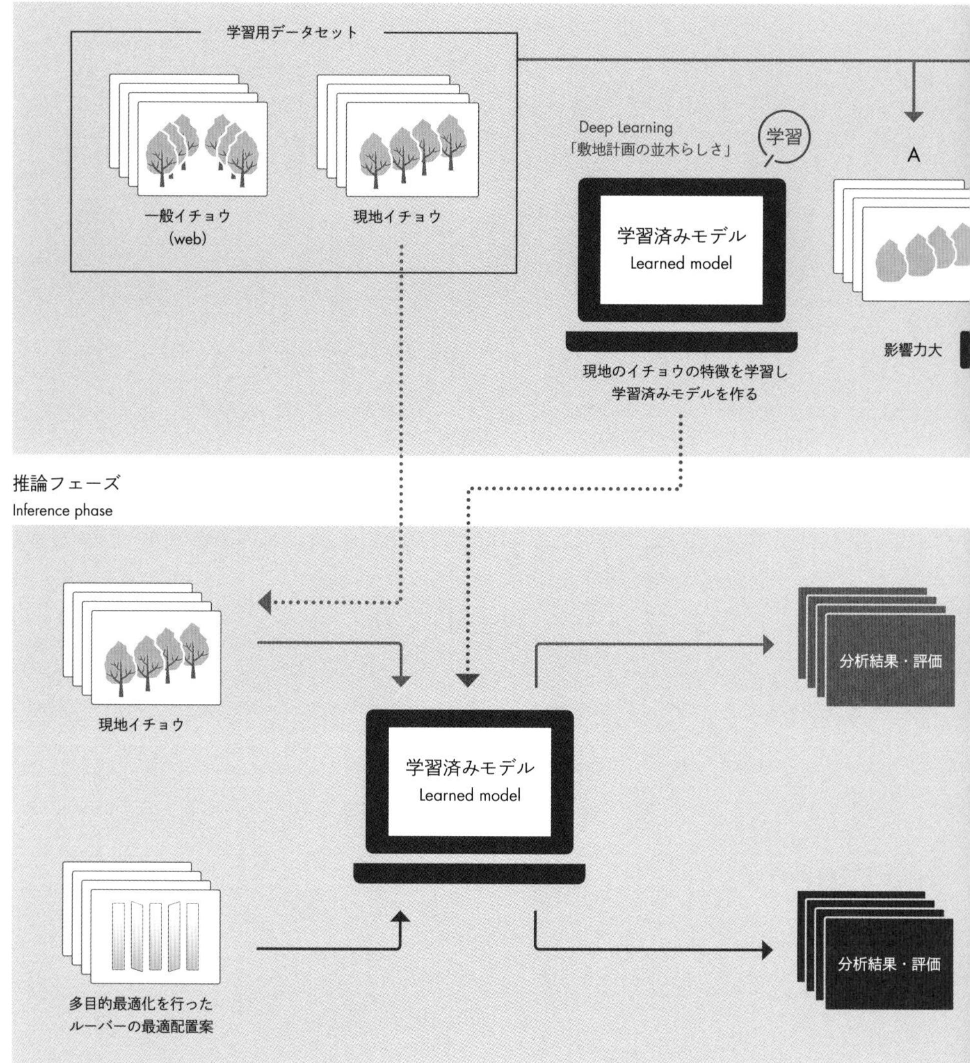

機械学習による「現地らしさ」の評価
Evaluation of "local-ness" via machine learning

機械学習の技術を用いて、計画敷地周辺の「イチョウ並木の風景」を学習させる。抽出された特徴を「現地らしさ」とし、候補のCLTパネル配置から1案を選定した。

"Streetscapes of ginkgo trees" around the site were learned using machine learning technology. Extracted features that represent "local-ness" were used as one of the determining factors for CLT panel arrangement.

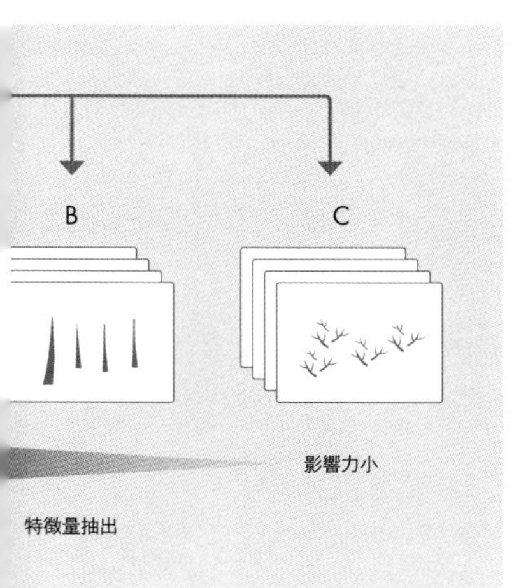

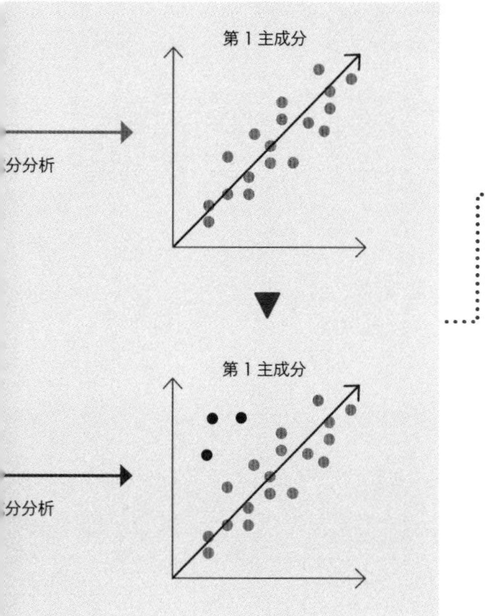

選定フェーズ
Selection phase

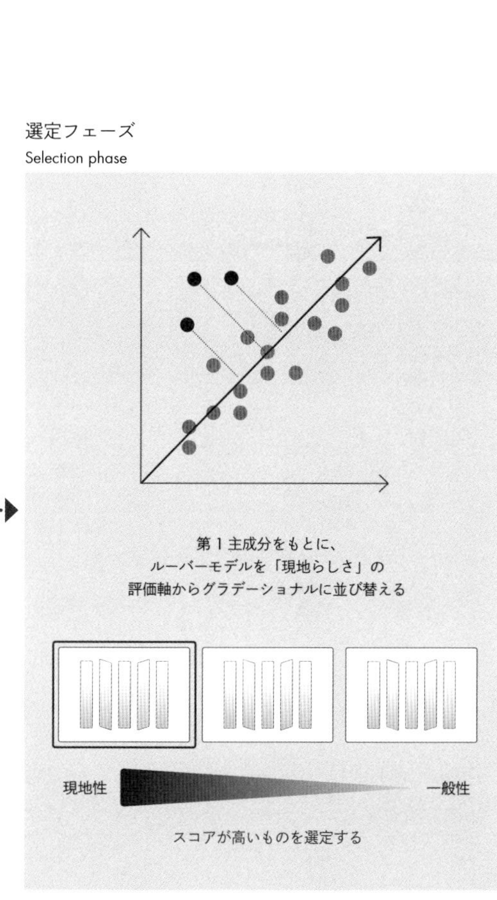

A.webスクレイピングにより収集したイチョウ並木
Rows of ginkgo trees collected through web scraping

「一般イチョウ」と「現地イチョウ」の学習
Learning of "general gingko" versus "local gingko"

「イチョウ並木の風景」の学習には画像データが用いられた。web上に多数存在するイチョウ並木画像を「一般イチョウ」[A]、敷地内で撮影されたイチョウ並木画像を「現地イチョウ」[B]とし、大量の画像が入力された。Pythonの機械学習ライブラリであるLIMEを利用し、その差異を推量する試みがなされた。

Image data was used for learning "streetscapes of ginkgo trees." Numerous images of ginkgo trees available online were categorized as "general ginkgo" [A], and images of ginkgo photographed on site were categorized as "local ginkgo" [B]. Using LIME, a Python machine learning library, we aimed to approximate their differences.

B. 設計者が撮影した、設計敷地に植生するイチョウ並木
Rows of ginkgo trees on the site, photographed by the designers

Python による AI プログラム開発
AI development via Python

プログラミング言語には、Keras、scikit-learn、LIME といった機械学習用ライブラリが豊富に用意されている Python が採用された。開発環境は Anaconda。

Python, which has a plenty of machine learning libraries including Keras, scikit-learn, and LIME, was adopted as the programming language. Anaconda was used for the development environment.

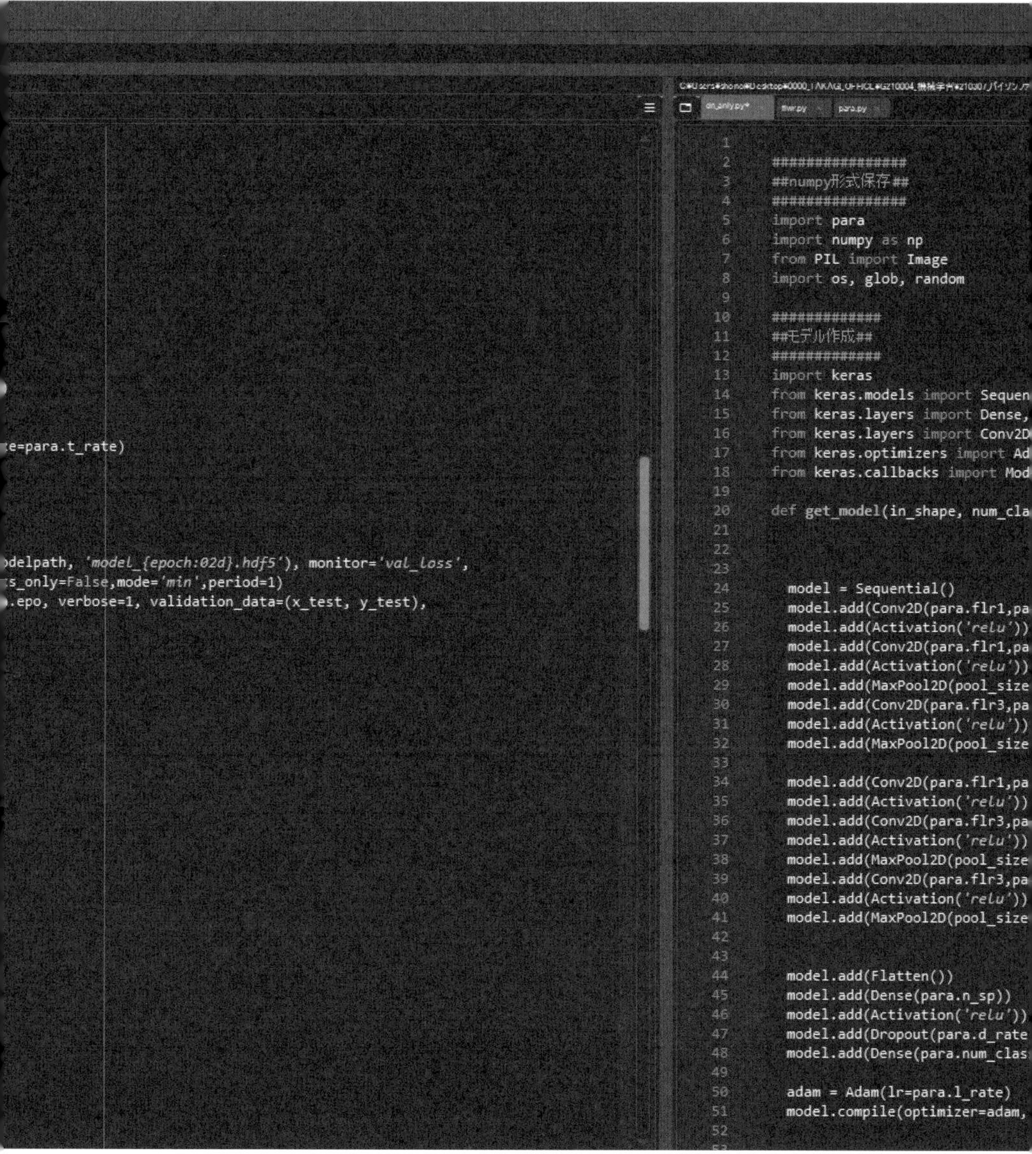
e=para.t_rate)
odelpath, 'model_{epoch:02d}.hdf5'), monitor='val_loss',
s_only=False,mode='min',period=1)
.epo, verbose=1, validation_data=(x_test, y_test),
cnn_only.py*
trwr.py
para.py
################
##numpy形式保存##
################
import para
import numpy as np
from PIL import Image
import os, glob, random
#############
##モデル作成##
#############
import keras
from keras.models import Sequen
from keras.layers import Dense,
from keras.layers import Conv2D
from keras.optimizers import Ad
from keras.callbacks import Mod
def get_model(in_shape, num_cla
model = Sequential()
model.add(Conv2D(para.flr1,pa
model.add(Activation('relu'))
model.add(Conv2D(para.flr1,pa
model.add(Activation('relu'))
model.add(MaxPool2D(pool_size
model.add(Conv2D(para.flr3,pa
model.add(Activation('relu'))
model.add(MaxPool2D(pool_size
model.add(Conv2D(para.flr1,pa
model.add(Activation('relu'))
model.add(Conv2D(para.flr3,pa
model.add(Activation('relu'))
model.add(MaxPool2D(pool_size
model.add(Conv2D(para.flr3,pa
model.add(Activation('relu'))
model.add(MaxPool2D(pool_size
model.add(Flatten())
model.add(Dense(para.n_sp))
model.add(Activation('relu'))
model.add(Dropout(para.d_rate
model.add(Dense(para.num_clas
adam = Adam(lr=para.l_rate)
model.compile(optimizer=adam,

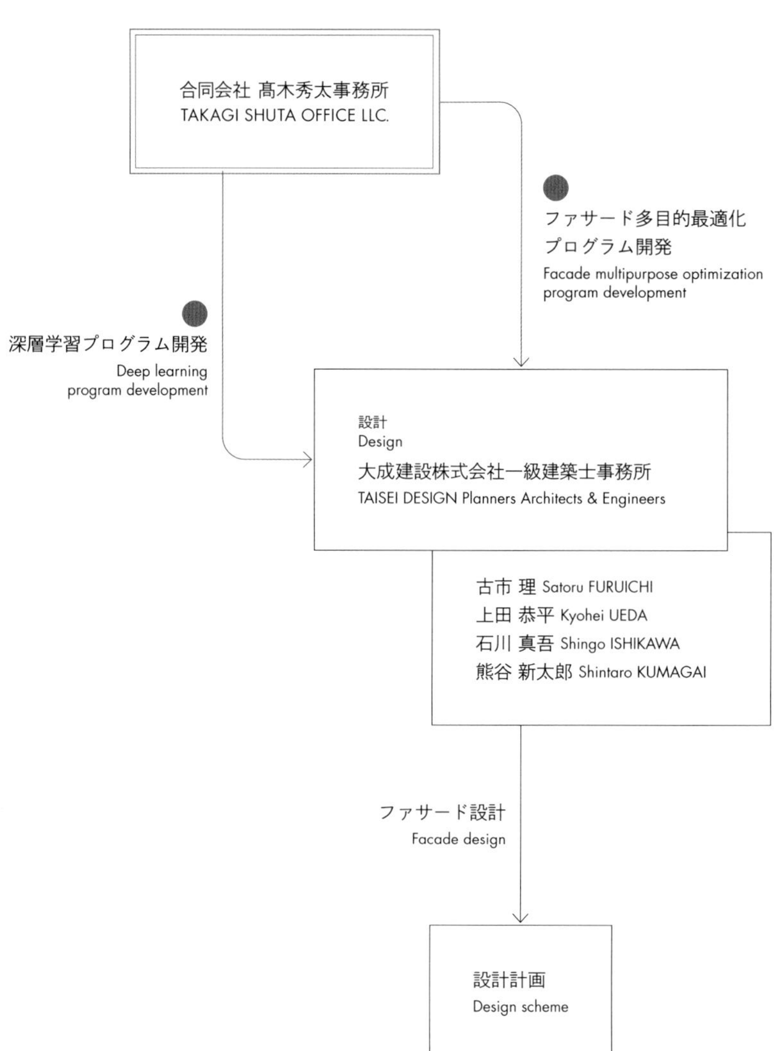

髙木秀太事務所においては、初の機械学習技術を取り入れたプロジェクトである。コンピューターによる画像認識とヒトによる風景の知覚に関して、数多くの研究的知見も得た。

It was the first project for Takagi Shuta Office to employ machine learning technology. We gained a multitude of research knowledge regarding image recognition by computers and human perception of sceneries.

プロジェクトID プロジェクト期間	200041 2020.12–2021.07
クライアント	沖電気工業株式会社
設計 担当	大成建設株式会社一級建築士事務所 古市 理、上田 恭平、石川 真吾、熊谷 新太郎
プロジェクトマネージメント メインプログラマー アシスタントスタッフ	高木 秀太、布井 翔一郎 高木 秀太、布井 翔一郎、竹中 虎太郎 川西 愛子、野末 誠斗
ソフトウェア / 開発環境 プログラミング言語 キーワード	Rhinoceros, Octopus, Ladybug, Anaconda Grasshopper, Python (Keras, scikit-learn, LIME) ファサード設計、多目的最適化計算、深層学習、 主成分分析、CNN 学習、環境シミュレーション

Project ID Project term	200041 2020.12–2021.07
Client	Oki Electric Industry Co., Ltd.
Design Project team	TAISEI DESIGN Planners Architects & Engineers Satoru FURUICHI, Kyohei UEDA, Shingo ISHIKAWA, Shintaro KUMAGAI
Project management Main programmer Assistant staff	Shuta TAKAGI, Shoichiro NUNOI Shuta TAKAGI, Shoichiro NUNOI, Kotaro TAKENAKA Aiko KAWANISHI, Makoto NOZUE
Software / SDE Programming language Keywords	Rhinoceros, Octopus, Ladybug, Anaconda Grasshopper, Python (Keras, scikit-learn, LIME) Facade design, Multipurpose optimization, Deep learning, Principal component analysis, CNN learning, Environmental simulation

多目的最適化シミュレーションで採用された最適化エンジンはGrasshopperプラグインOctopus。数万個体のオーダーによって最適モデルの探索がなされた。

The optimization engine adopted in multipurpose optimization simulation was Octopus, a Grasshopper plug-in, in which the optimal model search could be conducted in the order of tens of thousands.

サンスターコミュニケーションパーク ファサード

SUNSTAR COMMUNICATION PARK FACADE

06

クライアント　サンスター株式会社
Client　Sunstar Inc.

デザイン　株式会社小林・槇デザインワークショップ（KMDW）
Design　Kobayashi Maki Design Workshop (KMDW)

大阪府高槻市に建設されたサンスターグループの地域交流機能を持つオフィスのファサードデザインである。建築設計事務所 KMDW とのコラボレーション。建物前面を往来する阪急京都線の車窓からの視線を考慮し、配置間隔の粗密をコントロールする縦ルーバーのデザインが採用された。高木秀太事務所はルーバー配置の最適化プログラムの作成とルーバーによる日射遮蔽効果の検証を担当した。

Facade design for Sunstar Group's office with a community exchange function, built in Takatsuki City, Osaka Prefecture, in collaboration with architectural design office KMDW. Considering the view from the Hankyu Kyoto Line trains that are running parallel to the building facade, vertical louver design with varying densities is adopted. Takagi Shuta Office was responsible for creating an optimization program for the louver arrangement and verifying the effectiveness of sunlight deflection by the louvers.

建物正面向かって左右の端は密なルーバー配置だが、建物の入り口に向かってグラデーショナルに間隔が広がってゆく。視点場や時間帯によって異なる表情を見せる造形となった。

Louvers on the left and right ends of the facade are dense, and the spacing increases gradually towards the entrance of the building. The pattern creates varied expressions depending on the viewpoint and time of day.

06_SUNSTAR COMMUNICATION PARK FACADE

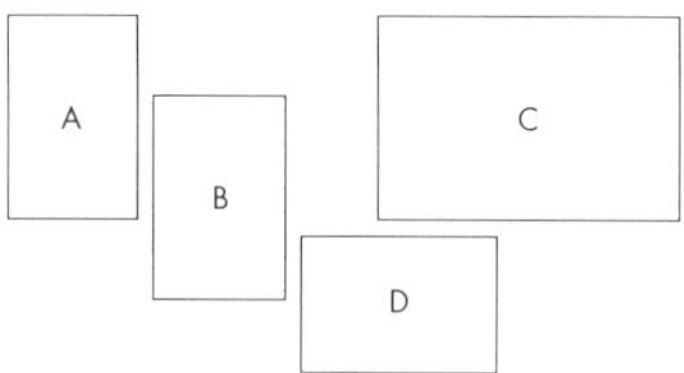

1本1本のルーバーは左右の面で塗装色を塗り分けられた。建物をどこから望むかによってイメージが異なる[A][B]。夜はライトアップが施され、シルエットがより際立つ[C][D]。

Since each louver was painted with different colors on its left and right surfaces, impressions of the building differ depending on one's viewpoint [A][B]. At night, they are lit up and the silhouette becomes more prominent [C][D].

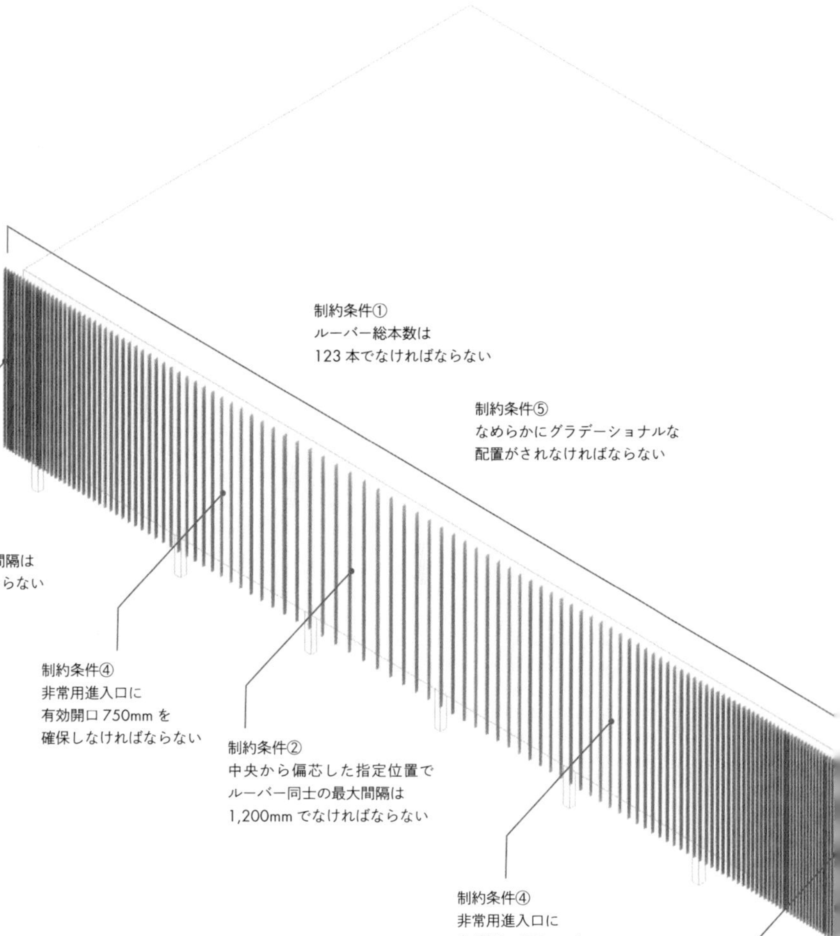

制約条件①
ルーバー総本数は
123本でなければならない

制約条件⑤
なめらかにグラデーショナルな
配置がされなければならない

制約条件③
ルーバー同士の最小間隔は
250mm でなければならない

制約条件④
非常用進入口に
有効開口 750mm を
確保しなければならない

制約条件②
中央から偏芯した指定位置で
ルーバー同士の最大間隔は
1,200mm でなければならない

制約条件④
非常用進入口に
有効開口 750mm を
確保しなければならない

制約条件③
ルーバー同士の
最小間隔は
250mm で
なければならない

ルーバー配置最適化計算

Louver arrangement optimization calculations

ルーバーの①総本数、②最大間隔、③最小間隔、④非常用進入口確保、⑤グラデーショナルな配置、これらの制約条件 [A] をすべて満たす配置間隔を繰り返し演算で最適化した [B]。

Louver pattern that meets all required conditions; ①total number, ②maximum spacing, ③minimum spacing, ④clearance for emergency entry points, and ⑤smooth interval gradation [A] was optimized through sequential operations [B].

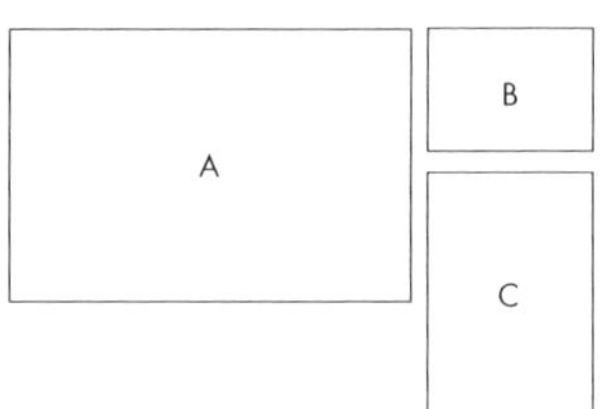

最適化シミュレーションUI
Optimization simulation UI

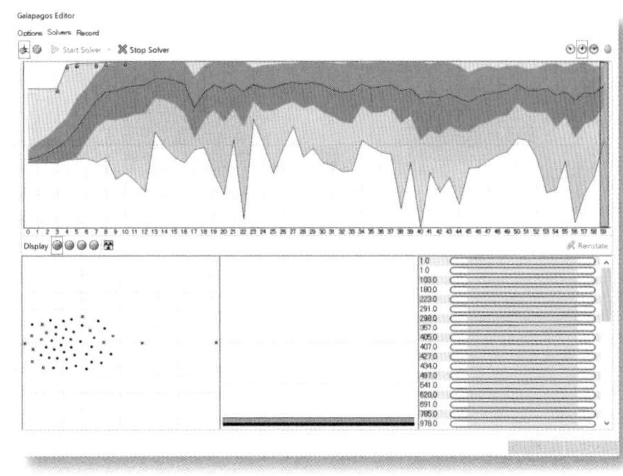

ルーバーモジュール
Louver module

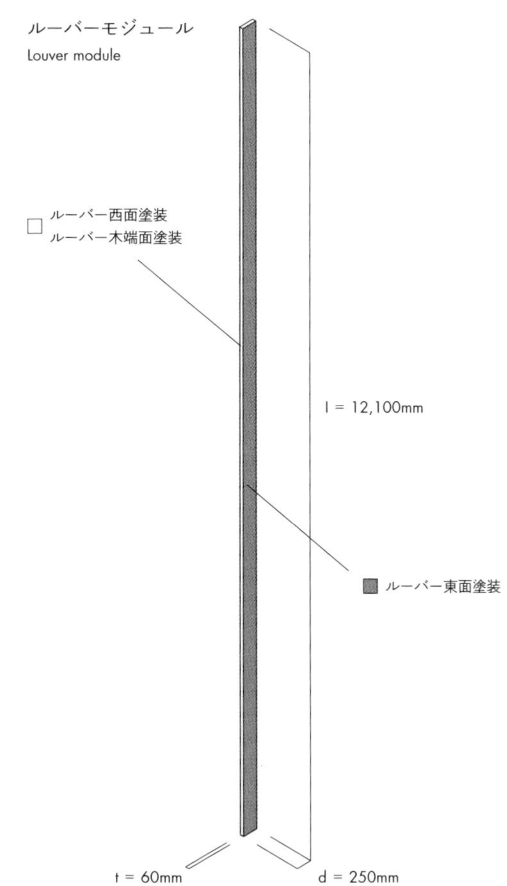

本数スタディ
Number studies

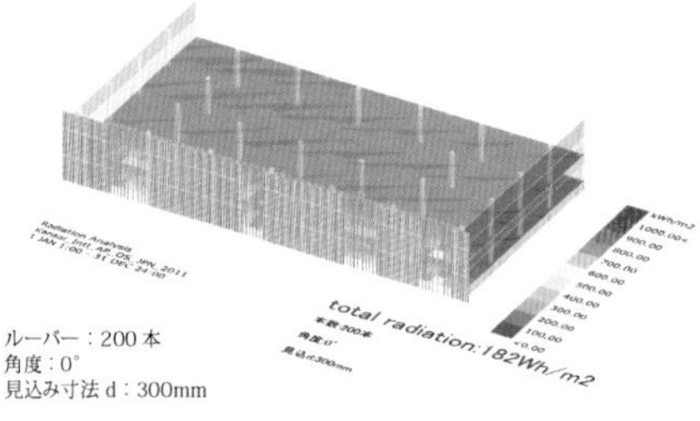

ルーバー：200本
角度：0°
見込み寸法 d：300mm

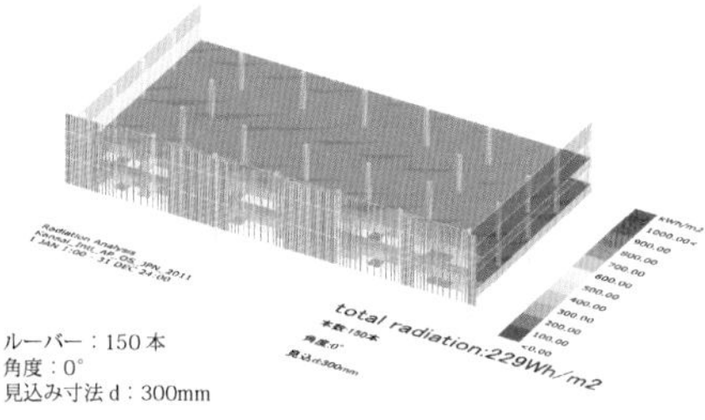

ルーバー：150本
角度：0°
見込み寸法 d：300mm

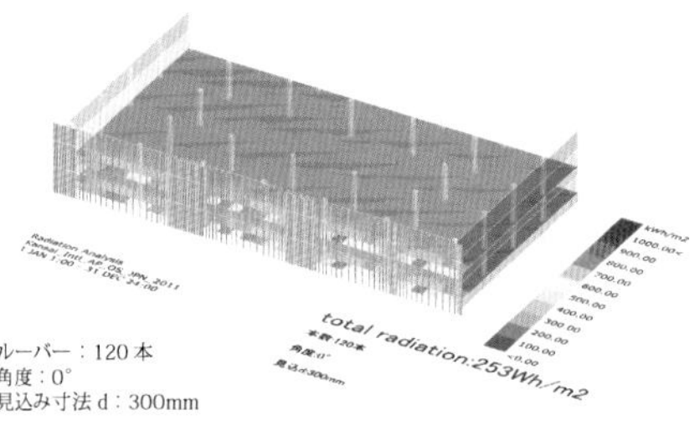

ルーバー：120本
角度：0°
見込み寸法 d：300mm

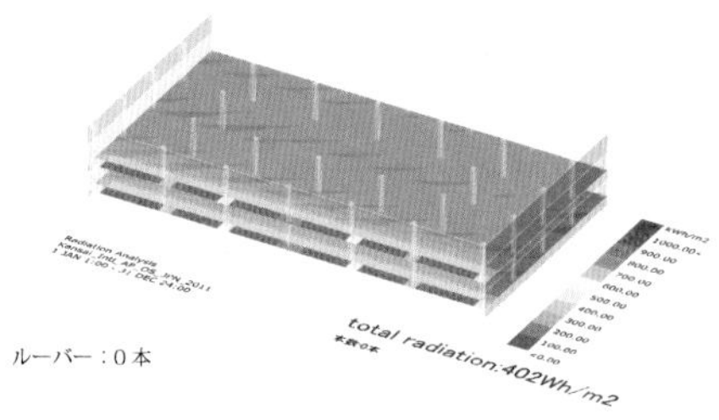

ルーバー：0本

（見込300mm、0°で）200本は0本の50%の日射量
（見込300mm、0°で）200本は120本の75%の日射量

見込み寸法スタディ
Depth dimension studies

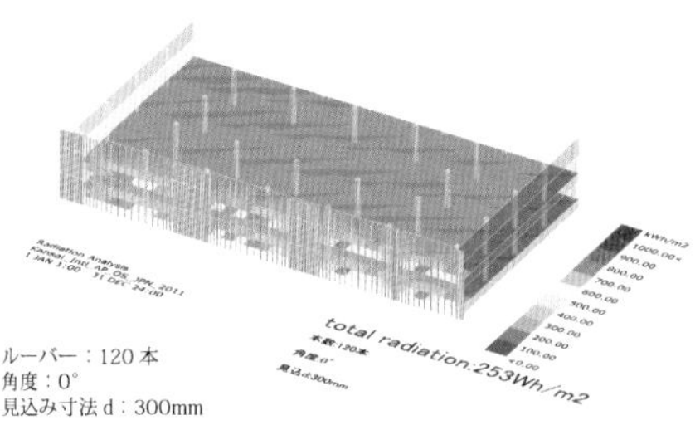

ルーバー：120本
角度：0°
見込み寸法 d：300mm

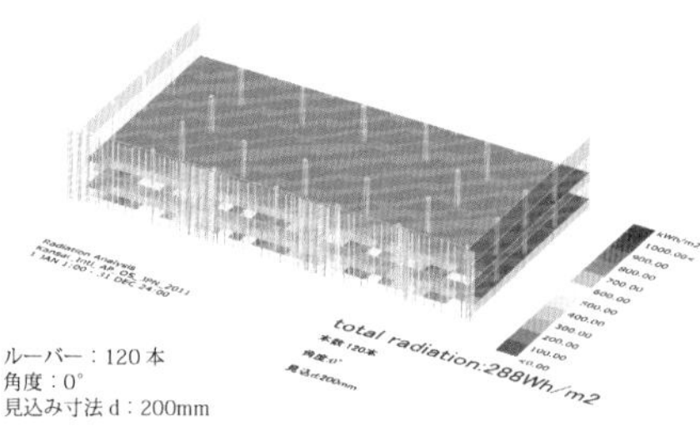

ルーバー：120本
角度：0°
見込み寸法 d：200mm

ルーバー日射遮蔽シミュレーション
Louver sunlight deflection simulations

検討されたルーバーの日射遮蔽性能シミュレーション。ルーバーに遮られた窓面に対する年間日射量を算出する。プロジェクトの初期段階においては大量の比較検討がなされた。

Simulations of the louvers' sunlight deflection performance. Annual solar radiation on the window surface behind the louvers was calculated for each pattern. Extensive comparative studies were made in the early stage of the project.

角度スタディ
Angle studies

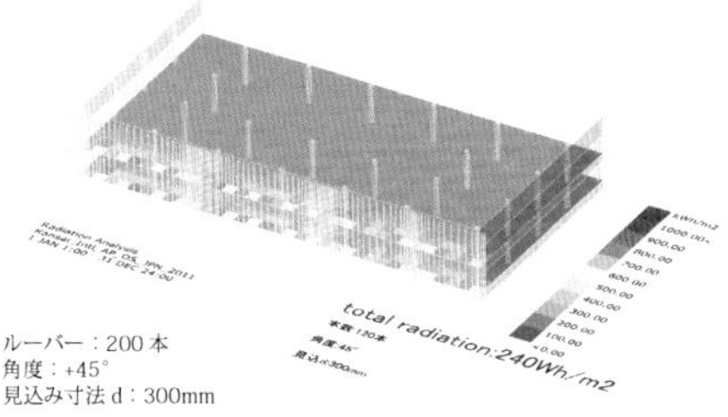

ルーバー：200本
角度：+45°
見込み寸法 d：300mm

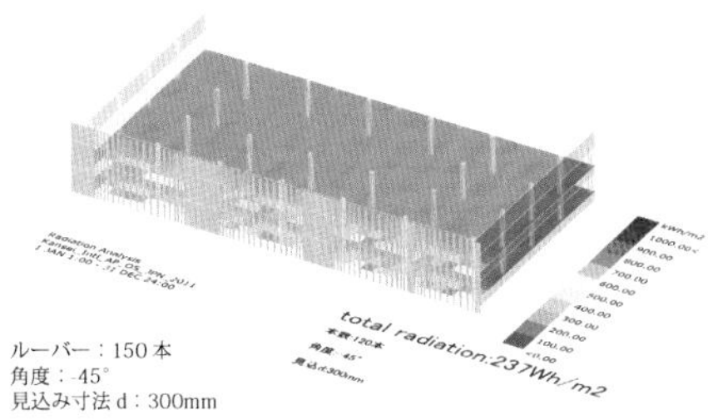

ルーバー：150本
角度：-45°
見込み寸法 d：300mm

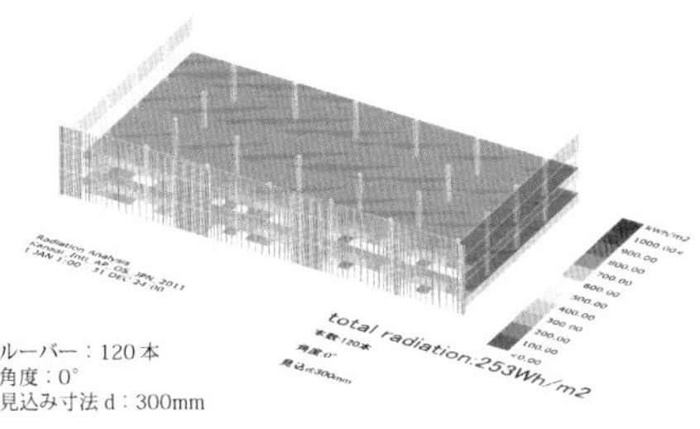

ルーバー：120本
角度：0°
見込み寸法 d：300mm

（見込 300mm、120本で）+45° or-45°は0°の95%の日射量
「朝の時間に強い角度」「昼の時間に強い角度」など要検討

見込み寸法スタディ＋本数スタディ
Depth dimension studies + Number studies

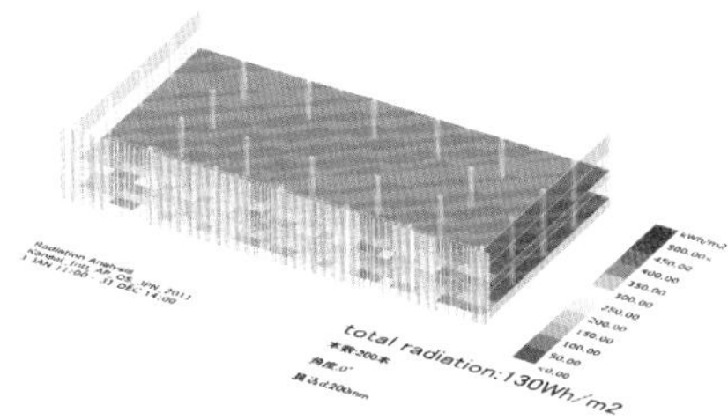

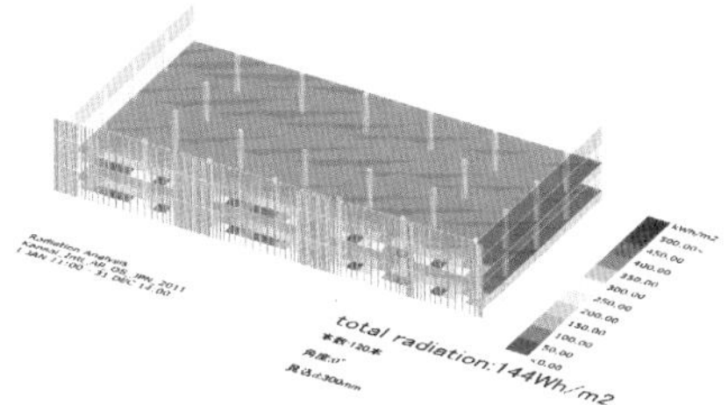

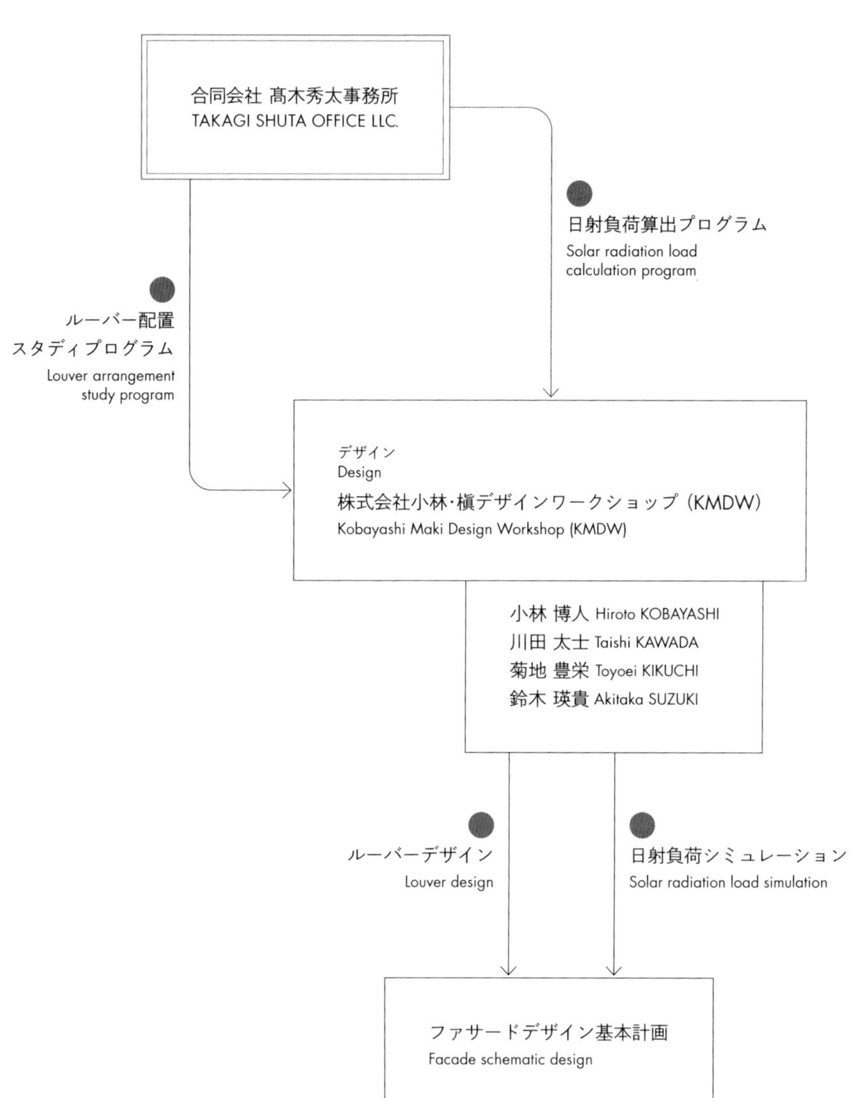

建築デザインは、建築設計事務所 株式会社小林・槇デザインワークショップ（KMDW）。高木秀太事務所はルーバーファサードデザインに特化し、デジタルサポートを行った。

Kobayashi Maki Design Workshop (KMDW) was in charge of architectural design. Takagi Shuta Office provided digital support specifically for the louver design of the facade.

プロジェクトID	180011
プロジェクト期間	2018.03–2021.03
クライアント	サンスター株式会社
デザイン	株式会社小林・槇デザインワークショップ（KMDW）
担当	小林 博人、川田 太士、菊地 豊栄、鈴木 瑛貴
プロジェクトマネージメント	髙木 秀太
メインプログラマー	髙木 秀太
アシスタントプログラマー	髙塚 悟、竹中 美穂、南 佑樹
ソフトウェア / 開発環境	Rhinoceros, Galapagos, Ladybug
プログラミング言語	Grasshopper, Python
キーワード	建築設計、最適化計算、 環境シミュレーション

Project ID	180011
Project term	2018.03–2021.03
Client	Sunstar Inc.
Design	Kobayashi Maki Design Workshop (KMDW)
Project team	Hiroto KOBAYASHI, Taishi KAWADA, Toyoei KIKUCHI, Akitaka SUZUKI
Project management	Shuta TAKAGI
Main programmer	Shuta TAKAGI
Assistant programmer	Satoru TAKATSUKA, Miho TAKENAKA, Yuki MINAMI
Software / SDE	Rhinoceros, Galapagos, Ladybug
Programming language	Grasshopper, Python
Keywords	Architectural design, Optimization calculation, Environmental simulation

3Dモデリングプログラムは Rhinoceros+Grasshopperを採用。ルーバー配置の最適化エンジンにはGalapagosを、日射量計算にはLadybugをそれぞれ接続した。

Rhinoceros and Grasshopper were used for 3D modeling. Galapagos and Ladybug were connected to them for the louver placement optimization engine and solar radiation calculation, respectively.

ヤギのいる庭

A GARDEN WITH A GOAT

クライアント / ディレクター / 設計　**佐倉 弘祐**
Client / Director / Design　Kosuke SAKURA

設計　**香川 翔勲**
Design　Shokun KAGAWA

長野県長野市の住宅と畑の計画プロジェクトである。「畑を地域に開放する」というユニークなコンセプトをもとに展開される。施主は信州大学 助教で都市計画学者の佐倉 弘祐氏。計画敷地は同氏の自邸でもある。計画は建築家の香川 翔勲氏。

髙木秀太事務所では畑部分の計画のシミュレーションを担当。計画全体における初期検討で主にサポートを遂行した。

A project for a residence and vegetable garden in Nagano City, Nagano Prefecture, based on a unique concept of "opening the garden to the community." The client was Kosuke Sakura, an assistant professor at Shinshu University and researcher of urban planning. The site had also been his home. Architectural design by Shokun Kagawa.

Takagi Shuta Office was in charge of simulating the planning of the vegetable garden, providing support particularly in the early phase of the planning.

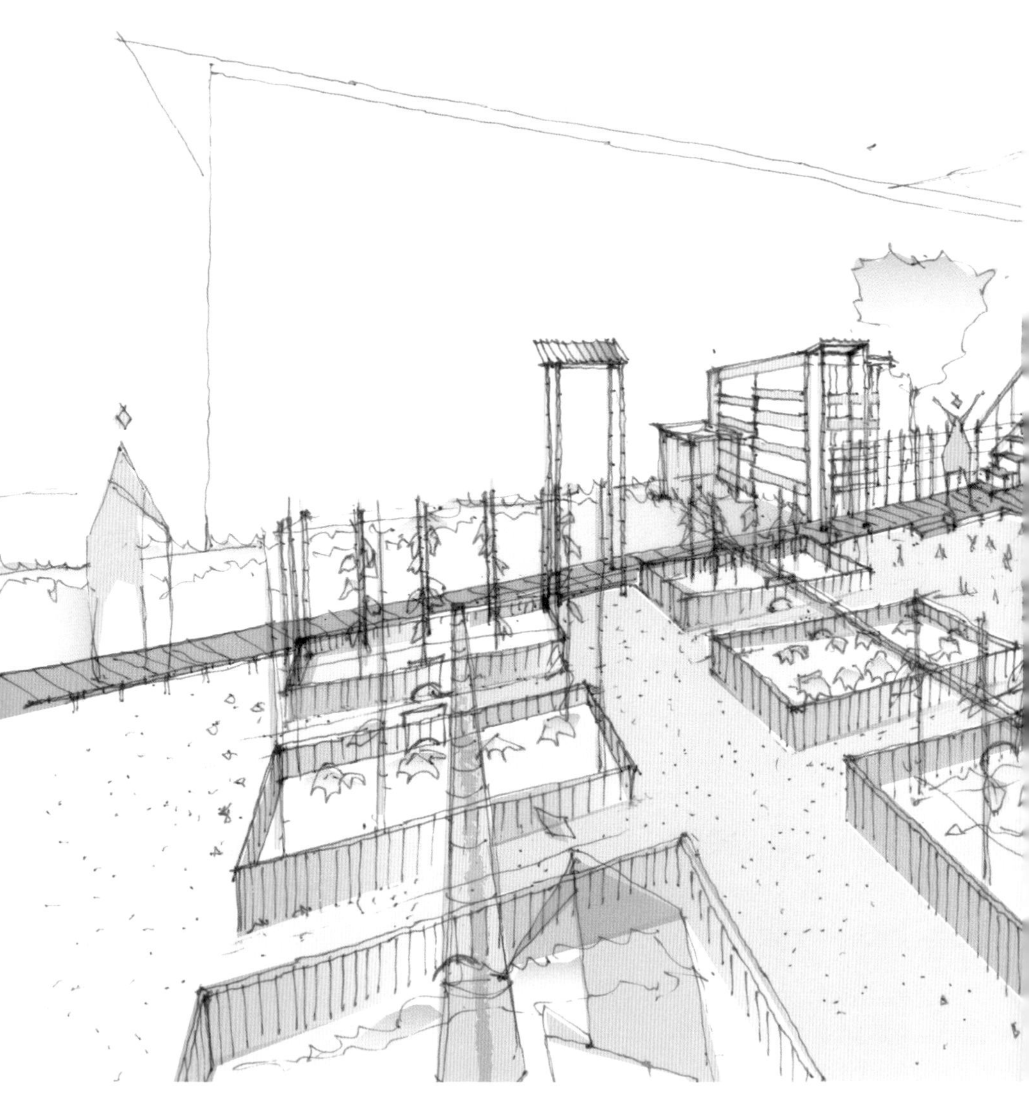

信州大学 佐倉弘祐研究室によるイメージパース。ヒトを引き込みやすい通路や屋根、そして、マスコットとしてのヤギ。ヤギは畑という小さな生態系のコントロールにも一役を買っている。

Perspective image by Sakura Laboratory at Shinshu University. Pathways and roofs help entice people in. The goats play a role as mascots, while also assisting in controlling the small ecosystem of the vegetable garden.

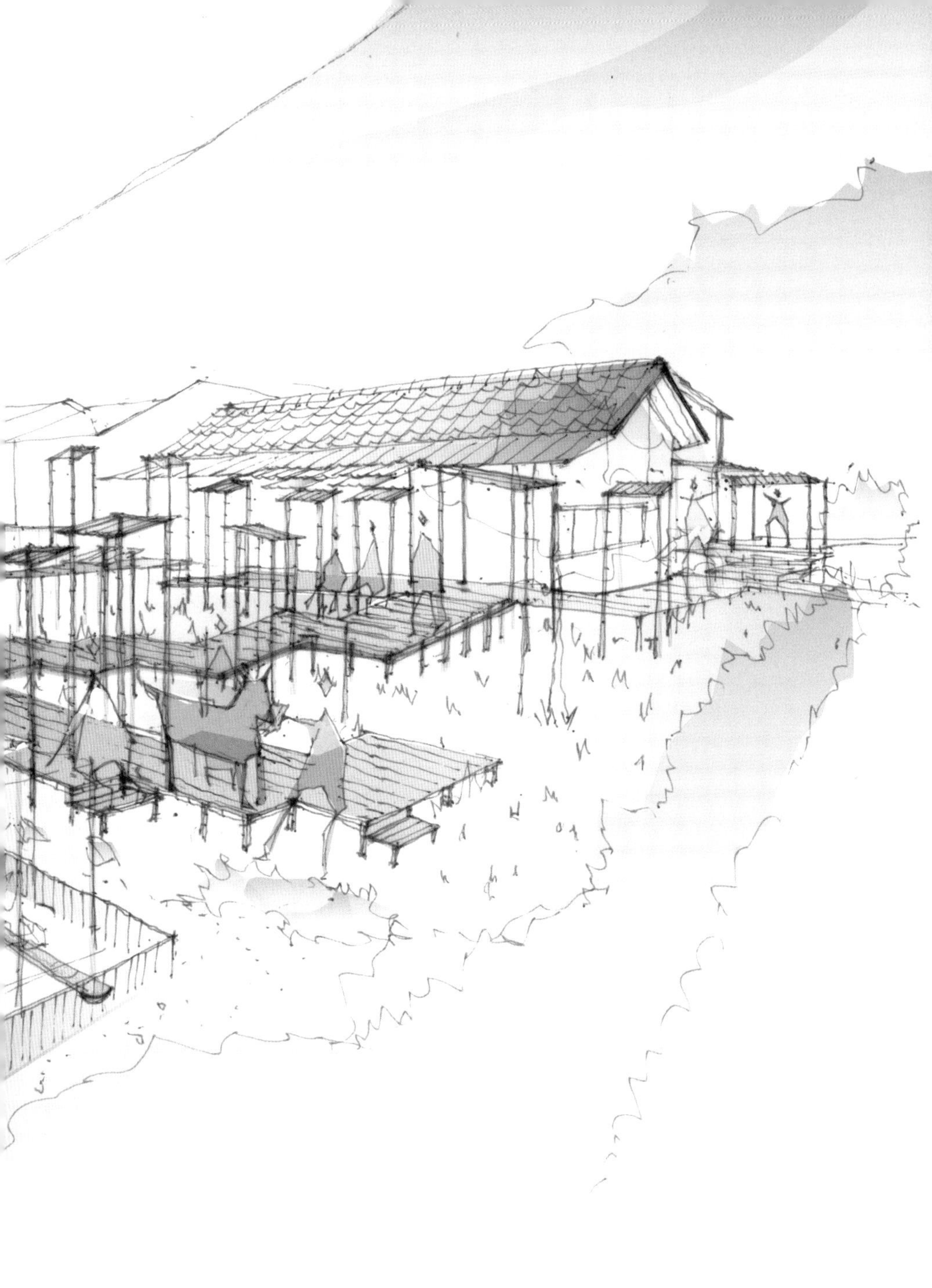

07_A GARDEN WITH A GOAT

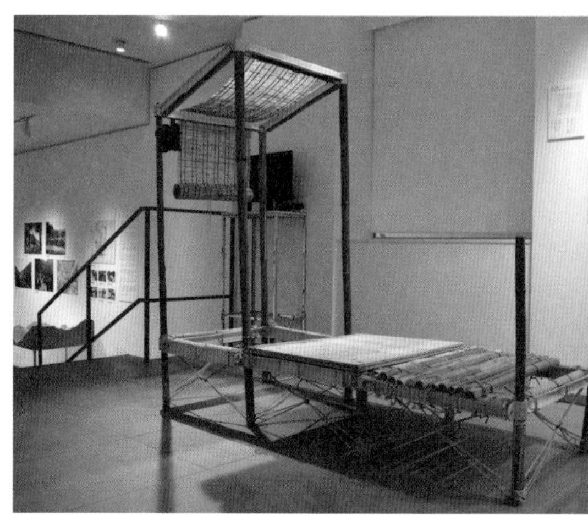

SD レビュー 2018 展示
SD Review 2018 exhibition

本計画は SD レビュー 2018 で入選し、展示が行われた。髙木秀太事務所は展示レイアウトの計画補助も担当。計画のモックアップ [A] や模型 [B][C] などが展示された [D]。会場は代官山ヒルサイドテラス。

The project was awarded and exhibited at SD Review 2018. Takagi Shuta Office was also responsible for aiding in the planning of its exhibition design. A mock-up [A] and models [B][C] were exhibited at Daikanyama Hillside Terrace [D].

A	B
D	C

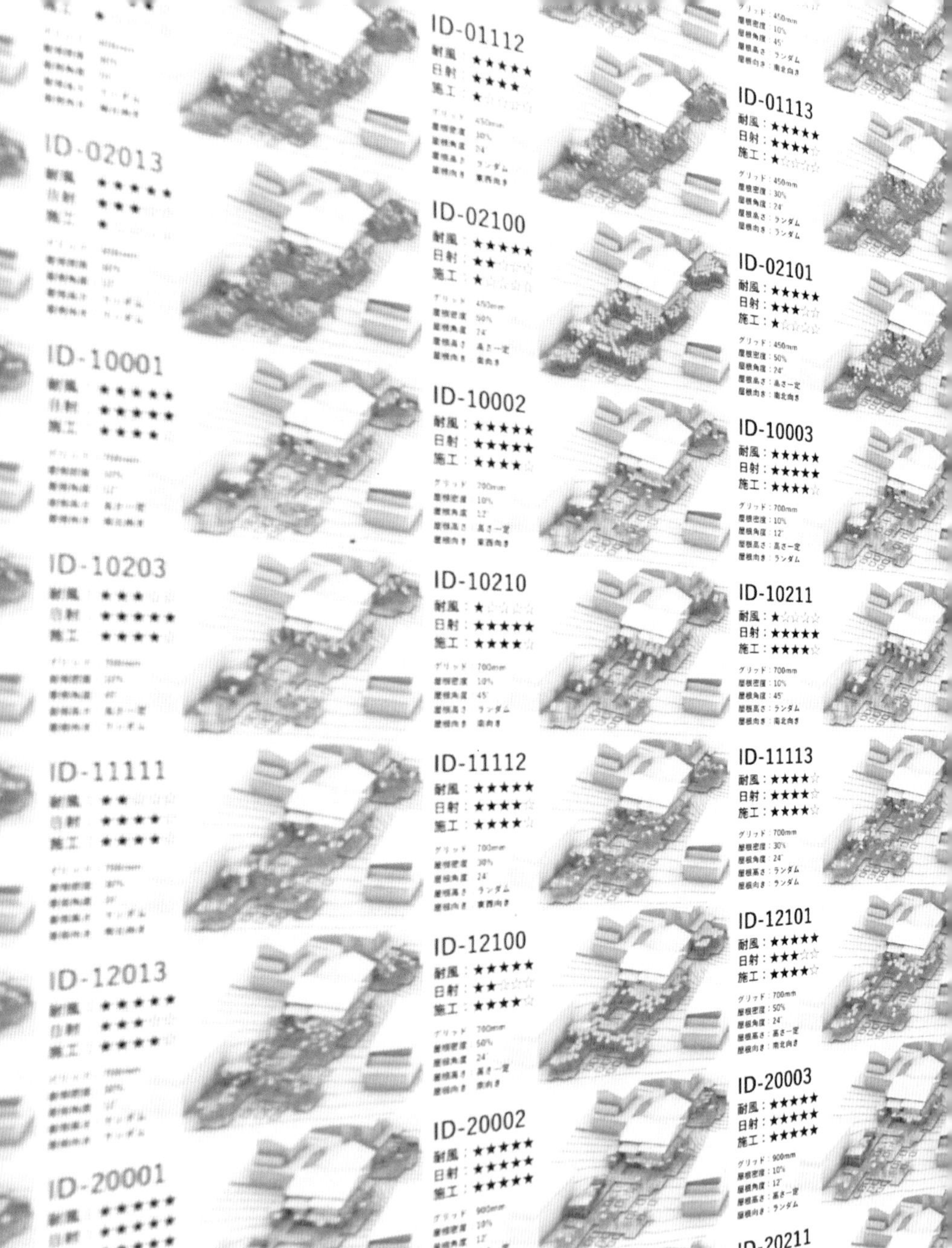

本プロジェクトでの初期検討用シミュレーター。通路幅や屋根の数・形状などをあらゆる可能性をしらみ潰しに生成し、都度 ①耐風 ②日射 ③施工コスト の評価を行った。プログラムによるスタディ数は数万件に及ぶ。

Initial studies of the simulator, in which every possibility regarding pathway widths, number and shape of the roofs, etc. were generated exhaustively. Each result was evaluated for ①wind resistance; ②solar radiation; and ③construction cost. Tens of thousands of studies were conducted in the program.

ID-00213
ID-01201
ID-02103
ID-10011
ID-10213
ID-11201
ID-12103
ID-20011
ID-20213
ID-01000
ID-01202
ID-02110
ID-10012
ID-11000
ID-11202
ID-12110
ID-20012
ID-21000
ID-21202
ID-01001
ID-01203
ID-02111
ID-10013
ID-11001
ID-11203
ID-12111
ID-20013
ID-21001
ID-21203

1. コンセプト
Concept

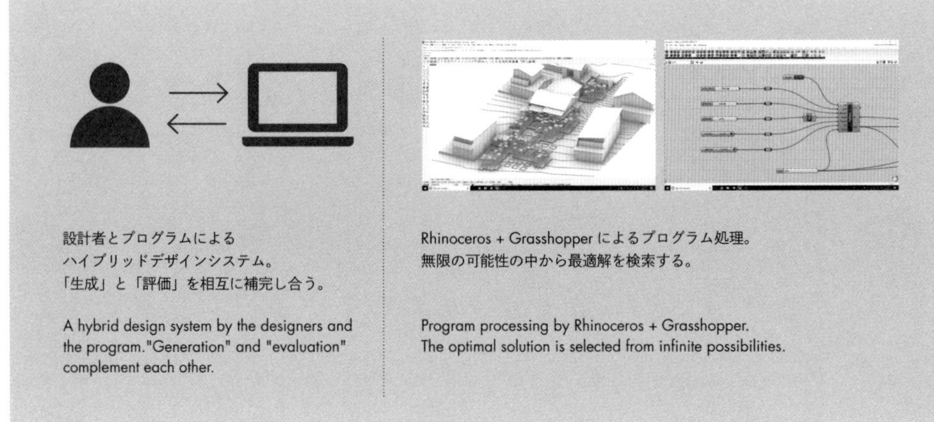

2. 生成と評価の手法
Generation and evaluation methods

役割 Role	生成 Generation	評価 Evaluation 意匠 Design	構造 Structure	法規 Regulation	環境 Environment	施工 Construction	総合 Overall
設計者 Designer	パラメーター制御 Parameter control	○					○
プログラム Program	造形アルゴリズム処理 Modeling algorithm processing		○		○	○	

シミュレーションアルゴリズム
Simulation algorithms

設計者とコンピューターがデザインスタディを協力し合うハイブリッドな設計手法 [1]。生成と評価を何万回と繰り返し [2][3]、配置計画の下敷きが決定された [4]。

Designers and computers collaborated in design studies in this hybrid design method [1]. By repeating tens of thousands of generations and evaluations [2][3], a draft for the architectural layout was determined [4].

3. プログラム評価の詳細
Details of program evaluation

A 構造評価
暴風時の柱の変形

Structural evaluation
Deformation of columns during a storm

★☆☆☆☆ : 0 ≦ X ≦ 0.2
★★☆☆☆ : 0.2 ≦ X ≦ 0.4
★★★☆☆ : 0.4 ≦ X ≦ 0.6
★★★★☆ : 0.6 ≦ X ≦ 0.8
★★★★★ : 0.8 ≦ X ≦ 1.0

※南北方向の風に対して、
変形が規定値を満たす柱の割合 X

B 環境評価
畑への年間平均日射量

Environmental evaluation
Average annual solar radiation to the vegetable garden

★☆☆☆☆ : 〜 3900h
★★☆☆☆ : 3,900 〜 4,000h
★★★☆☆ : 4,000 〜 4,100h
★★★★☆ : 4,100 〜 4,200h
★★★★★ : 4,200h 〜

※ Ladybug による日影解析

C 施工評価
施工時間

Construction evaluation
Construction duration

★☆☆☆☆ : 200h 〜
★★☆☆☆ : 150 〜 200h
★★★☆☆ : 100 〜 150h
★★★★☆ : 50 〜 100h
★★★★★ : 〜 50h

※ 5 人工で総施工時間を予測

4. 結果
Result

モジュールスタディの結果、

グリッドサイズ	750mm
屋根密度	30%
屋根角度	12%
屋根高さ	1,800-2,400mmの範囲
屋根向き	東西南北

を設計者の評価によって決定

As a result of the module study,

Grid size	750mm
Roof density	30%
Roof angle	12%
Roof height	Range of 1,800-2,400mm
Roof orientation	East, West, South, North

Determined by the designer's evaluation

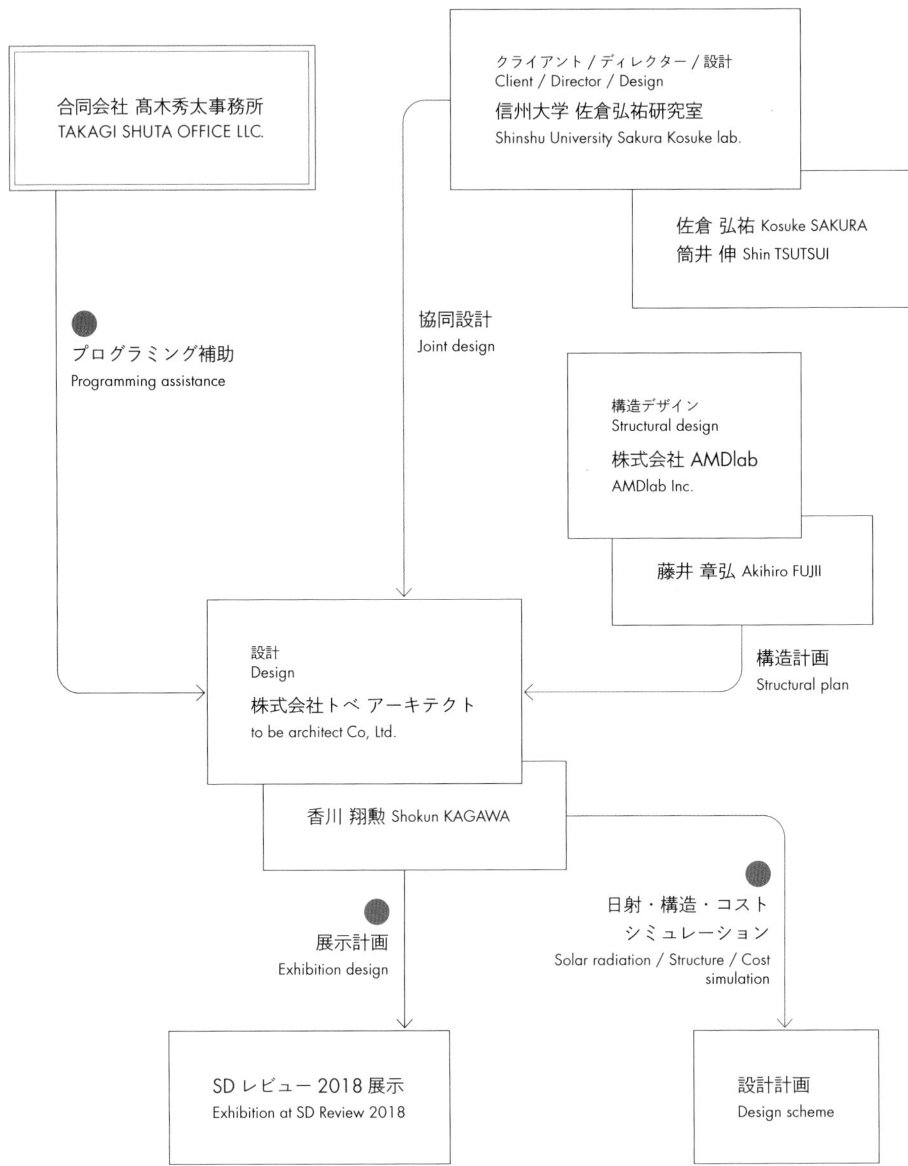

高木秀太事務所はプロジェクトにおいて日照負荷・構造計算・コスト算出の統合型シミュレーターの開発を担当。構造シミュレーション開発の協力は株式会社 AMDlab の藤井 章弘氏。

Takagi Shuta Office oversaw the development of integrated simulator for solar load, structural calculations, and cost calculations. Structural simulation development was conducted in cooperation with Akihiro Fujii of AMDlab.

プロジェクトID プロジェクト期間	170028 2017.12–2018.10
クライアント / ディレクター / 設計	佐倉 弘祐
設計	香川 翔勲（株式会社トベ アーキテクト） 筒井 伸（信州大学 佐倉弘祐研究室）
構造デザイン	藤井 章弘（株式会社 AMDlab）
プロジェクトマネージメント メインプログラマー アシスタントプログラマー	髙木 秀太 髙木 秀太、髙塚 悟 南 佑樹、布井 翔一郎、飛田 剛太
ソフトウェア / 開発環境 プログラミング言語 キーワード	Rhinoceros, Ladybug, Adobe Illustrator Grasshopper, Python 建築設計、展示計画、多目的最適化計算、 環境シミュレーション

Project ID Project term	170028 2017.12–2018.10
Client / Director	Kosuke SAKURA
Design	Shokun KAGAWA (to be architect Co, Ltd.) Shin TSUTSUI (Shinshu University Sakura Kosuke lab.)
Structural design	Akihiro FUJII (AMDlab Inc.)
Project management Main programmer Assistant programmer	Shuta TAKAGI Shuta TAKAGI, Satoru TAKATSUKA Yuki MINAMI, Shoichiro NUNOI, Gota HIDA
Software / SDE Programming language Keywords	Rhinoceros, Ladybug, Adobe Illustrator Grasshopper, Python Architectural design, Exhibition, Multipurpose optimization, Environmental simulation

日射シミュレーションはGrasshopperプラグインLadybugで開発。「畑の計画」という性質上、日射シミュレーションは本プロジェクトにおいて必須であった。

Solar radiation simulations were developed with Grasshopper plug-in Ladybug. These simulations were crucial to this project, due to its nature of "planning for a vegetable garden."

慶應義塾大学 SFC ORF 2017

KEIO UNIVERSITY SFC ORF 2017

クライアント　慶應義塾大学 SFC 研究所
Client　Keio Research Institute at SFC

設計　慶應義塾大学 SFC 鳴川肇研究室
Design　Keio Research Institute at SFC Hajime Narukawa Laboratory

慶應義塾大学 SFC のイベント Open Research Forum (ORF) 2017 の会場構成プロジェクトである。本イベントは産官学連携による研究成果の発表の場として毎年企画される。同大学 准教授 鳴川 肇氏のマスタープランニングのもと、髙木秀太事務所は会場レイアウト計画をデジタルサポートした。

A venue design project for Open Research Forum (ORF) event in 2017 at Keio University SFC. This annual event is an occasion to present research results of industry-academia-government collaboration. Under the masterplan by Hajime Narukawa, associate professor at the university, Takagi Shuta Office provided digital support for the venue design.

鳴川 肇氏デザインの「イーゼル」と呼ばれる展示用什器を各出展者に割り当て、会場を構成した。会場は東京ミッドタウン ホール＆カンファレンス。

Exhibition furniture called "easels" designed by Hajime Narukawa were assigned to each exhibitor to comprise the venue, which was held at Tokyo Midtown Hall & Conference.

A56
筧康明研究室
YASUAKI KAKEHI LAB.
筧康明
YASUAKI KAKEHI
A36
Abstract
Implementation
ORF

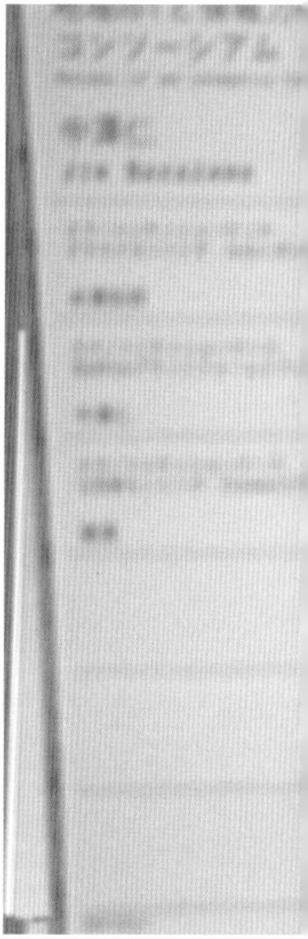

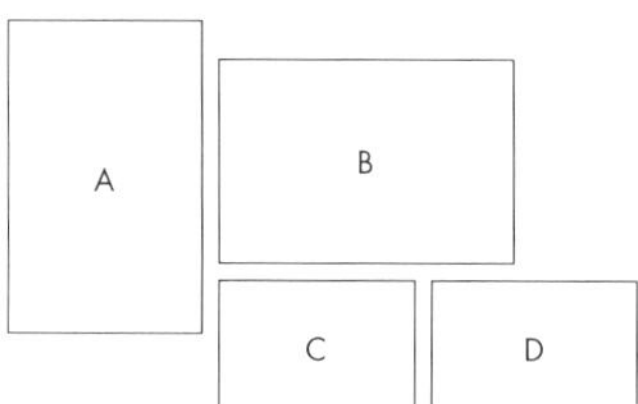

無機質な会場に「イーゼル」の木質マテリアルが映える。規則正しくも離散的な展示ができるようにレイアウトされた [A][B]。サインデザイン・構成も髙木秀太事務所の担当 [C][D]。

The wood texture of "easels" stand out inside the inanimate venue space, and their layout creates a consistent yet discrete exhibition [A][B]. Takagi Shuta Office was also in charge of signage design and configuration [C][D].

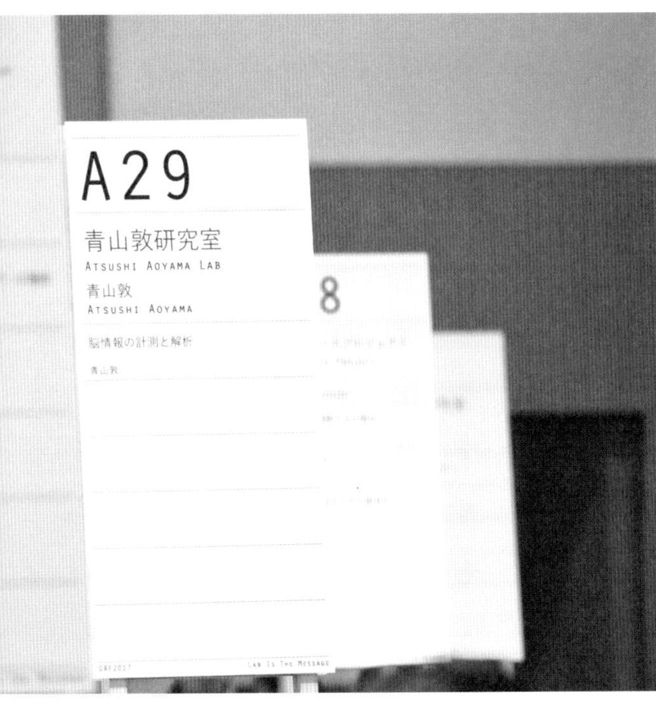
A29
青山敦研究室
ATSUSHI AOYAMA LAB
青山敦
ATSUSHI AOYAMA
脳情報の計測と解析
青山敦
ORF2017
LAB IS THE MESSAGE

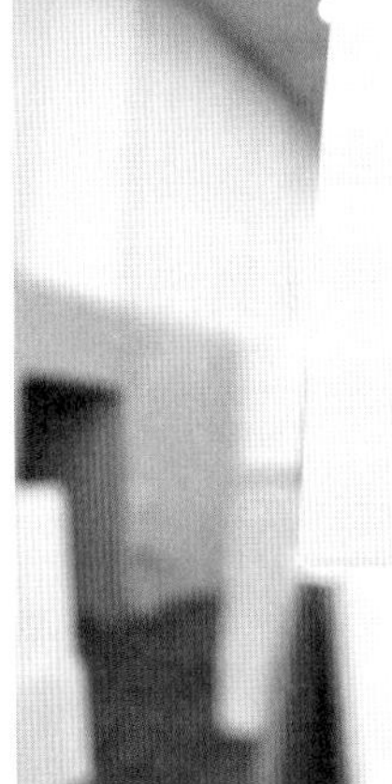

サインレイアウトプログラム
Signage layout program

サインデザインはGrasshopperによるパラメトリックスタディにより決定した。フォントサイズや文字間隔などをパラメーター化することによって100枚以上のサインを一括して管理する体制とした。

Signage design was determined through parametric studies in Grasshopper. By parametrizing font sizes and letter spacing, more than 100 signage displays could be managed at once.

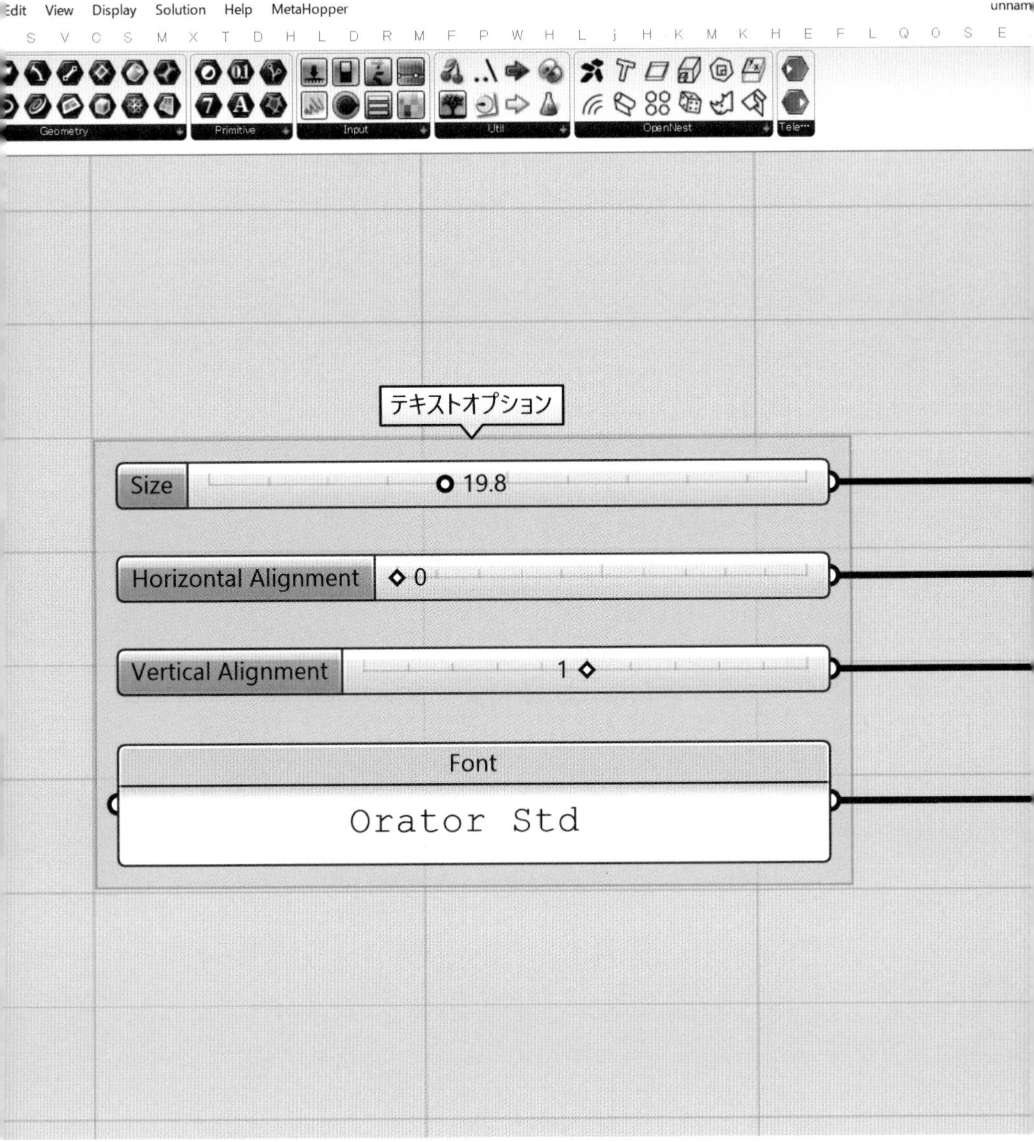
Edit View Display Solution Help MetaHopper
Geometry
Primitive
Input
Util
OpenNest
テキストオプション
Size
19.8
Horizontal Alignment
0
Vertical Alignment
1
Font
Orator Std

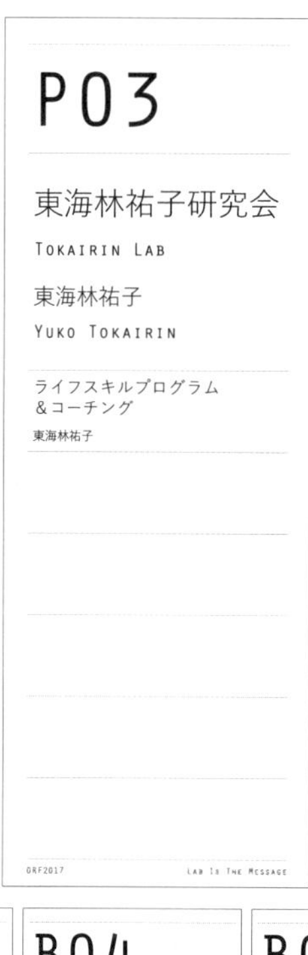

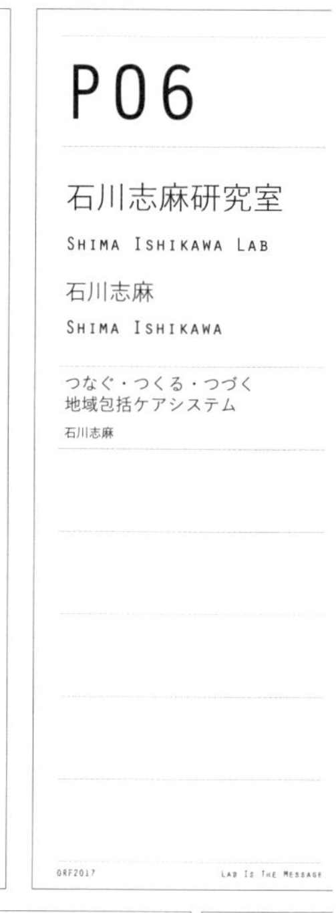

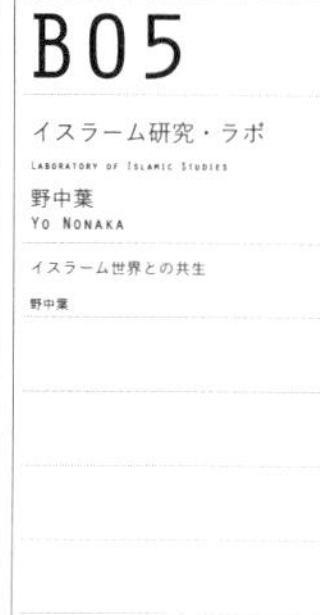

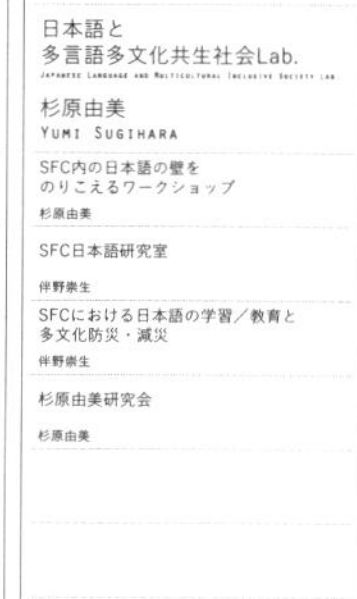

入稿サインデータ
Signage draft data

サインデザインの決定稿。ポスターで使用されたフォント、キーカラーの踏襲などデザインコントロールに工夫がなされた。各種テキストも徹底されたデジタルデータによって管理されたので誤植の報告はゼロであった。

Final version of the signage design. Design was worked out and controlled in terms of fonts and accompanying key colors. Since all text data were managed digitally, there were no typographical errors.

07
護100年
業委員会
F KEIO NURSING
IVERSARY
子
KOMATSU
どる慶應看護100年
LAB IS THE MESSAGE

P08
野中葉研究会
NONAKA SEMINAR
野中葉
YO NONAKA
現代東南アジア研究
横井伶衣菜
東南アジア共生プロジェクト
真貝佳夏子
マレー・インドネシア語研究室
柿沼真奈
ORF2017
LAB IS THE MESSAGE

P09
山岸学生プロジェクト
支援制度
YAMAGISHI STUDENT PROJECT
SUPPORT PROGRAM
高汐一紀
KAZUNORI TAKASHIO
山岸学生プロジェクト支援制度
高汐一紀
ORF2017
LAB IS THE MESSAGE
P10
慶應義塾湘南藤沢
中等部・高等部
KEIO SHONAN FUJISAWA JUNIOR
AND SENIOR HIGH SCHOOL
会田一雄
KAZUO AIDA
生徒の作品
会田一雄
ORF2017
LAB IS THE MESSAGE

P1
SFCス
開発コ
SMART LIV
DEVELOPER
池田靖
YASUSH
SFCスマ
コンソー
池田靖史
ORF2017

B10
保史生研究会
MPO LAB
保史生
IO SHIMPO
バー法プロジェクト
LAB IS THE MESSAGE

B11
宮代康丈研究室
MIYASHIRO LAB
宮代康丈
YASUTAKE MIYASHIRO
政治哲学・倫理学
宮代康丈
ORF2017
LAB IS THE MESSAGE
B12
ことばとメディア
-藁谷郁美研究会-
藁谷郁美
IKUMI WARAGAI
メディアと宗教言語
-日独米 3.11 報道比較-
ゲームのローカライゼーション:
日本発デジタルゲームの発信・受容分析
ステファン・ブリュックナー
ドイツ語教材開発研究プロジェクト
藁谷郁美
ORF2017
LAB IS THE MESSAGE

B13
SFCコタン
～アイヌ語と口承文芸～
藤田護
MAMORU FUJITA
SFCコタン
～アイヌ語と口承文学を通じて～
藤田護
ORF2017
LAB IS THE MESSAGE

B14
働き方改革
より働きやすい職場へ
千谷真美子
MAMIKO CHIYA
フレックスタイム制
好きな時間に働ける職場へ
ORF2017
LAB IS THE MESSAGE

B15
鈴木寛研究会
SUZUKAN LAB
鈴木寛
KAN SUZUKI
情報社会における
ソーシャル・プロデュース
鈴木寛
ORF2017
LAB IS THE MESSAGE

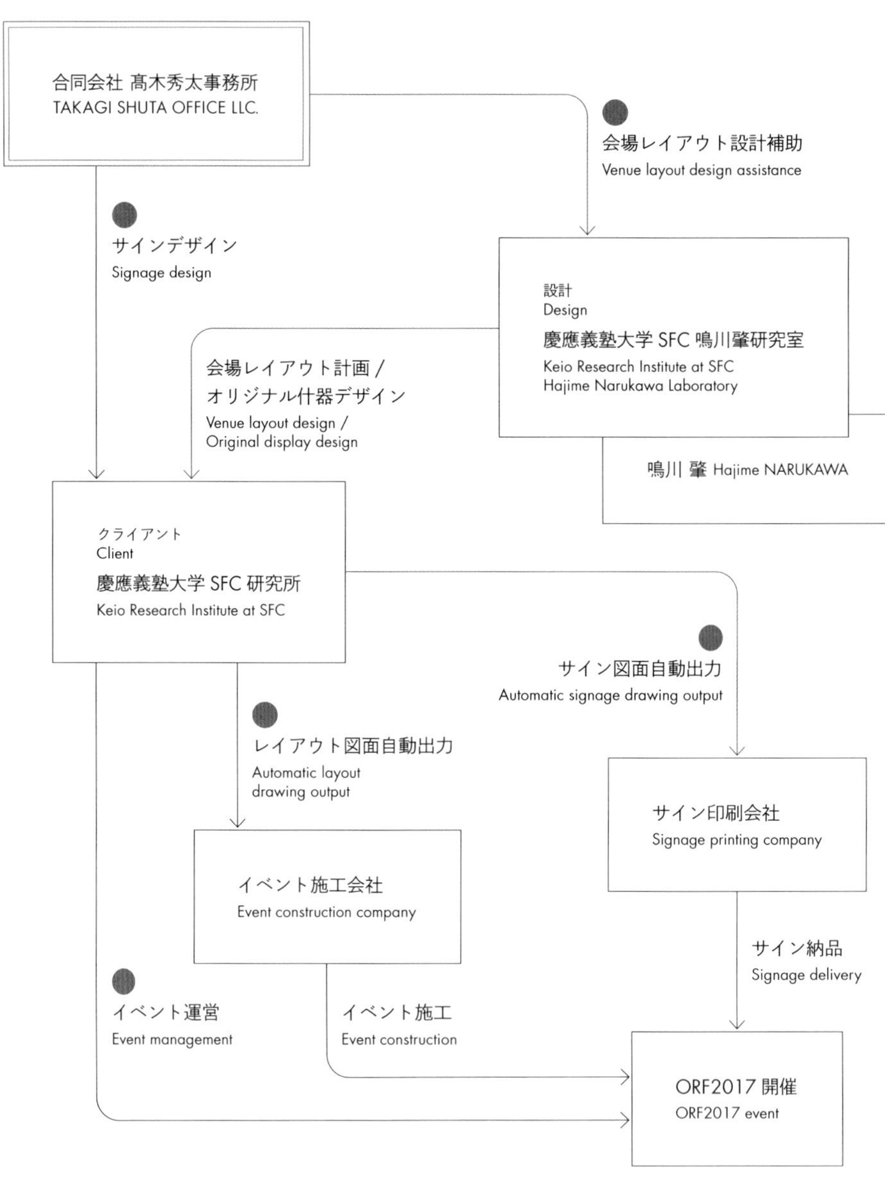

髙木秀太事務所の主なミッションは鳴川 肇氏と施工会社、各種制作会社との橋渡しである。同氏のアイデア実現のためにデジタルツールを駆使し計画をサポートした。イベントの主催は慶應義塾大学 SFC 研究所。

The key mission of Takagi Shuta Office was to be a bridge between Hajime Narukawa, fabricators, and various production companies. To bring Mr. Narukawa's ideas into fruition, we made full use of digital tools. The event was hosted by Keio Research Institute at SFC.

プロジェクト ID プロジェクト期間	170011 2017.04–2017.11
クライアント	慶應義塾大学 SFC 研究所
設計	鳴川 肇 慶應義塾大学 SFC 鳴川肇研究室
プロジェクトマネージメント メインプログラマー アシスタントプログラマー	髙木 秀太、髙塚 悟 髙木 秀太、髙塚 悟 菊池 毅
ソフトウェア / 開発環境 プログラミング言語 キーワード	Rhinoceros, Adobe Illustrator, Excel Grasshopper, Python, JavaScript 展示計画、サインデザイン、図面自動出力

Project ID Project term	170011 2017.04–2017.11
Client	Keio Research Institute at SFC
Design	Hajime NARUKAWA Keio Research Institute at SFC Hajime Narukawa Laboratory
Project management Main programmer Assistant programmer	Shuta TAKAGI, Satoru TAKATSUKA Shuta TAKAGI, Satoru TAKATSUKA Tsuyoshi KIKUCHI
Software / SDE Programming language Keywords	Rhinoceros, Adobe Illustrator, Excel Grasshopper, Python, JavaScript Exhibition planning, Signage design, Automatic drawing output

　サインデザインの納入は、Adobe Illustrator ファイルでの指定があった。デザインの最終出力には JavaScript プログラミングによる自動データ変換・自動出力がなされた。

For the delivery of signage design, the specified file format was Adobe Illustrator. The final data of the design was automatically converted and output using JavaScript programming.

東京大学 T-ADS まちめぐりアプリケーション

THE UNIVERSITY OF TOKYO T-ADS STREET WALKING APPLICATION

09

クライアント / ディレクター　東京大学 T-ADS Design Think Tank
Client / Director　T-ADS Design Think Tank, the University of Tokyo

（東京大学・NTT 都市開発株式会社・株式会社新建築社共同研究「都市空間生態学」研究 2017 ～ 2019 にて）

東京大学 T-ADS Design Think Tank（DTT）による社会実験のためのアプリケーション開発である。都市の隠れた魅力を歩きながら探索するためのタブレット用地図アプリ開発を髙木秀太事務所で担当した。シェアサイクルを用いた、まちめぐりワークショップ「ツギ__ツギ」（2017 年、2018年）で運用され、参加者の行動履歴や散策経路が記録された。

Application development for a social experiment by T-ADS Design Think Tank (DTT) at the University of Tokyo. Takagi Shuta Office was in charge of the map application development for tablet computers to explore the hidden charms of the city through walking. It was applied in shared-bike city exploration workshop "Tsugi_Tsugi" (2017, 2018), in which participants' activities and walking routes were recorded.

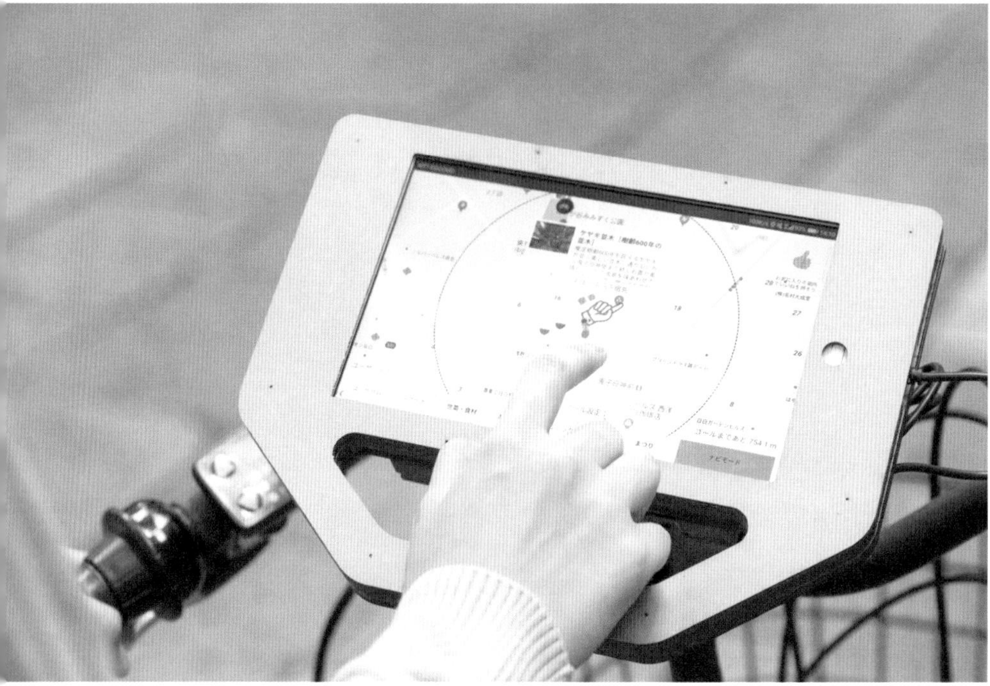

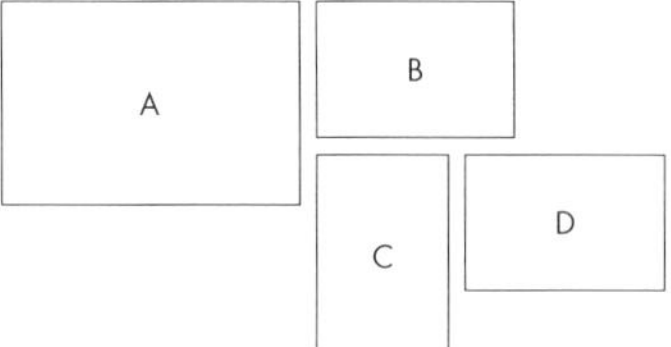

2017年東京都台東区 三筋・小島・鳥越、2018年 豊島区 東池袋でまちめぐりのワークショップが企画され、シェアサイクルと地図アプリケーションを連動させた社会実験が企画された [A]-[D]。

2017 in Misuji, Kojima, and Torigoe, Taito-ku; 2018 in Higashi-Ikebukuro, Toshima-ku. City exploration workshops were organized, in which social experimentation linking shared bicycles and map applications were planned [A]-[D].

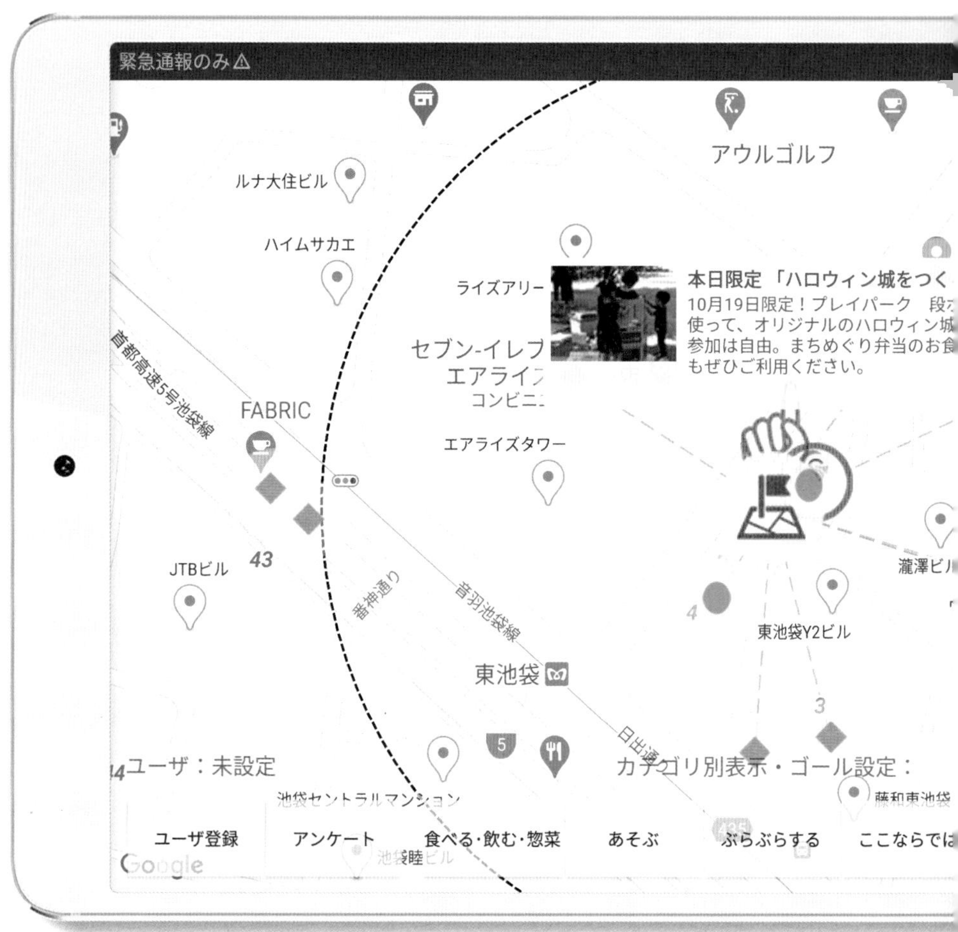

アプリ上でゴール地点は設定するが、経路は提示しない。ゴール方向のみ示し、自由な散策を促すインターフェースが求められた [A]。まちのスポットを 5 つのジャンルにカテゴライズし、マッピングした [B]-[F]。

While a target point could be set on the map, the route was purposely not shown, so as to encourage free strolls via its interface [A]. City sights were categorized into five genres and mapped [B]-[F].

A	B
	C
	D
	E
	F

97% 15:39
お気に入りの場所
でいいねを押そう
4丁目
30
ほいっぽ東池袋
17
ディクオーレ
ゴールまであと 0.0 m
ナビモード
都電荒川線

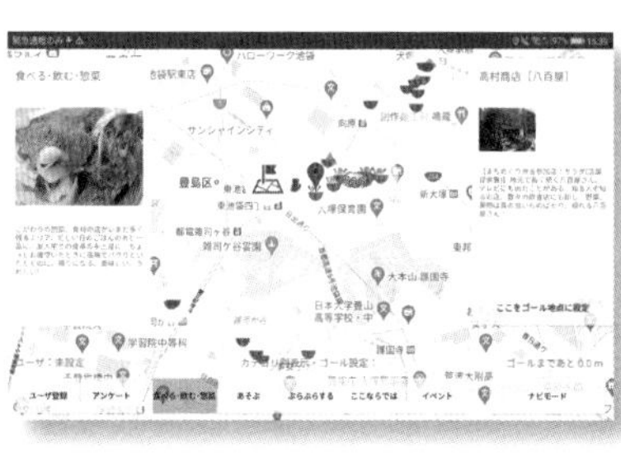

開発環境

Development environment

Android タブレットでの運用を想定。プログラム開発言語はJava、開発環境はAndroid Studioを採用した。地図 API は Google マップを用い、タブレットの各種センサーとも対応させた。

Operation on Android tablet was presumed. Java was selected as the program development language and Android Studio as the development environment. Map API uses Google Maps to support various sensors on tablets.

takagishuta 〉 maps 〉 MapsActivity   app   Pixel_3a_API_30_x86

psActivity.java

```
//マーカーのタップ設定
mMap.setOnMarkerClickListener((marker) → {
        return true;
});

mMap.setOnMapClickListener((tapLocation) → {

        showMessage("ゴール設定をしました。ナビモードに戻ります。");

        button2.setBackgroundColor(Color.argb( alpha: 80, red: 255, green: 0, blue: 0));
        //button1.setBackgroundColor(Color.argb(180,255,255,255));

        buttonFav.setVisibility(View.VISIBLE);
        textFav.setVisibility(View.VISIBLE);

        //tapされた位置の緯度経度をゴール地点に
        goal.change(tapLocation.latitude, tapLocation.longitude, myLocation);

        //ゴール地点のグローバル変数保存
        globalApp.setlatG(tapLocation.latitude);
        globalApp.setlngG(tapLocation.longitude);

        //位置情報の送信(Amazon)
        if(sendGPS_G == true) {
            runnable = (Runnable) () → {
                    //Goal情報の送信
                    long time = System.currentTimeMillis();
                    GoalSender gs = new GoalSender();
                    gs.setProject("-");
                    gs.setId(String.valueOf(2147483647 - time / 1000).concat("-").concat(serialI
                    gs.setDev_id(serialId);
                    gs.setMyLat(myLocation.latitude);
                    gs.setMyLng(myLocation.longitude);
                    gs.setGoalLat(goal.pos.latitude);
                    gs.setGoalLng(goal.pos.longitude);
                    gs.setTimestamp(time);
                    mapper.save(gs);
            };
            Thread myThread = new Thread(runnable);
            myThread.start();
        }

        for (int i = 0; i < spots.length; i++) {
            spots[i].red.setVisible(false);
            spots[i].white.setVisible(true);
            spots[i].marker.setVisible(true);
```

GPS データ　1 回 / 2 秒
GPS data once / 2 seconds

アンドロイド アプリ
Android app

- ナビモード
  Navigation mode
- ゴール地点設定モード
  Goal point setting mode
- アンケートモード
  Questionnaire mode
- ユーザー登録モード
  User registration mode

アマゾンウェブサービス
DynamoDB
Amazon Web Services DynamoDB

- 位置座標データ
  Location coordinate data

- 時刻データ
  Time data

- ユーザー情報
  User information

システムフロー
System flow

モバイルネットワークを通じて２秒に１回のペースでクラウドデータベースに位置情報などを記録。データベースはアマゾンウェブサービスのDynamoDB を採用した。

Through the mobile network, location information was recorded every 2 seconds on the cloud database. The database service used was DynamoDB of Amazon Web Services.

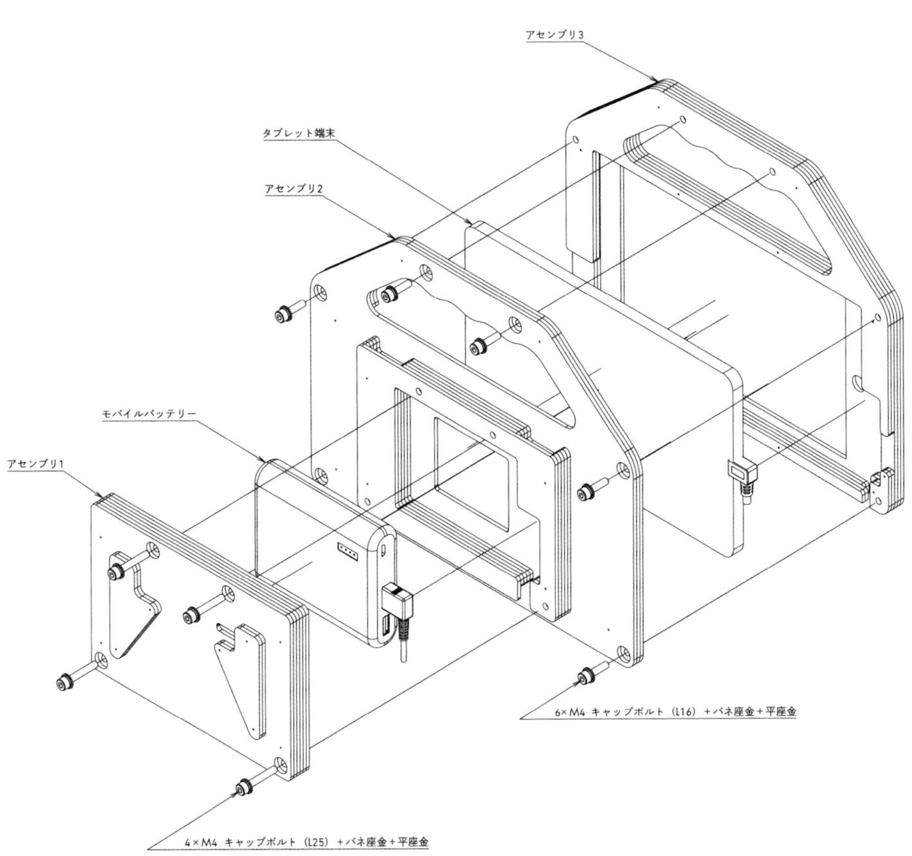

タブレットケース

Tablet carrying case

タブレットを携帯するためのケース。レーザー加工されたMDFの積層構造によって構成された。バッテリーを同梱する仕様も求められた。株式会社ノメナとのコラボレーション。

The carrying case for the tablet was composed of laminated layers of laser-cut MDF with additional space to encase a mobile battery. Produced in collaboration with nomena inc.

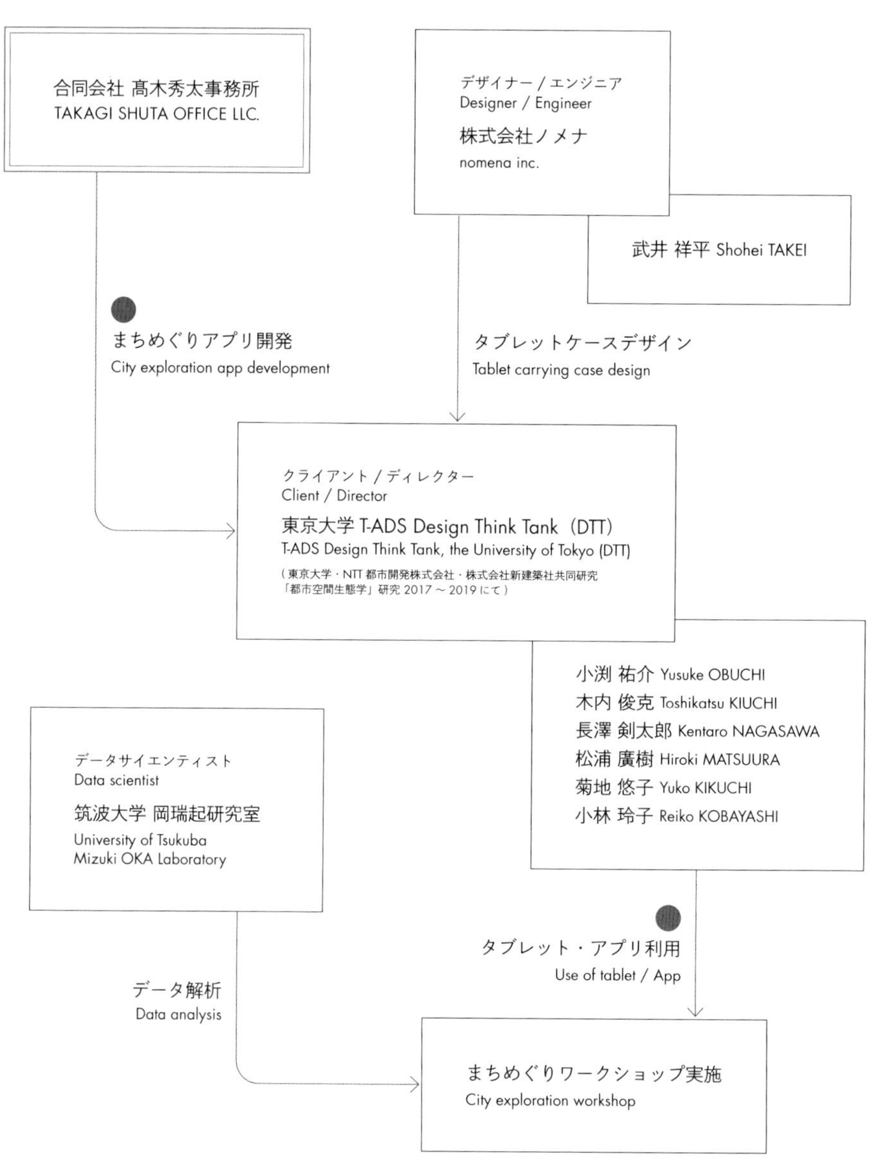

東京大学 T-ADS (Advanced Design Studies) 内で各種研究を都市デザインへの応用に取り組むグループ Design Think Tank(DTT) の企画。アプリのコンセプト発案はプロジェクトリーダー・木内 俊克氏。

Design Think Tank (DTT), a group engaged in various research projects to urban design within T-ADS (Advanced Design Studies) at the University of Tokyo, was planned. Concept of the application originated from Toshikatsu Kiuchi, the project leader.

プロジェクト ID	180041
プロジェクト期間	2017.04–2019.10
クライアント / ディレクター	東京大学 T-ADS Design Think Tank (DTT) （東京大学・NTT 都市開発株式会社・株式会社新建築社共同研究「都市空間生態学」研究 2017〜2019 にて）
担当	小渕 祐介、木内 俊克、長澤 剣太郎、 松浦 廣樹、菊地 悠子、小林 玲子
共同研究ディレクター	隈 研吾、小渕 祐介（東京大学） 楠本 正幸、篠原 宏年（エヌ・ティ・ティ都市開発株式会社） 吉田 信之、四方 裕（株式会社新建築社）
プロジェクトマネージメント	髙木 秀太
メインプログラマー	髙木 秀太、髙塚 悟
アシスタントスタッフ	永井 宏
ソフトウェア / 開発環境	Android Studio, Amazon DynamoDB
プログラミング言語	Java
キーワード	アプリケーション開発、ワークショップ、 デジタルファブリケーション

Project ID	180041
Project term	2017.04–2019.10
Client / Director	T-ADS Design Think Tank, the University of Tokyo (DTT)
Project team	Yusuke OBUCHI, Toshikatsu KIUCHI, Kentaro NAGASAWA, Hiroki MATSUURA, Yuko KIKUCHI, Reiko KOBAYASHI
Co-developed director	Kengo KUMA, Yusuke OBUCHI (The University of Tokyo) Masayuki KUSUMOTO, Hirotoshi SHINOHARA (NTT Urban Development Corporation) Nobuyuki YOSHIDA, Yutaka SHIKATA (Shinkenchiku-Sha Co., Ltd.)
Project management	Shuta TAKAGI
Main programmer	Shuta TAKAGI, Satoru TAKATSUKA
Assistant staff	Hiroshi NAGAI
Software / SDE	Android Studio, Amazon DynamoDB
Programming language	Java
Keywords	Application development, Workshops, Digital fabrication

膨大な量の参加者の行動履歴や散策経路がデータベースに記録され、まちの隠れた魅力を統計解析するための情報として活用された。解析の担当は筑波大学 岡瑞起研究室。

Vast amounts of data related to participants' activity histories and walking routes were recorded in the database, which were then used for statistical analysis of the hidden charms of the city. Data analysis was managed by Mizuki Oka Laboratory at Tsukuba University.

都市×公園データビジュアライゼーション

CITY×PARK DATA VISUALIZATION

ディレクター　株式会社 船場
Director　SEMBA CORPORATION

株式会社 船場による「公共空間における商業開発」を対象とした都市情報のデータビジュアライゼーションプロジェクト。とある地方都市に多数存在する都市公園において、暗黙知化されている「(周辺環境含む)公園の特性」を探索する課題が与えられ、髙木秀太事務所では都市という情報の海の中から、公園に関する有益な情報をデジタルメソッドであぶり出す試みがなされた。株式会社船場は出力されたデータセットの中から特性を分析し、現状に関する認識の統一を行うことで開発着手につながる提案を行政に対して行った。

A data visualization project for urban information by SEMBA CORPORATION. In targeting "commercial development in public spaces", we were tasked with finding "appealing parks (including its surrounding environment)" amongst the numerous existing parks in a certain local city. From the sea of information, Takagi Shuta Office embarked on extracting useful information related to parks using digital methods. From our dataset, SEMBA CORPORATION analyzed the characteristics, discerned the current situation, and made proposals for development to the municipal government.

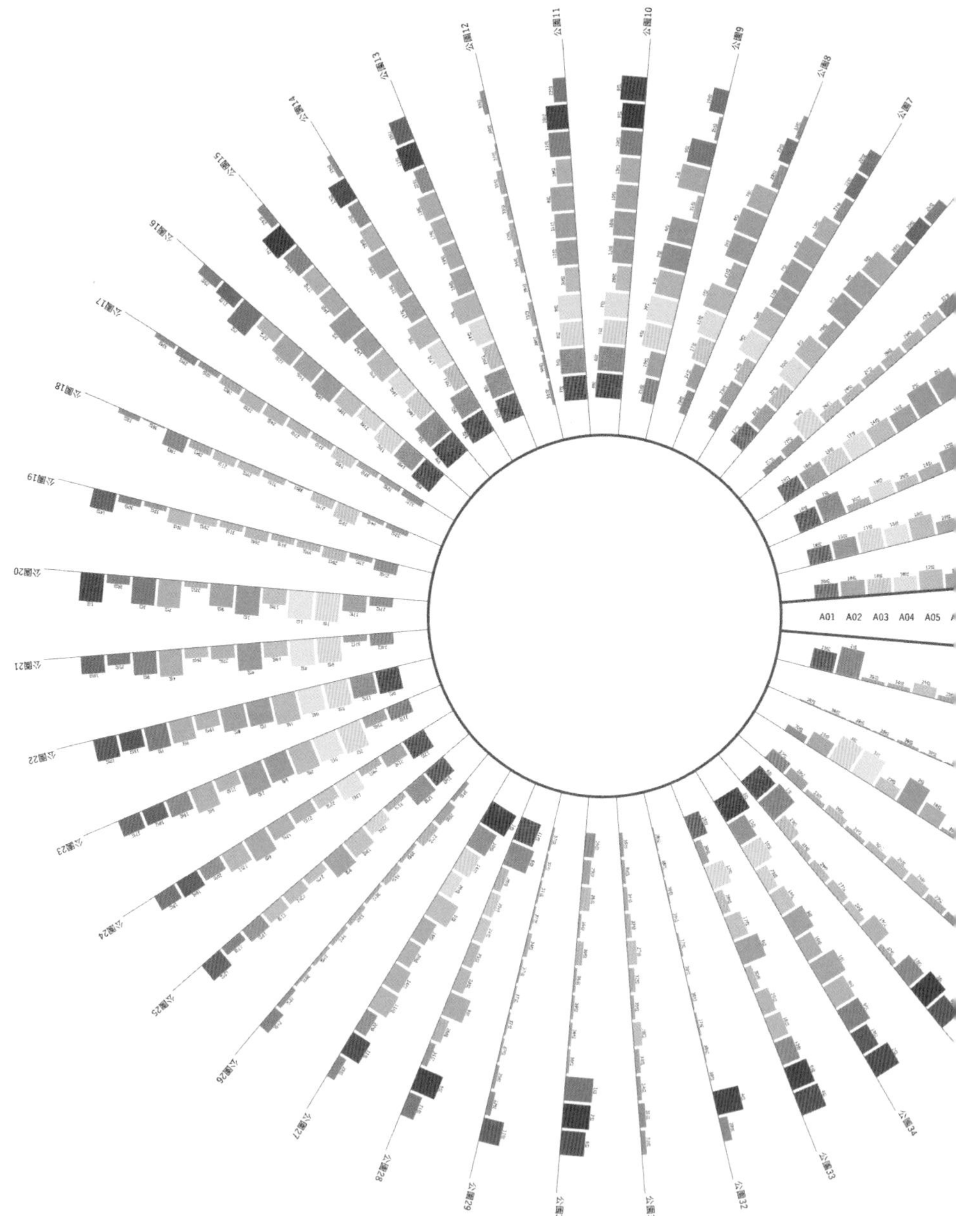

公園の価値分類と多軸グラフ

Value classification of parks and multi-axis graph

株式会社 船場は商業コンサルタントとしての経験値から公園の価値を評価分類し、それらに影響する都市要素を抽出、各要素の重みを設定した。

SEMBA CORPORATION, based on their expertise as commercial consultants, assessed and categorized the value of the parks, extracting urban elements that affect them and setting the importance for each element.

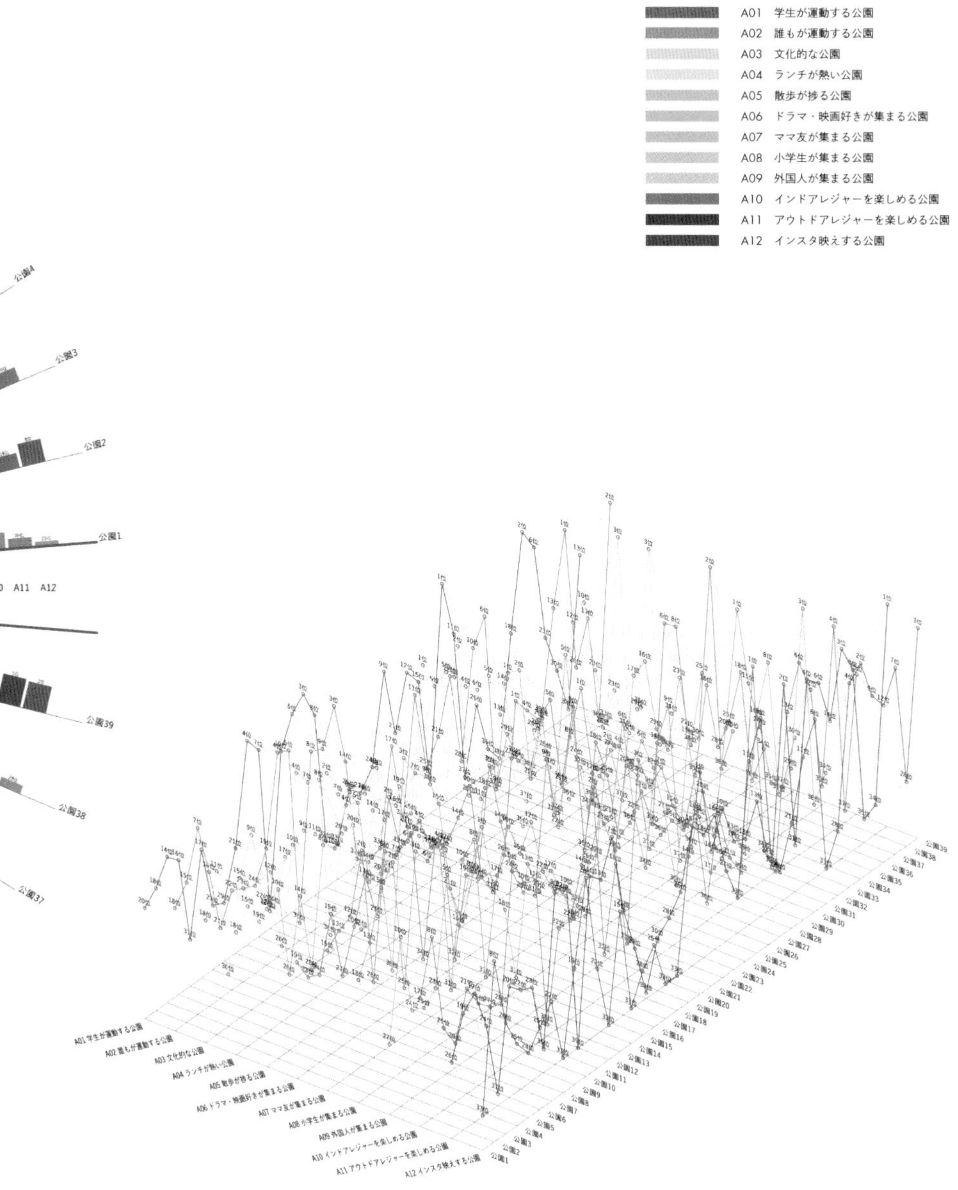

高木秀太事務所では、データの収集、比較、出力を半自動化することで、これまで現地調査することでかかっていた労力コストを大幅にカットした。また、関係者間での先入観に左右されない現状理解、情報共有にも寄与した。

Takagi Shuta Office substantially reduced labor costs related to conventional site survey by semi-automating the process of data collection, comparison, and output. It also contributed to unbiased understanding of the current situation and information sharing among the related parties.

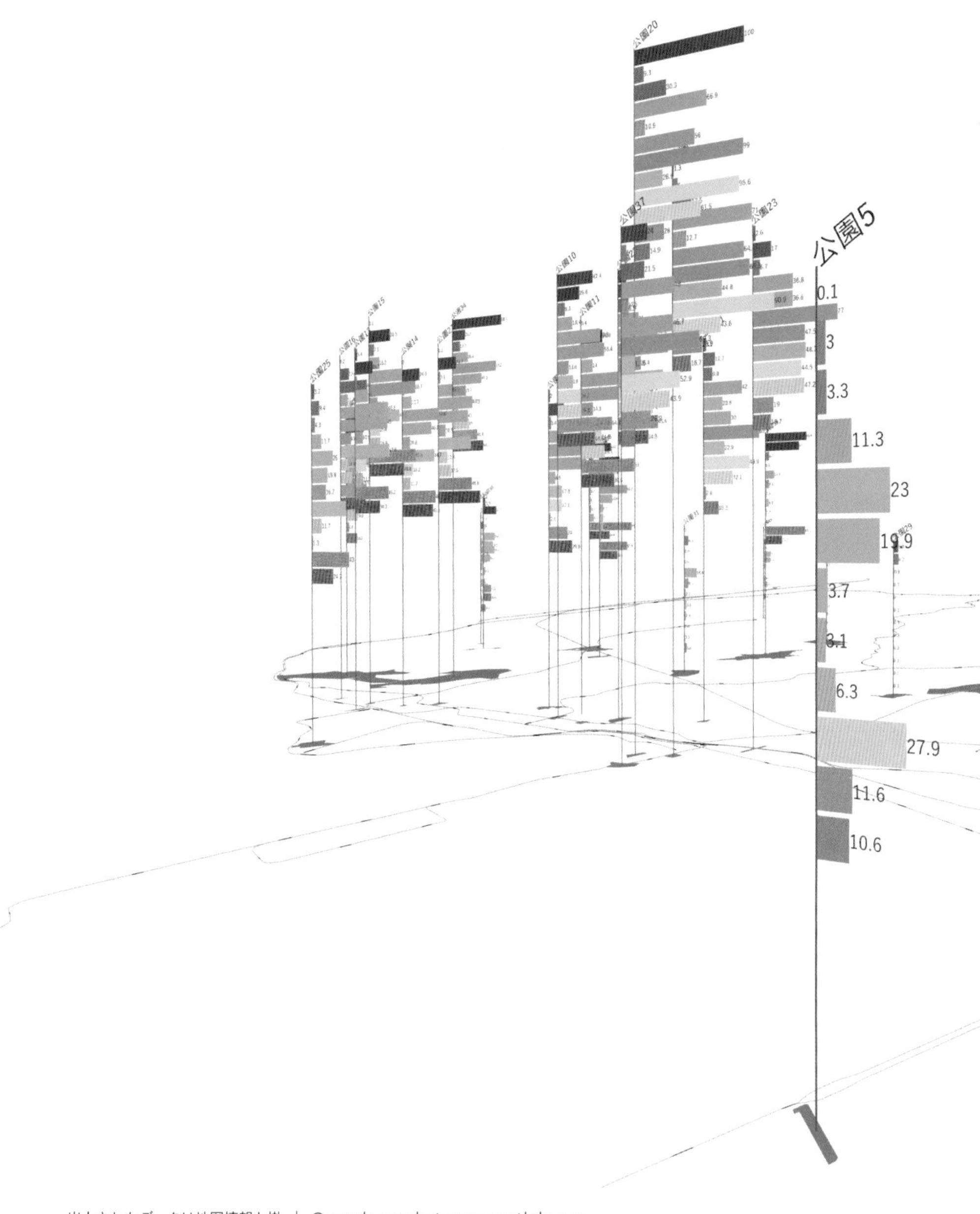

出力されたデータは地図情報と掛け合わせてマッピングビジュアライゼーションすることも可能。どの公園がどのような特性を持っているのか、連携の可能性はあるのか、俯瞰的に眺めることでエリアマネジメント視点での事業検討に資する。

Output data can be interwoven with the map information to produce map data visualization. Through a comprehensive review of the characteristics for each park and whether there is an opportunity for cooperation, potential business considerations can be made through an area management perspective.

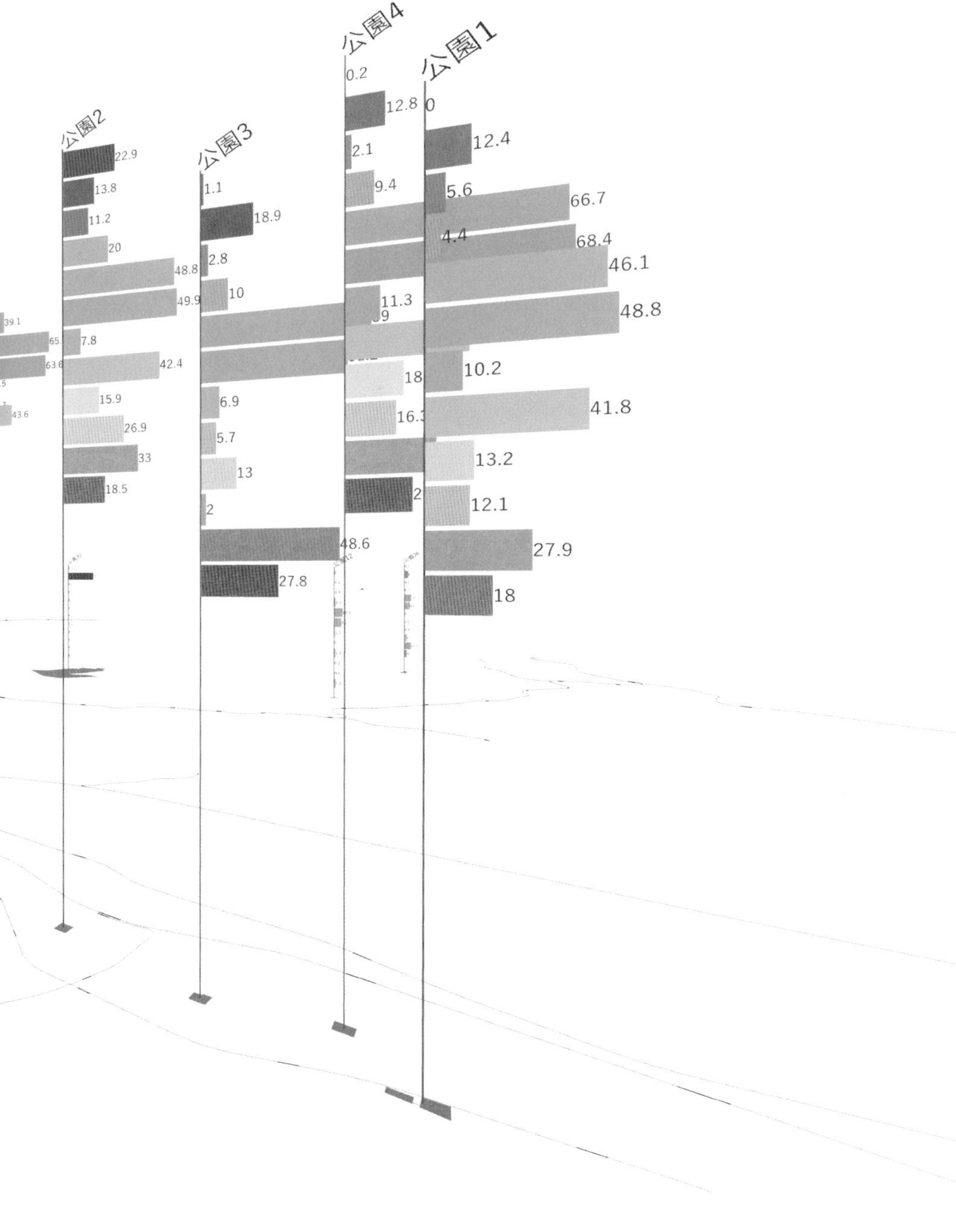
公園4
公園1
公園2
公園3
0.2
12.8
0
12.4
22.9
1.1
2.1
13.8
9.4
5.6
66.7
11.2
18.9
4.4
68.4
20
2.8
46.1
48.8
10
49.9
11.3
48.8
39.1
7.8
42.4
10.2
18
15.9
6.9
16.3
41.8
43.6
26.9
5.7
33
13.2
13
18.5
2
12.1
48.6
27.9
27.8
18

GIS ソフトウェア：QGIS
GIS software: QGIS

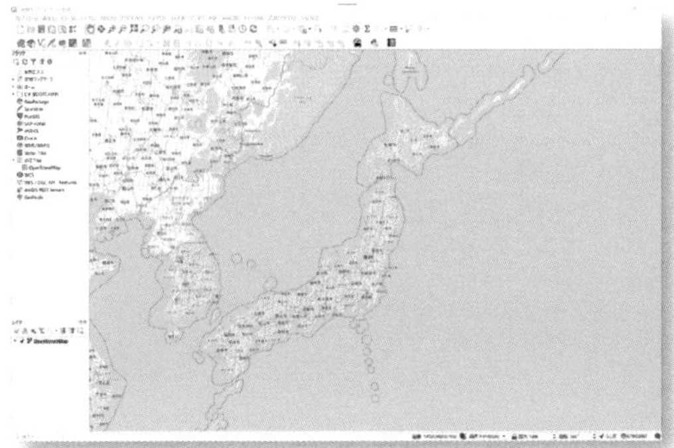

施設・スポット一覧
List of facilities / Spots

ジャンル	軸番	評価軸	データ名	施設件数
スポーツ	A01	学生が運動する公園	スポーツ施設	53
			公園内スポーツ施設	32
			大学・短大	33
			高校	38
			全国大会出場高校	15
			複数部活全国大会出場高校	6
			中学校	99
			バス停	1521
			駅	139
	A02	誰もが運動する公園	スポーツ施設	53
			公園内スポーツ施設	32
			バス停	1521
			駅	139
憩い・散策	A03	文化的な公園	観光資源	34
			美術館	7
			文化施設	27
			図書館	42
			スターバックス	22
			バス停	1521
			駅	139
	A04	ランチが熱い公園	食べログ上位100店	100
			バス停	1521
			駅	139
			昼間人口	39公園
	A05	散歩が捗る公園	総合病院	14
			ペット可飲食店	108
			ペットホテル・サロン・動物病院	41
			ドッグラン・ペット可宿	4
			駐車台数	39公園
	A06	ドラマ・映画好きが集まる公園	ロケ地	88
			バス停	1521
			駅	139
コミュニティ	A07	ママ友が集まる公園	幼稚園・保育施設	623
			買い物施設	166
			カフェチェーン	105
			バス停	1521
			駅	139
			25-39歳女性人口	39公園
	A08	小学生が集まる公園	児童館・学童保育	218
			小学校	171
			公文式	109
			ヤマハ音楽教室	20
			ニュータウン	63
			5-14歳人口	39公園
	A09	外国人が集まる公園	日本語学校	20
			宗教施設	150
			領事館・国際センター	3
			インターナショナルスクール	14
			バス停	1521
			駅	139
レジャー	A10	インドアレジャーを楽しめる公園	動植物園	3
			水族館	1
			文化施設	27
			バス停	1521
			駅	139
			駐車台数	39公園
	A11	アウトドアレジャーを楽しめる公園	公園内レジャー施設	38
			スポーツ系レジャー施設	5
			キャンプ場	4
			バス停	1521
			駅	139
			駐車台数	39公園
その他	A12	インスタ映えする公園	Instagram投稿数	39公園
	EX	公示地価ボロノイ	公示地価	1194地点

地図情報
Map information

施設・スポット プロット
Facilities / Spots plotted

バッファ解析
Buffer analysis

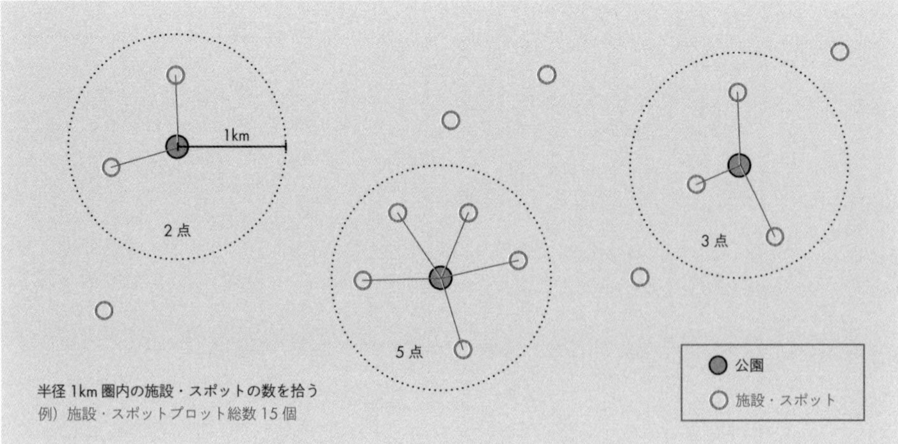

バッファ解析ランキング
Buffer analysis ranking

公園名称	A01 学生が運動する公園	A02 誰もが運動する公園	A03 文化的な公園	A04 ランチが熱い公園	A05 散歩が捗る公園	A06 ドラマ・映画好きが集まる公園	A07 ママ友が集まる公園	A08 小学生が集まる公園	A09 外国人が集まる公園	A10 インドアレジャーを楽しめる公園	A11 アウトドアレジャーを楽しめる公園	A12 インスタ映えする公園
公園1	18.0	27.9	12.1	13.2	41.8	10.2	48.8	46.1	4.4	5.6	12.4	0.0
公園2	18.5	33.0	26.9	15.9	42.4	7.8	49.9	48.8	20.0	11.2	13.8	22.9
公園3	27.8	48.6	2.0	13.0	5.7	6.9	51.2	59.0	10.0	2.8	18.9	1.1
公園4	21.4	28.5	16.3	18.6	38.4	11.3	68.4	66.7	9.4	2.1	12.8	0.2
公園5	10.6	11.6	27.9	6.3	3.1	3.7	19.9	23.0	11.3	3.3	3.0	0.1
公園6	19.9	23.0	10.3	20.5	43.6	9.9	63.6	65.6	39.1	2.8	13.5	0.2
公園7	13.6	22.5	8.3	22.5	42.4	12.3	60.7	56.0	17.8	2.4	13.1	0.4
公園8	13.5	22.2	14.6	19.7	47.0	8.6	61.7	61.5	27.1	2.2	12.9	0.0
公園9	16.7	26.9	43.6	90.9	44.8	69.3	64.4	12.7	71.4	17.5	5.0	1.3
公園10	44.6	64.3	28.8	28.2	19.0	13.6	55.4	50.8	18.4	9.3	26.6	42.4
公園11	39.5	63.0	28.1	24.6	19.0	14.3	52.6	54.1	14.0	8.4	25.8	0.4
公園12	1.8	0.6	0.3	1.9	0.0	1.1	8.7	10.4	1.9	0.4	0.4	0.0
公園13	34.3	46.2	11.2	16.2	47.6	10.9	45.0	46.2	18.4	3.1	24.7	3.4
公園14	42.5	46.1	11.2	15.2	44.7	10.8	40.8	50.8	13.3	3.1	24.6	0.0
公園15	49.6	65.8	15.9	15.4	43.5	11.9	65.7	46.5	15.2	7.5	30.5	0.1
公園16	36.8	38.9	17.7	11.9	32.1	15.9	49.1	49.5	11.4	40.1	13.4	0.2
公園17	10.6	2.1	1.1	8.3	0.6	3.7	21.1	30.6	2.8	1.5	6.8	0.0
公園18	4.5	1.6	11.7	5.5	0.0	2.8	17.8	19.1	2.5	5.1	1.0	0.0
公園19	15.9	1.8	7.4	4.1	0.6	6.3	10.3	17.9	11.8	1.4	6.7	3.5
公園20	14.9	28.0	61.5	95.6	26.9	99.0	56.0	10.5	66.9	30.3	9.3	100.0
公園21	16.3	2.6	32.1	49.9	22.9	60.1	30.0	20.8	42.0	9.9	12.7	3.1
公園22	34.8	45.6	40.0	35.6	51.4	26.4	56.9	45.6	24.0	12.5	20.5	9.6
公園23	16.7	19.0	47.2	44.5	48.3	47.5	77.0	36.6	36.8	6.7	17.0	2.6
公園24	29.9	24.0	2.5	17.1	17.3	8.6	47.8	56.0	19.2	3.4	19.5	2.0
公園25	24.7	43.0	1.3	11.7	39.5	16.7	18.8	25.0	11.7	4.3	9.4	3.7
公園26	4.0	10.1	4.0	0.9	0.6	1.0	8.5	10.2	0.3	0.6	6.0	0.3
公園27	57.3	45.8	17.6	12.8	44.8	10.3	41.0	47.3	19.8	3.1	24.7	0.1
公園28	32.6	50.9	2.9	6.8	7.0	6.7	23.6	51.2	5.8	1.6	37.2	0.8
公園29	0.1	0.1	0.1	0.2	0.3	0.3	0.1	0.0	0.1	0.8	6.2	5.9
公園30	15.3	9.9	7.0	0.4	1.2	0.7	0.3	1.7	0.2	40.2	43.8	26.2
公園31	3.6	1.3	0.6	2.4	3.5	2.2	6.4	18.9	0.8	0.9	6.3	0.0
公園32	0.0	0.0	0.0	0.0	0.1	0.0	0.0	0.0	0.0	0.2	41.4	0.1
公園33	18.5	4.5	19.9	5.4	28.6	29.5	14.9	39.3	16.8	8.0	30.9	46.7
公園34	50.1	40.4	27.0	8.9	31.3	21.7	47.9	71.2	25.4	12.7	20.7	80.1
公園35	39.9	83.1	9.4	3.9	3.0	3.7	17.9	46.9	1.3	8.2	43.2	13.5
公園36	16.4	16.5	0.8	4.3	0.3	2.9	20.6	24.6	2.5	1.8	27.7	4.6
公園37	12.9	26.9	43.9	52.9	12.6	69.3	46.7	6.9	48.0	21.5	5.0	24.0
公園38	0.0	0.0	0.0	0.1	0.2	0.1	0.0	0.0	0.0	0.4	5.8	0.1
公園39	28.2	67.1	0.5	1.7	6.2	1.9	6.6	15.6	0.6	6.7	57.0	69.6

解析結果
Analysis results

魅力度スコアリング手法
Appeal level scoring method

各評価分類での比較には、スコアリングの手法が必要不可欠である。本プロジェクトでは、多くの都市解析で使用される「バッファ解析」を採用した [A]-[C]。各テーマに関係する施設・スポットの座標情報をプロットし、カウントすることで魅力度評価とした [D]。

A scoring method is crucial in creating a ranking. This project adopted a "buffer analysis" that is often used in urban analysis [A]-[C]. The coordinate information of the facilities and spots related to each theme were plotted and counted to evaluate the appeal level [D].

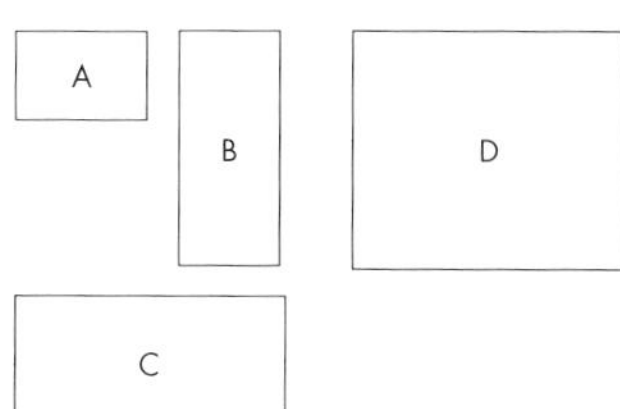

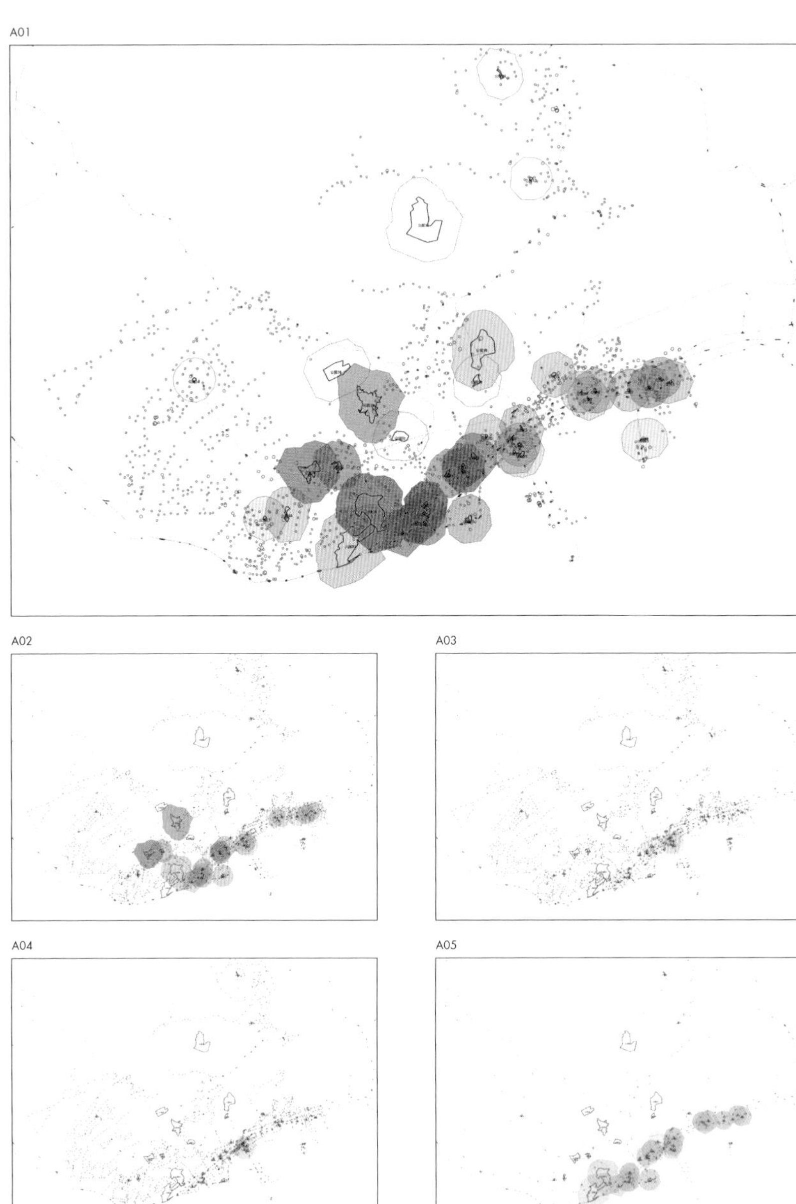

バッファ解析の実行画面。表示されている無数の赤点が各テーマに関連する施設・スポットのプロットである。これらの座標データベースの構築にはwebスクレイピングの技術が用いられ、半自動化のシステムが構築された。

Screenshots of buffer analysis execution. Countless red dots represent facilities and spots related to each theme. Web scraping technology was adopted to create the coordinates database, and a semi-automated system was built.

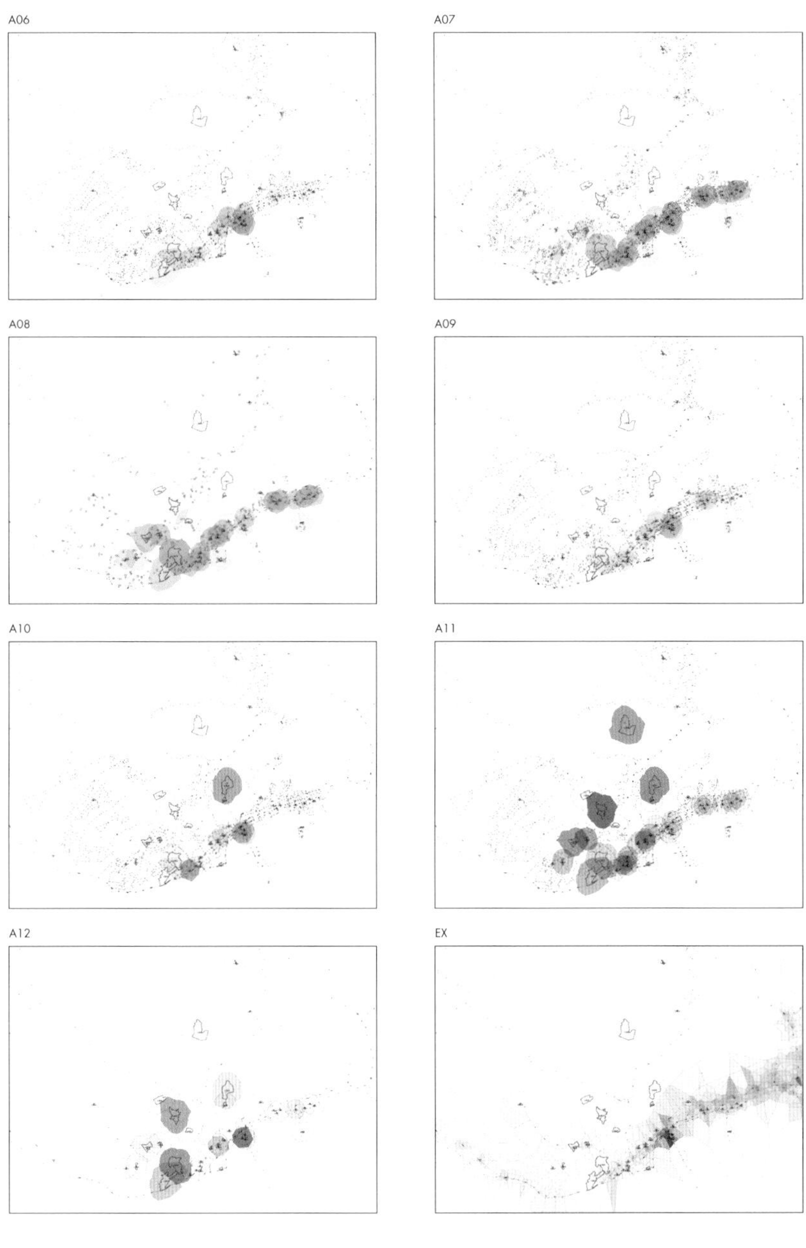

A01　学生が運動する公園
A02　誰もが運動する公園
A03　文化的な公園
A04　ランチが熱い公園
A05　散歩が捗る公園
A06　ドラマ・映画好きが集まる公園
A07　ママ友が集まる公園
A08　小学生が集まる公園
A09　外国人が集まる公園
A10　インドアレジャーを楽しめる公園
A11　アウトドアレジャーを楽しめる公園
A12　インスタ映えする公園
EX　公示地価ボロノイマップ

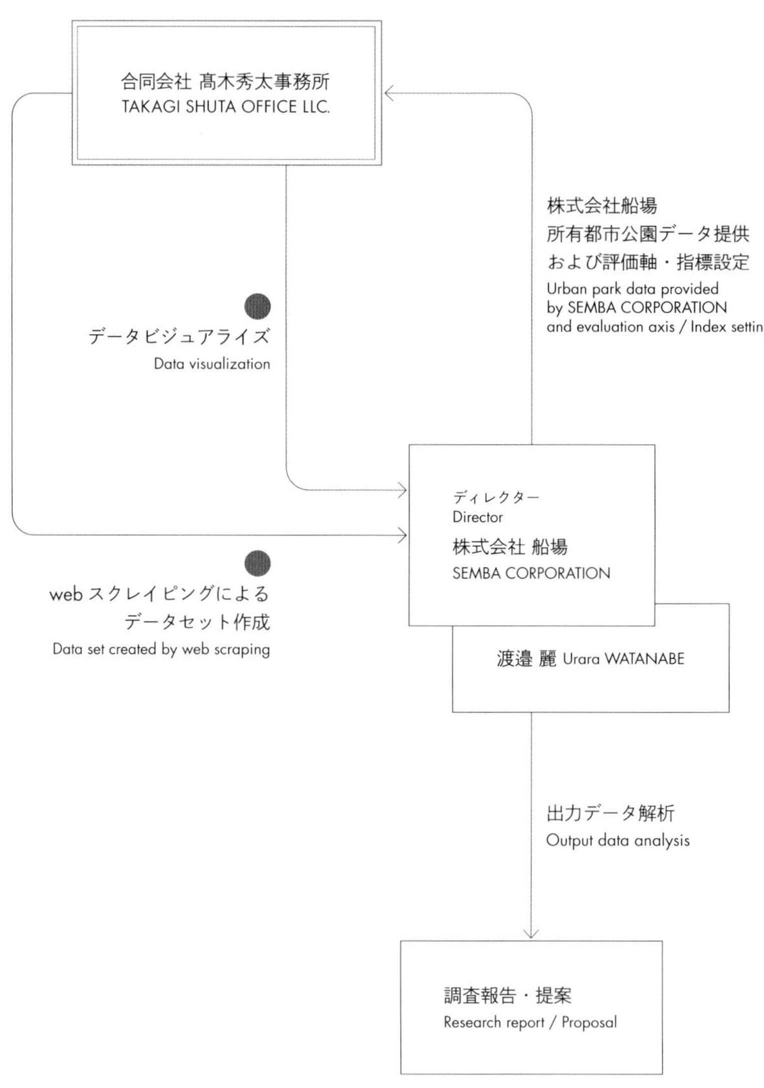

都市および公園に関する各種情報は株式会社 船場が有する情報と、高木秀太事務所が収集した情報がハイブリッドに掛け合わされた。多様な情報の重ね合わせとプロフェッショナルな視点でのレビューが出力の精度を上げた。

Miscellaneous information on cities and parks was a result of hybridization of data held by SEMBA CORPORATION and data collected by Takagi Shuta Office. Overlapping of diverse information and reviews from professional perspectives increased the output accuracy.

プロジェクトID	170030
プロジェクト期間	2017.11–2018.03
ディレクター	株式会社 船場
担当	渡邉 麗
プロジェクトマネージメント	髙木 秀太、髙塚 悟
メインプログラマー	髙木 秀太、髙塚 悟
アシスタントプログラマー	南 佑樹、三原 義弘、菊池 毅
ソフトウェア / 開発環境	Rhinoceros, QGIS, Excel
プログラミング言語	Grasshopper, Python
キーワード	都市解析、データビジュアライゼーション、webスクレイピング

Project ID	170030
Project term	2017.11–2018.03
Director	SEMBA CORPORATION
Project leader	Urara WATANABE
Project management	Shuta TAKAGI, Satoru TAKATSUKA
Main programmer	Shuta TAKAGI, Satoru TAKATSUKA
Assistant programmer	Yuki MINAMI, Yoshihiro MIHARA, Tsuyoshi KIKUCHI
Software / SDE	Rhinoceros, QGIS, Excel
Programming language	Grasshopper, Python
Keywords	Urban analysis, Data visualization, Web scraping

地図情報の取得にはオープンソースGISソフトウェアQGISが使用された。取り込まれた国土地理院の地図情報を座標系変換処理した後、以降のバッファ解析へとつなげた。

Open source GIS software "QGIS" was used to obtain map information. After converting the map information from Geospatial Information Authority of Japan into coordinate system, subsequent buffer analysis were made.

千葉工業大学 折り紙ワークショップ

CHIBA INSTITUTE OF TECHNOLOGY ORIGAMI WORKSHOP

運営　　千葉工業大学 創造工学部 デザイン科学科

Management　Department of Design, Chiba Institute of Technology

千葉工業大学 創造工学部 デザイン科学科で行われたワークショップである。折り紙というプロダクトデザインを通じた制作課題であるが、コンピューテーショナルデザインに関する思考実験的な側面が強い。

コンピューターが自動的・網羅的に構築した「デザインのデータベース」から有効な組み合わせを抽出する、というユニークな課題設定となった。

The workshop was held at the Department of Design, Chiba Institute of Technology. While the assignment dealt with the product design of origami and its making, it also incorporated a vigorous thought experiment on computational design.

The unique framing of the assignment challenged students to extract effective combinations from "design database" assembled automatically and comprehensively by the computer.

制作の対象は鶴の折り紙。ひとつの鶴を構成する色は2色で限定されているが、色の種類は25色。その組み合わせは全部で25×25で625通りである。

The task was to make a crane out of origami. The colors that make up each crane was limited to two colors, to be selected from 25 colors. 25 x 25 combinations amount to 625 possible variations.

ID:479-B

Key Color:
ネイビー

Accent Color:
赤

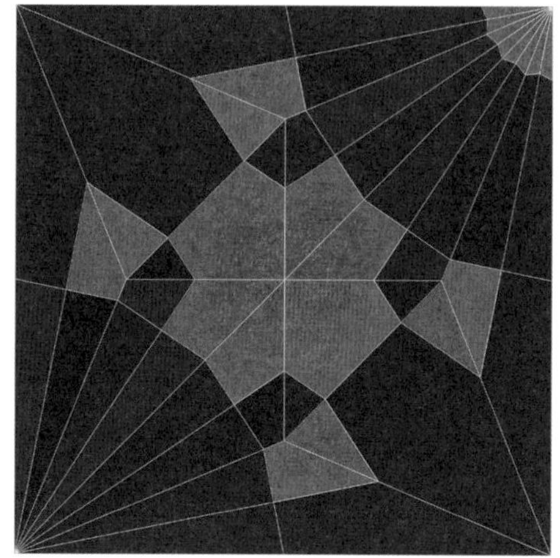

Digital Origami Maker for Chiba Institute of Technology

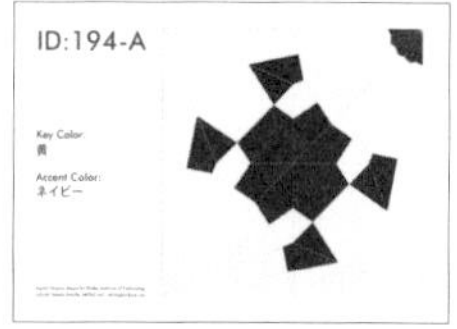

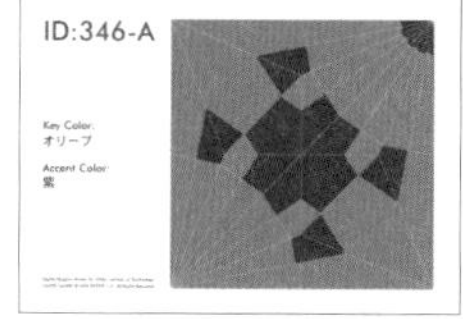

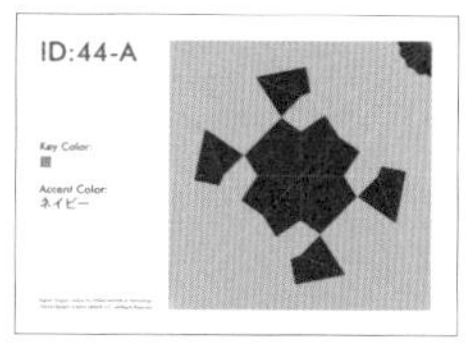

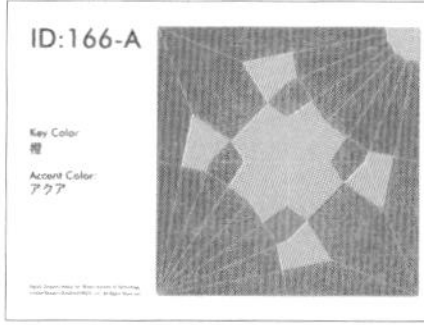

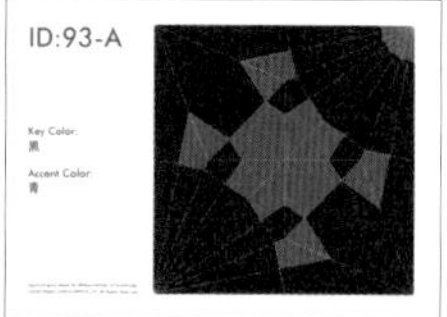

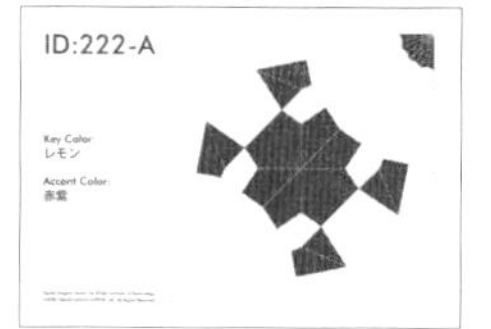

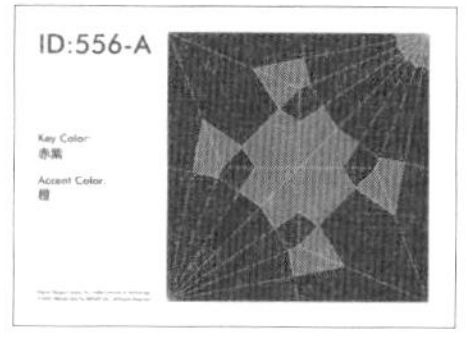

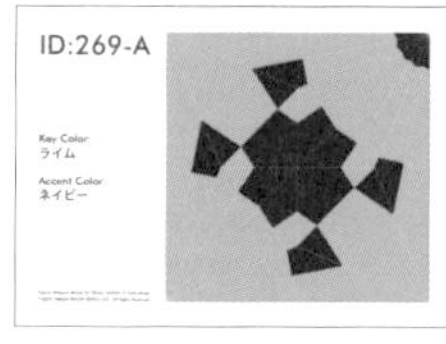

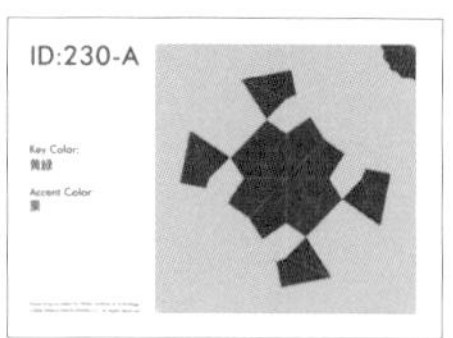

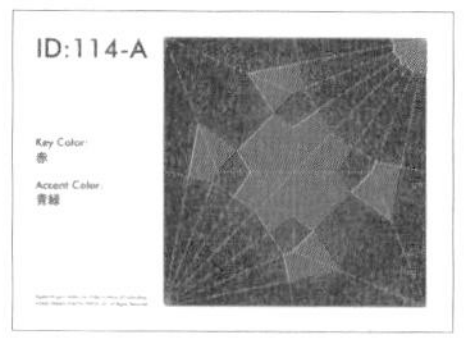

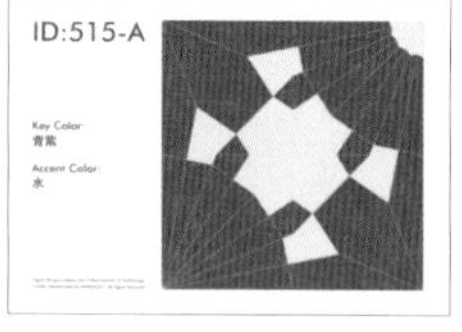

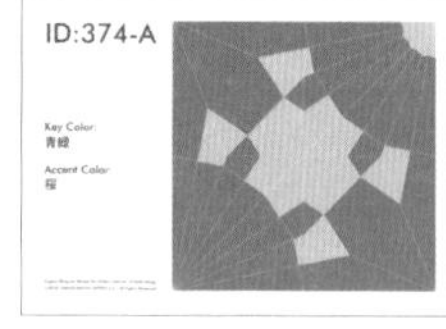

　コンピュータープログラムによって事前に用意された折り紙の展開図の一部。この中から自身の設定したコンセプトに合った色合いのものを探索し、拾い上げていく。

A few examples of geometric nets of origami, produced by a computer program in advance. Users can explore and choose color combinations that match their concept.

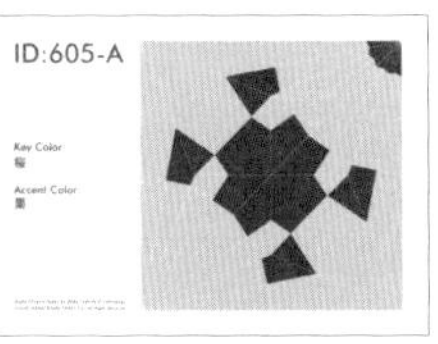
ID:605-A

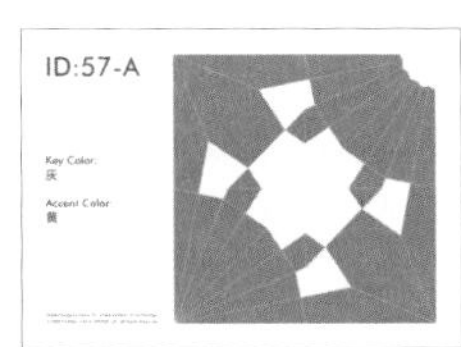
ID:57-A

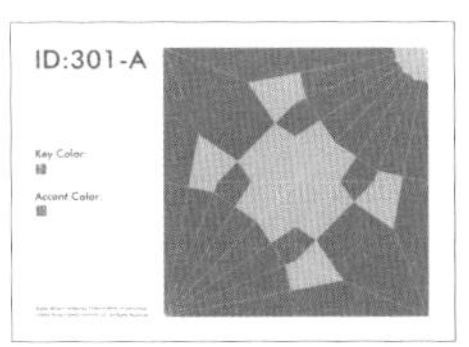
ID:301-A

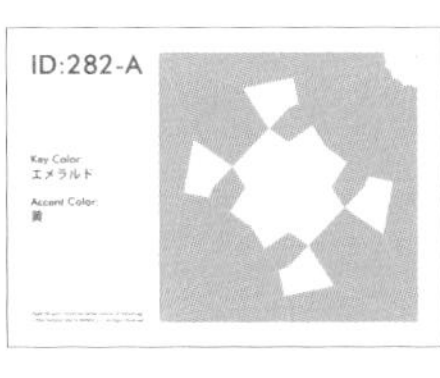
ID:282-A

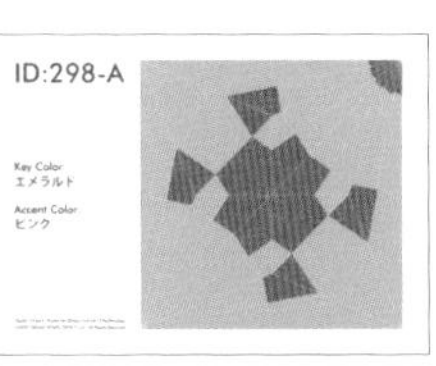
ID:298-A

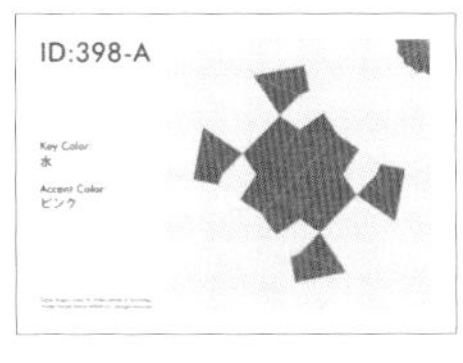
ID:398-A

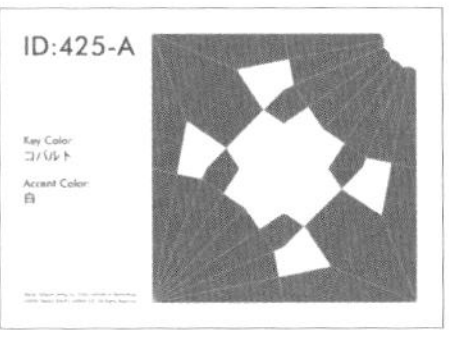
ID:425-A

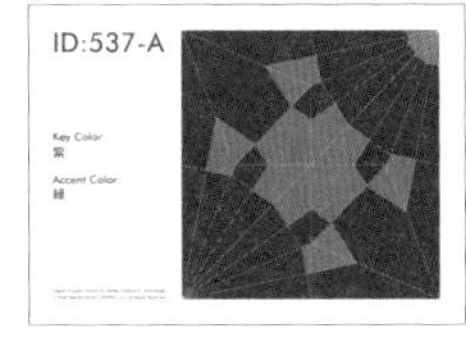
ID:537-A

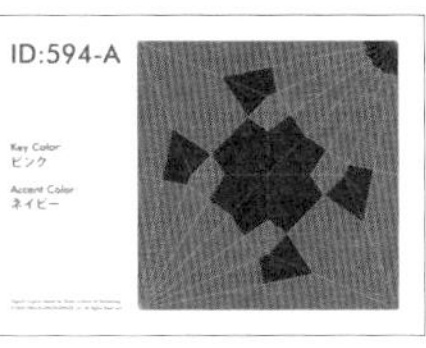
ID:594-A

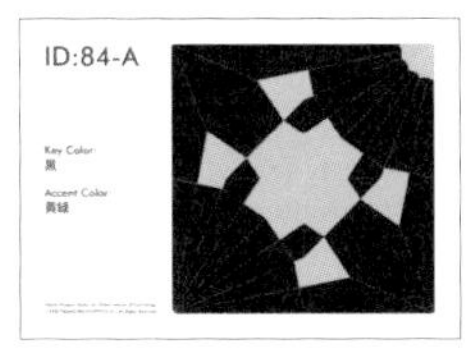
ID:84-A

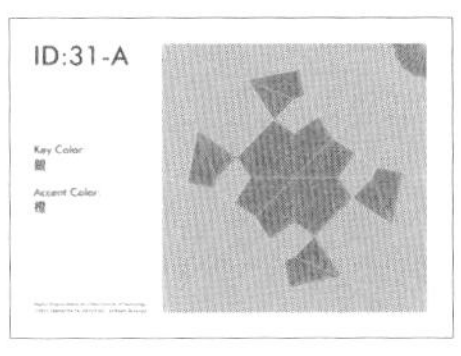
ID:31-A

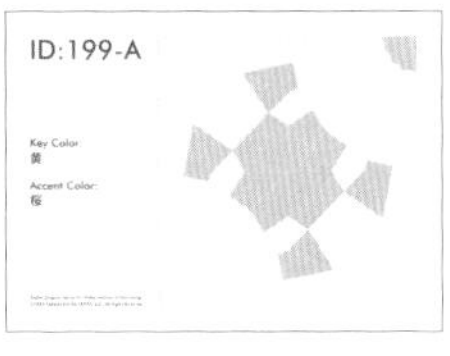
ID:199-A

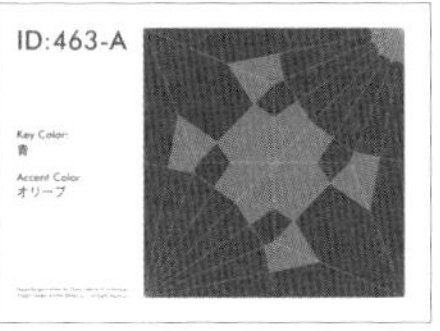
ID:463-A

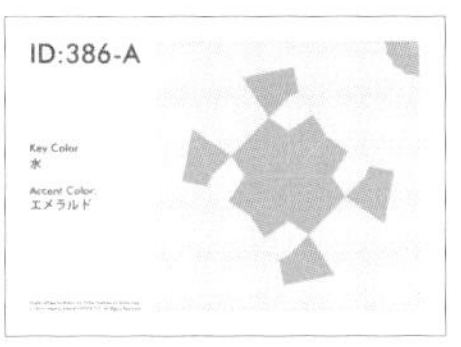
ID:386-A

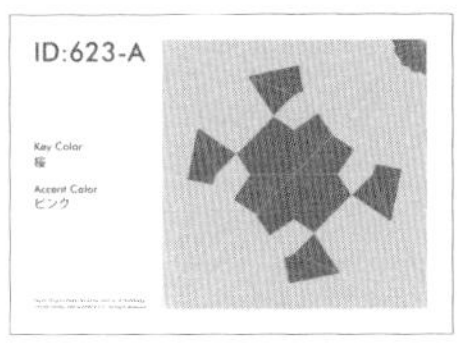
ID:623-A

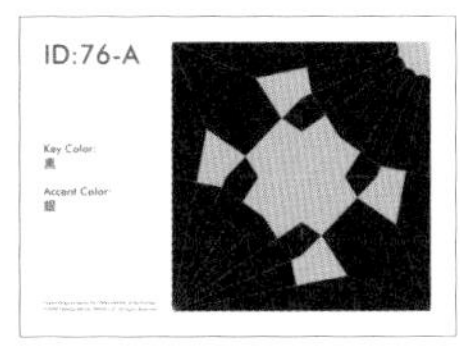
ID:76-A

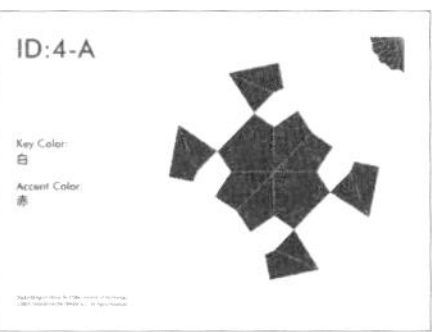
ID:4-A

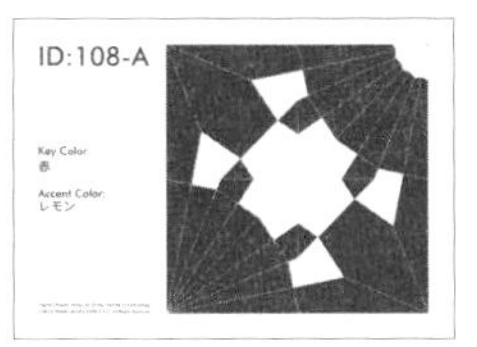
ID:108-A

ID:3-A

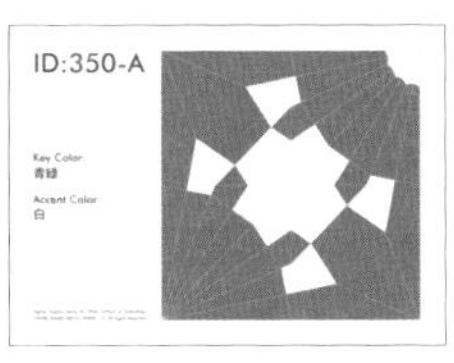
ID:350-A

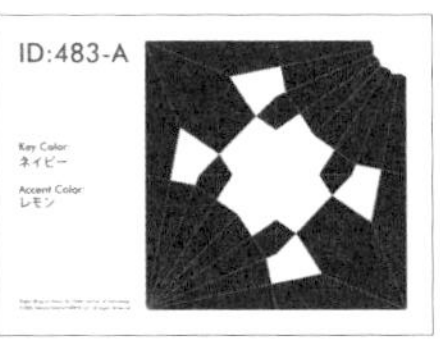
ID:483-A

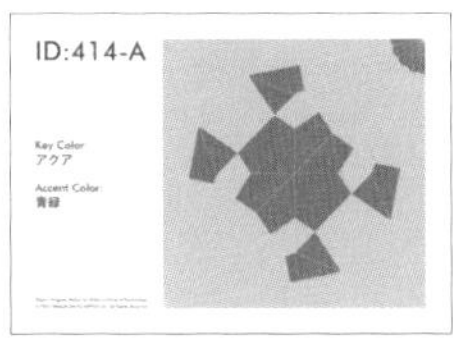
ID:414-A

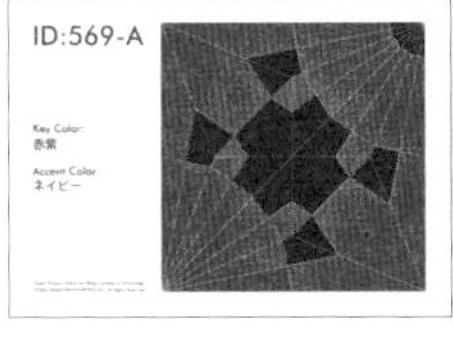
ID:569-A

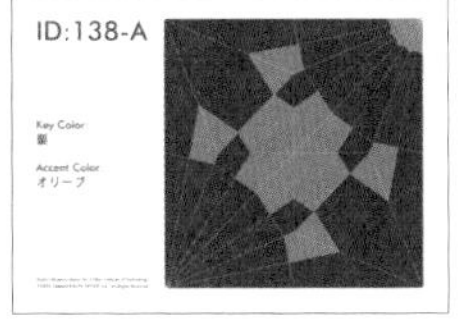
ID:138-A

1. 課題出題

Course assignment

　みなさんは日本のオリガミメーカーの企画者です。ある日、あなたは「そうだ、〇〇をテーマにしたオリガミセットを企画しよう！」と思いつきました。その〇〇とは一体どのようなもの（テーマ、モチーフ、コンセプト）で、そこから想起されるような色合いのオリガミは一体どんなものでしょうか。会社には、コンピューターパターンナーが作りあげた様々な色の組み合わせから成る「鶴のオリガミ」の展開図が、大量にインデックスされています。あなたは早速、自身が設定したテーマから、イメージにぴったりなサンプルを探し始めるのでした…

*

　デザインとは、何もないところから価値あるものを「生み出す」ことにこそ真理があるのでしょうか。あるいは、無限の可能性のなかから価値あるものを「選び出す」ことにこそ真理があるのでしょうか。本課題では後者のスタディ手法をコンピューターの力を借りて思考実験してみます。

You are all planners of a Japanese origami manufacturer. One day, you came up with the idea, "Yes, let's plan an origami set with 〇〇 as the theme!" What kind of thing (theme, motif, concept) is that 〇〇, and what kind of color origami is evoked from it? The company has a large index of geometric net drawings of "crane origami" made up of various color combinations created by computer patterners. You immediately started looking for a sample that fits your image from the theme you set yourself.

*

Does the truth of design lie in "creating" something of value out of nothing? Or is there truth in "picking out" something of value from an infinite number of possibilities? In this assignment, we will use the power of a computer to conduct a thought experiment on the latter study method.

課題：「無価値」の海から「価値」を見つけ出す

Assignment: Finding "value" from a "valueless" sea

　授業の課題文。コンピュータープログラムによって事前に用意されたデータベースを「無価値の海」と呼び [1]、その中から価値のあるデザインを拾い上げる。データベースには検索システムが用意されているので探索がサポートされる状況とした [2]。デザインセットの企画書を最終提出物として指定した [3]。

Course Assignment. A database named "valueless sea" [1] was prepared in advance by a computer program, from which valuable designs would be picked out. A search system was provided in the database to support the exploratory process [2]. A design set plan was specified for the final submission [3].

2. 資料・素材

Documents / Materials

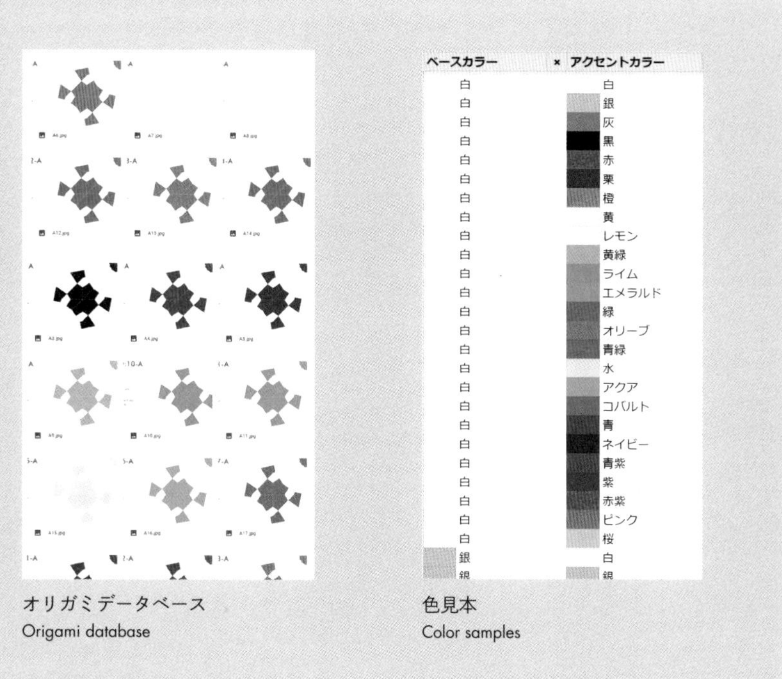

オリガミデータベース
Origami database

色見本
Color samples

3. 課題提出

Submission of the assignment

・オリガミサンプルから最低 3 枚以上を選択し、その選択理由を A3 プレゼンシート 1 枚にまとめる。

・選択したサンプルは（コンビニ / 自宅などで）A4 カラーでプリントアウトし、実際に鶴として折ること。

・折った鶴を綺麗にならべ写真を撮影し、プレゼンシートにレイアウトすること。（光の当て方や背景に気を使うこと）

・テーマ、モチーフ、コンセプトの情報をプレゼンシートに組み込むこと。
＊参照する画像などがある場合は出典を明記すること。

・タイトル（= 商品名）をつけることを忘れないこと。

·Select at least 3 origami samples, and summarize the reasons for their selection on a single A3 presentation sheet.

·Print out the selected sample in A4 color (at a convenience store / home, etc.) and fold it into a paper crane.

·Arrange the folded cranes neatly, take pictures, and lay them out on the presentation sheet. (Pay attention to lighting and background)

·Incorporate the theme, motif, and concept information into the presentation sheet.

·Don't forget to add a title (= product name).

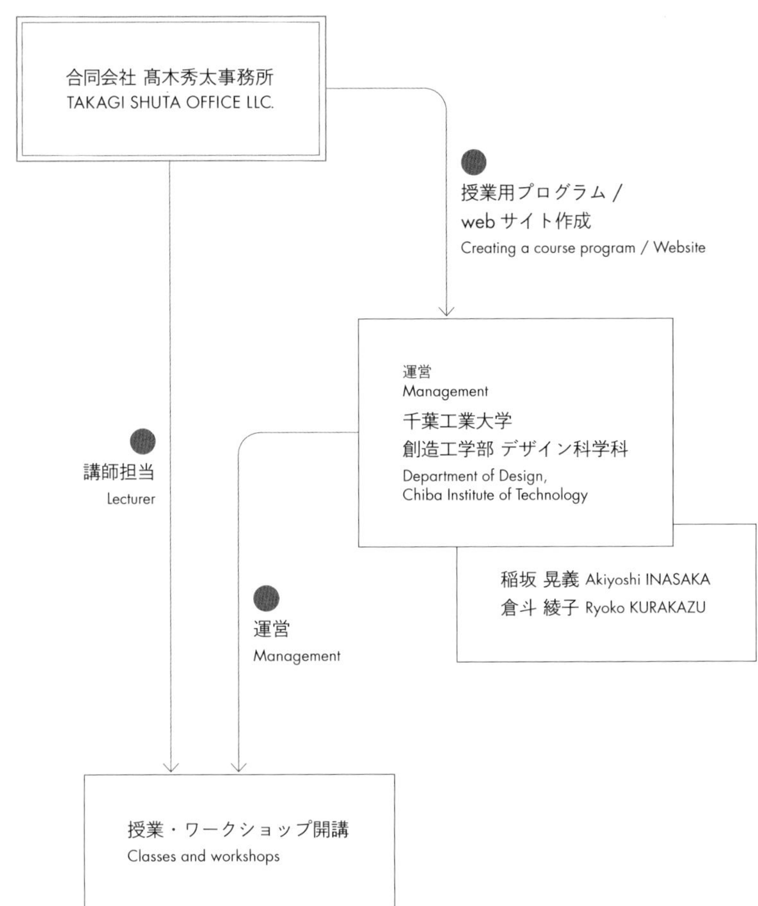

授業の運営担当は同学 准教授 稲坂 晃義氏、准教授 倉斗 綾子氏。両氏共に建築・都市計画を専門とするが、本授業は建築に限らずあらゆるデザインに関わる学生を対象とした。

The course was supervised by associate professors Akiyoshi Inasaka and Ryoko Kurakazu at Chiba Institute of Technology. They both specialize in architecture and urban planning, but this course was intended for students in all design fields, including architecture.

プロジェクトID	200025
プロジェクト期間	2020.05
運営	千葉工業大学 創造工学部 デザイン科学科
担当	稲坂 晃義、倉斗 綾子
プロジェクトマネージメント	髙木 秀太
メインプログラマー	髙木 秀太
ソフトウェア / 開発環境	Rhinoceros, Adobe Photoshop, WordPress
プログラミング言語	Grasshopper, Python
キーワード	教育、ワークショップ

Project ID	200025
Project term	2020.05
Operation	Department of Design, Chiba Institute of Technology
Project team	Akiyoshi INASAKA, Ryoko KURAKAZU
Project management	Shuta TAKAGI
Main programmer	Shuta TAKAGI
Software / SDE	Rhinoceros, Adobe Photoshop, WordPress
Programming language	Grasshopper, Python
Keywords	Education, Workshop

課題文の掲示や折り紙データベースの構築のためにワークショップ用のwebサイト／データベースを構築している。プラットフォームはWordPressを採用。

A website / database was built for the workshop to post course assignment and to construct the origami database. The platform used was WordPress.

RHINO-GH.COM

ディレクター　株式会社日建設計
Director　NIKKEN SEKKEI LTD

3Dモデリングソフトウェア Rhinoceros とビジュアルプログラミング言語 Grasshopper の独学 web サイトである。ディレクターである株式会社日建設計のツールノウハウを広く共有することを目的として 2016 年に一般公開された。髙木秀太事務所の記念すべき第一作でもある。

Self-learning website for 3D modeling software Rhinoceros and visual programming language Grasshopper. Aimed to widely share our client NIKKEN SEKKEI's technical expertise, it was made available to the general public in 2016. It is also the memorable first work of Takagi Shuta Office.

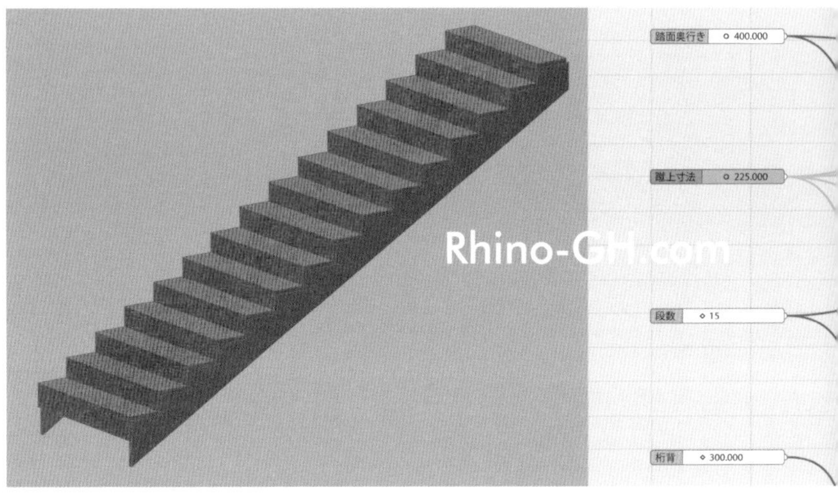

rhino-gh.com

本 web サイトは一切の広告が存在せず、会員登録も不要でフリーに利用ができる [A]。株式会社日建設計・髙木秀太事務所によって厳選された各種ツールがまとめて学習でき [B]、すべての教材は音声付きの動画によって提供されている [C]。

The website has no advertisement, does not require membership registration, and is available free of charge [A]. Tools carefully handpicked by NIKKEN SEKKEI and Takagi Shuta Office can be learned jointly [B] via audiovisual instructional materials [C].

A	B
	C
	D
	E

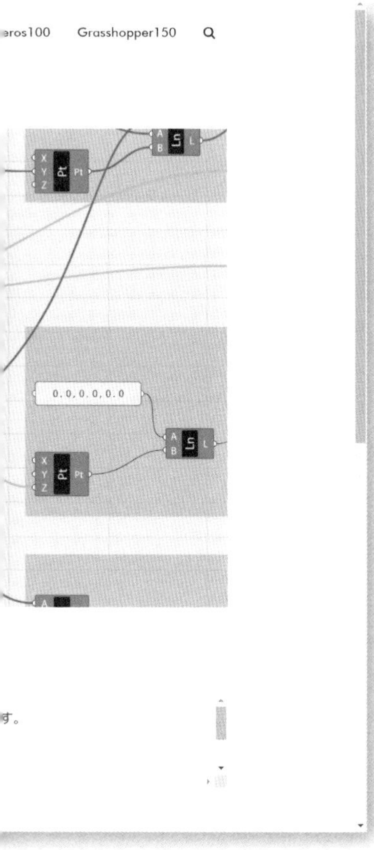
eros100
Grasshopper150
0.0,0.0,0.0
す。

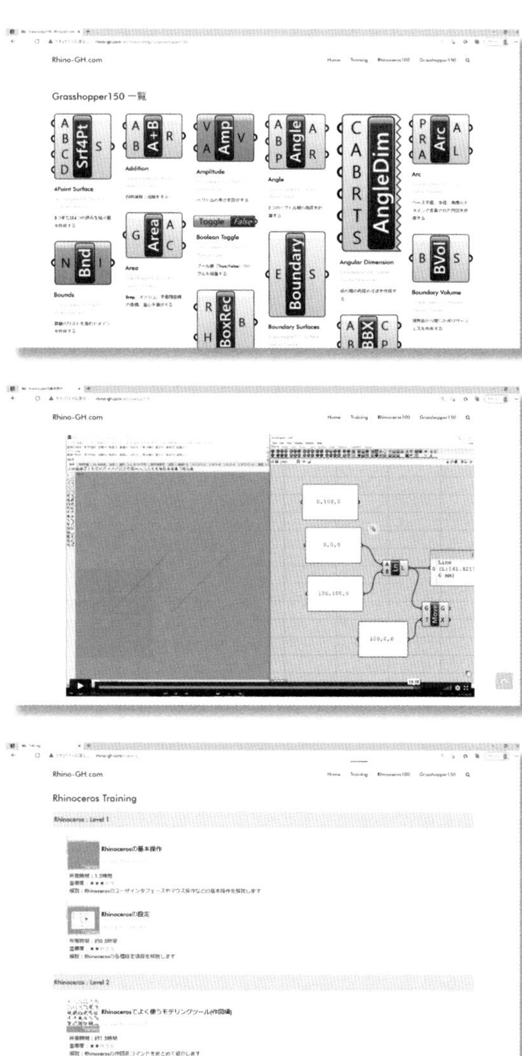
Rhino-GH.com
Grasshopper150 一覧
4Point Surface
Addition
Amplitude
Angle
Angular Dimension
Arc
Boolean Toggle
Bounds
Area
Boundary Surfaces
Boundary Volume
Rhinoceros Training
Rhinoceros : Level 1
Rhinocerosの基本操作
Rhinocerosの設定
Rhinoceros : Level 2
Rhinocerosでよく使うモデリングツール(作図編)

Rhino-GH.com

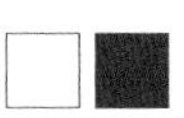

RG.
RG.

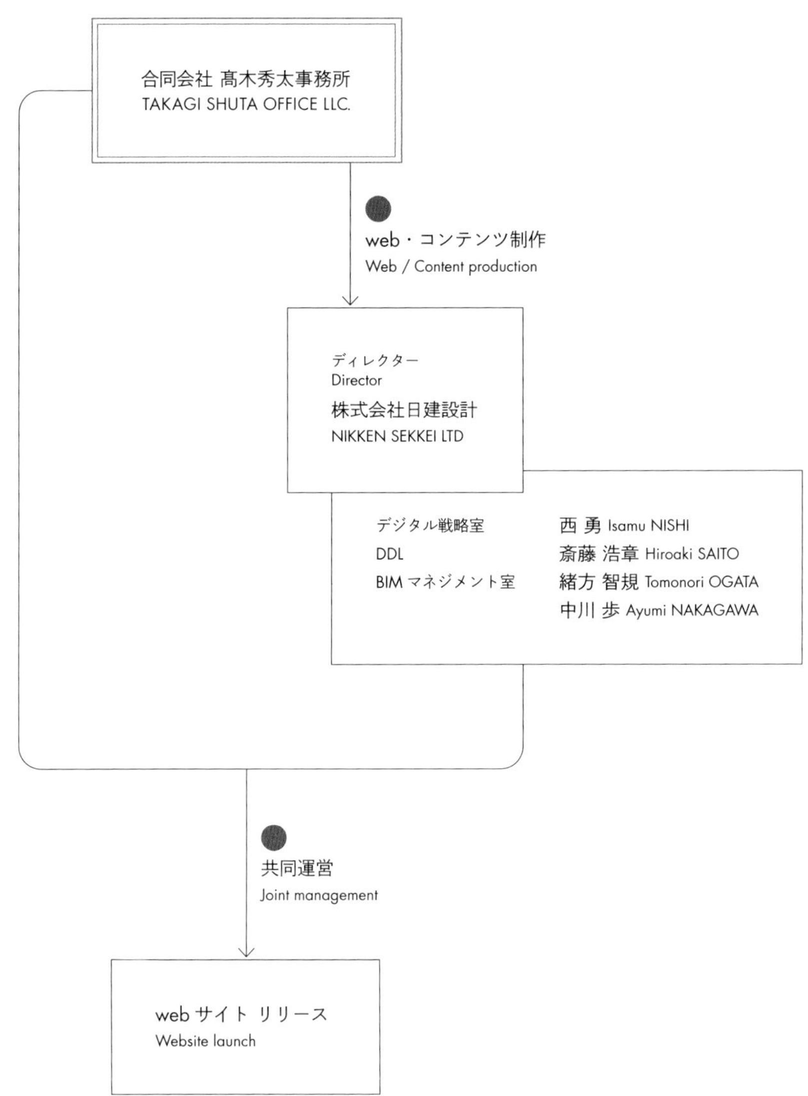

株式会社日建設計とのコラボレーション。髙木秀太事務所では動画・図版の作成から web 制作・運営までをトータルで担当した。レクチャー動画では講師役も務める。

In collaborating with NIKKEN SEKKEI, Takagi Shuta Office was in charge comprehensively from production of videos and diagrams to website creation and management. In the instructional videos, he also serves as a lecturer.

プロジェクト ID	160001, 220050
プロジェクト期間	2016.04–2017.03, 2022.09–
ディレクター	株式会社日建設計
担当	西 勇、斎藤 浩章、緒方 智規、中川 歩
プロジェクトマネージメント	髙木 秀太
メインプログラマー	髙木 秀太
アシスタントプログラマー	宮國 俊介、永井 宏
外部委託	トップ絵・アイコンデザイン：山口 幸宏
ソフトウェア / 開発環境	WordPress, Rhinoceros
プログラミング言語	HTML, PHP, JavaScript, CSS, Grasshopper
キーワード	web サイト、教育、動画制作

Project ID	160001, 220050
Project term	2016.04–2017.03, 2022.09–
Director	NIKKEN SEKKEI LTD
Project team	Isamu NISHI, Hiroaki SAITO, Tomonori OGATA, Ayumi NAKAGAWA
Project management	Shuta TAKAGI
Main programmer	Shuta TAKAGI
Assistant programmer	Shunsuke MIYAKUNI, Hiroshi NAGAI
Outsourcing	Main image / Icon design : Yukihiro YAMAGUCHI
Software / SDE	WordPress, Rhinoceros
Programming language	HTML, PHP, JavaScript, CSS, Grasshopper
Keywords	Website, Education, Video production

web プラットフォームは WordPress。動画プラットフォームは Vimeo を採用。公開から 5 年でページビューは 100 万ビュー、新規ユーザー数は 10 万人を突破している。

WordPress was used for the website platform, and Vimeo for the video platform. In the five years since its release, there has been more than 1 million page views and the number of first-time users has exceeded 100,000.

ARCHICAD-LEARNING.COM

13

ディレクター 株式会社日建設計
Director NIKKEN SEKKEI LTD

ディレクター グラフィソフトジャパン株式会社
Director Graphisoft Japan Co., Ltd.

建築設計BIMソフトウェアArchicadの独学webサイトである。Rhino-GH.comに続く独学webサイト第二弾として計画された。ディレクターは株式会社日建設計と同ソフトウェアの開発・販売メーカーであるグラフィソフトジャパン。実務を遂行する設計事務所、ソフトウェアを販売するメーカーとのコラボレーションとして三位一体体制のプロジェクトとなった。

A self-learning website of Archicad, a BIM software for architectural design, was planned as a follow-up to the self-learning website Rhino-GH.com. The clients were NIKKEN SEKKEI and Graphisoft Japan, developer and distributor of the software. In collaborating with the architectural firm with design practice and the manufacturer-distributor of the software, this project was realized through a triad structure.

ARCHICAD-Learning.com

Home

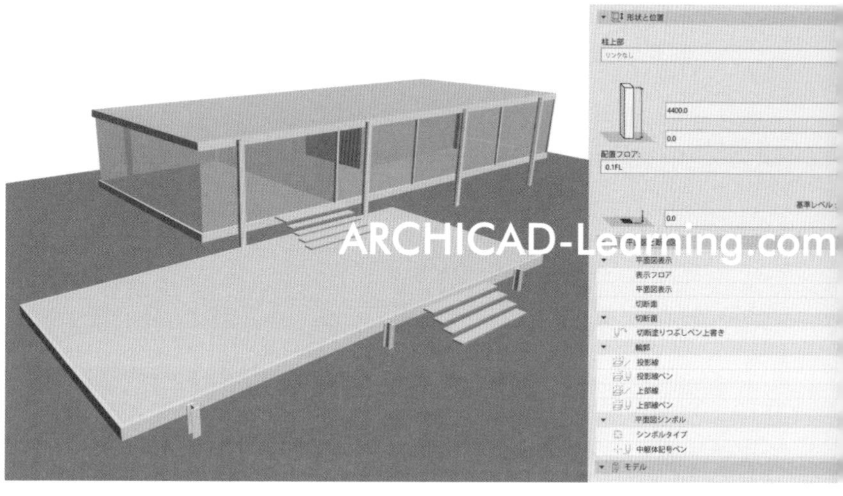

NEW!
Grasshopper — ARCHICAD Live Connection
待望の新コンテンツ ARCHICADをGrasshopperで制御してみましょう

お知らせ

サイトデザインはRhino-GH.comを踏襲しており[A]-[E]、両サイトそれぞれのユーザーがスムーズに双方を行き来できる構造となった。継続的な更新がなされており、2020年には大型アップデートが行われた。

Website design followed the precedent of Rhino-GH.com [A]-[E], and the structure allowed users to go back and forth between both sites smoothly. Continuous updates have been made since, and a major update was conducted in 2020.

A

B

C

D

E

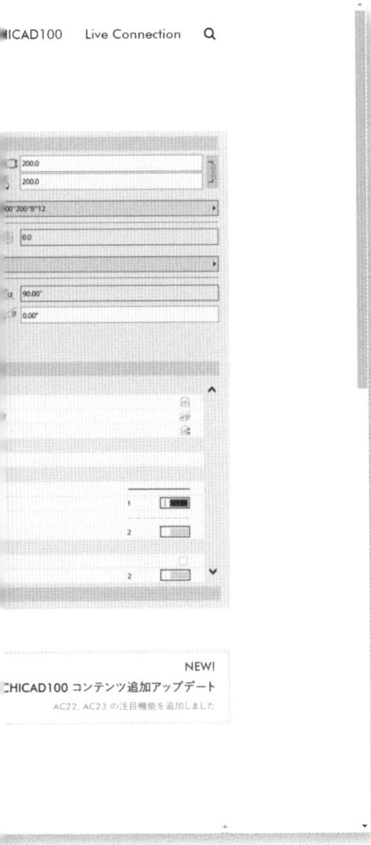

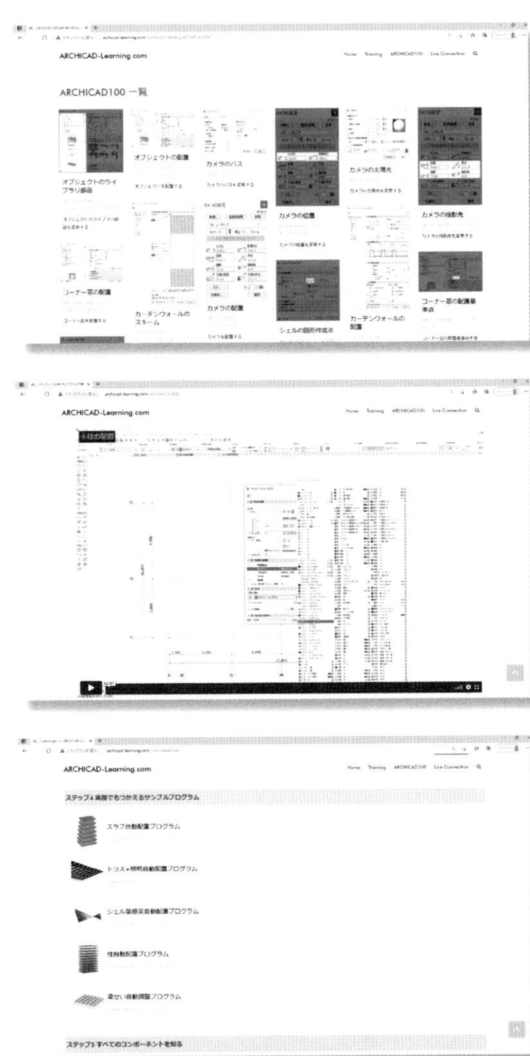

ARCHICAD-Learning.com

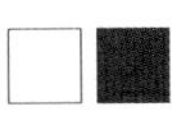

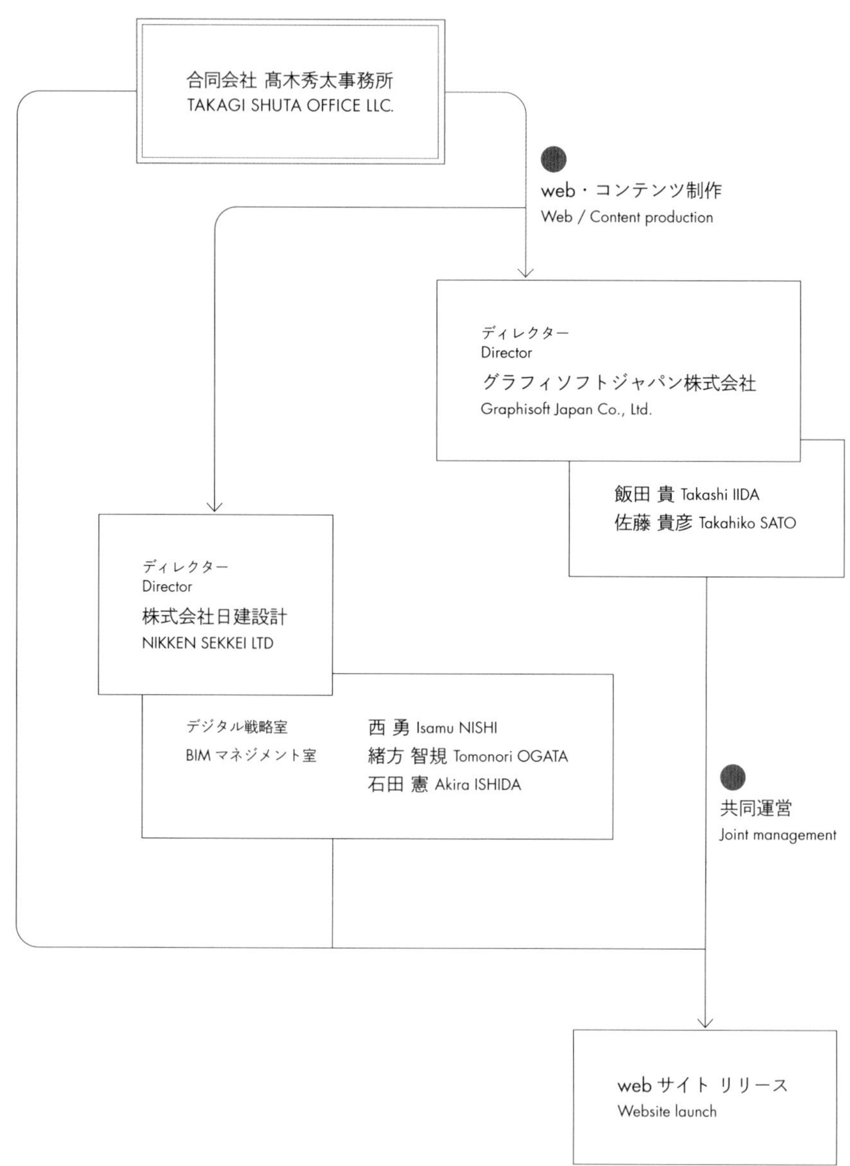

株式会社日建設計、グラフィソフトジャパン株式会社とのコラボレーション。髙木秀太事務所では引き続きwebサイトの全面的な制作・管理を担当している。

Working in collaboration with NIKKEN SEKKEI and Graphisoft Japan, Takagi Shuta Office continues to be fully in charge of production and management of the website.

プロジェクトID	170006, 200027, 220050
プロジェクト期間	2017.04–2017.10, 2020.04–2020.10, 2022.09–
ディレクター	株式会社日建設計
担当	西 勇、緒方 智規、石田 憲
ディレクター	グラフィソフトジャパン株式会社
担当	飯田 貴、佐藤 貴彦
プロジェクトマネージメント	髙木 秀太、髙塚 悟
メインプログラマー	髙木 秀太、髙塚 悟
アシスタントプログラマー	永井 宏、森 大樹、宮國 俊介
アシスタントスタッフ	川西 愛子、建道 佳一郎、野末 誠斗
外部委託	トップ絵・アイコンデザイン：山口 幸宏
ソフトウェア / 開発環境	WordPress, Archicad, Rhinoceros
プログラミング言語	HTML, PHP, JavaScript, CSS, Grasshopper
キーワード	web サイト、教育、動画制作

Project ID	170006, 200027, 220050
Project term	2017.04–2017.10, 2020.04–2020.10, 2022.09–
Director	NIKKEN SEKKEI LTD
Project team	Isamu NISHI, Tomonori OGATA, Akira ISHIDA
Director	Graphisoft Japan Co., Ltd.
Project team	Takashi IIDA, Takahiko SATO
Project management	Shuta TAKAGI, Satoru TAKATSUKA
Main programmer	Shuta TAKAGI, Satoru TAKATSUKA
Assistant programmer	Hiroshi NAGAI, Daiki MORI, Shunsuke MIYAKUNI
Assistant staff	Aiko KAWANISHI, Keiichiro KONDO, Makoto NOZUE
Outsourcing	Main image / Icon design : Yukihiro YAMAGUCHI
Software / SDE	WordPress, Archicad, Rhinoceros
Programming language	HTML, PHP, JavaScript, CSS, Grasshopper
Keywords	Website, Education, Video production

学習対象のArchicadはBIM (Building Information Modeling) と呼ばれる建築設計専用のモデリングソフトウェア。webサイトでは髙木秀太事務所作成の様々なサンプルファイルが公開されている。

Archicad is a BIM (Building Information Modeling) software dedicated to architectural design. On the website, diverse sample files created by Takagi Shuta Office have been made publicly available.

BUILDING ENVIRONMENT DESIGN.COM

14

クライアント　東京大学 前真之サステイナブル建築デザイン研究室
Client　MAE Lab for Sustainable Arch.Design, the University of Tokyo

ディレクター　合同会社スタジオノラ
Director　Studio Nora LLC.

建築設計における各種環境シミュレーションソフトウェアの独学webサイトである。東京大学 前真之サステイナブル建築デザイン研究室、合同会社スタジオノラとのコラボレーション。大学授業における環境シミュレーション教育のノウハウを一般公開していくことを目的とした。日射、日影、快適性、エネルギー、風、多種多様なシミュレーションをサポートしている。

A self-learning website for a wide variety of environmental simulation software in architectural design, in collaboration with Masayuki Mae Laboratory at the University of Tokyo and Studio Nora. The objective was to share the knowledge on environmental simulation education at the university with the general public. The website supports simulations involving sunlight, shadow, comfort, energy, wind, etc.

Building Environment Design.com

Ho

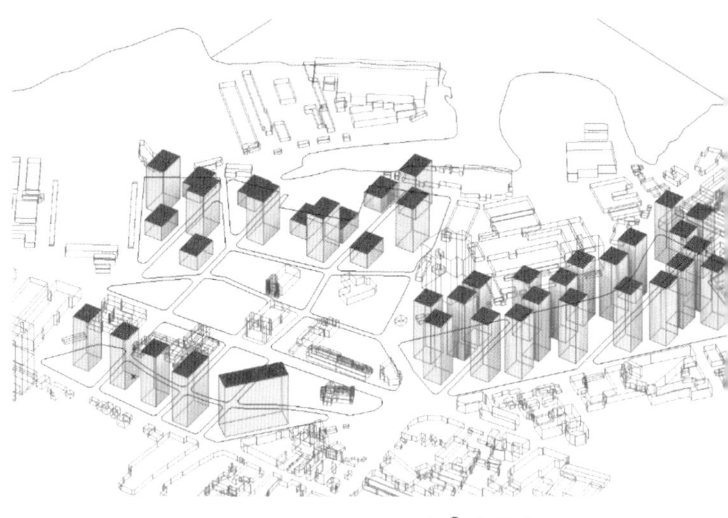

メンバーシップ制度を導入しました。レベル★★☆以上のプログラムDL及びフォーラムへの投稿はメンバー限定コンテンツとなりま
こちらでアカウントを作成できます。

[20/03/04] Training「Daylight Analysis 光環境解析 Honeybee (Radiance)」を公開しました。
[19/10/25] 風環境解析ページのGH2FDプラグインファイルを更新しました。
[19/10/25] 風環境解析ページに「屋内の風環境を解析するプログラム」「ループ解析機能の使い方」を追加しました。

webサイトのトップページ [A]。デザインフォーマットはRhino-GH.comとARCHICAD-Learning.comを踏襲している。環境設計の知識がない初心者でもわかりやすい入門編として各種コンテンツが用意された [B]-[D]。

Home page of the website [A]. The design format follows that of Rhino-GH.com and ARCHICAD-Learning.com. Various contents were prepared as a primer for beginners with little knowledge of environmental design [B]-[D].

A B C D E

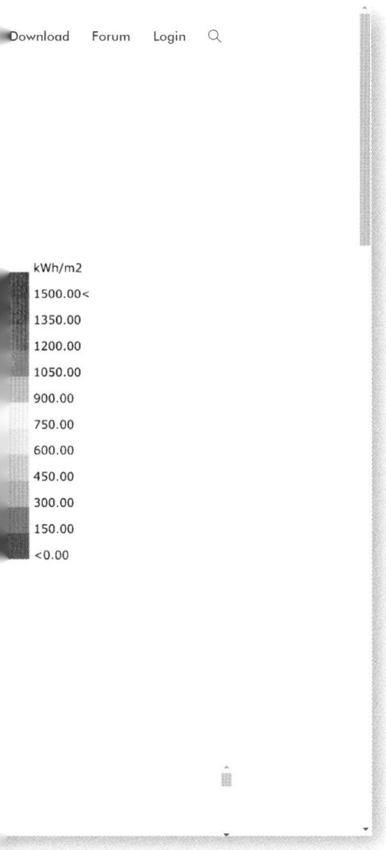

Download Forum Login

kWh/m2
1500.00<
1350.00
1200.00
1050.00
900.00
750.00
600.00
450.00
300.00
150.00
<0.00

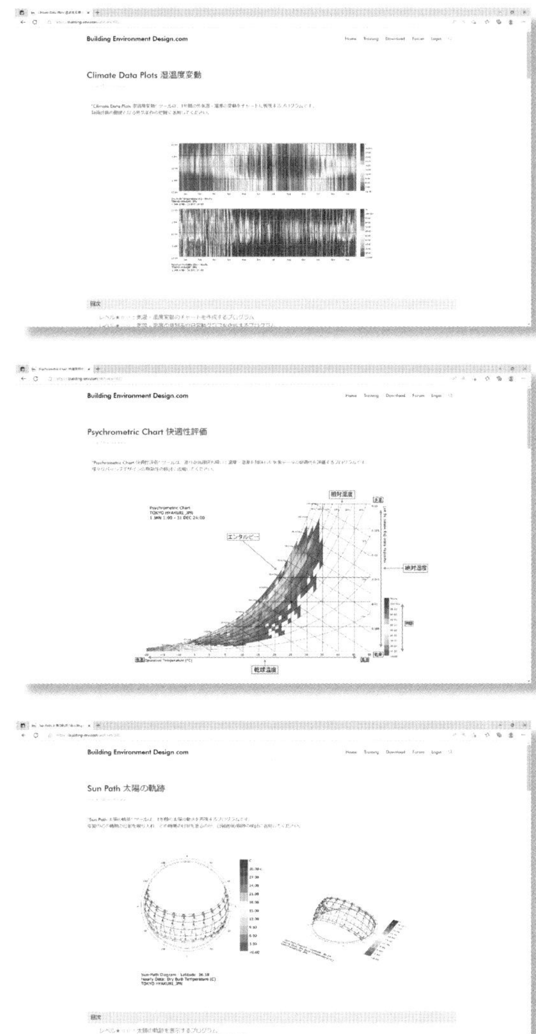

Building Environment Design.com

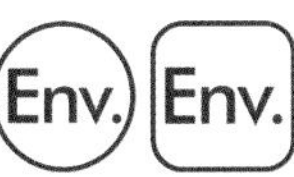

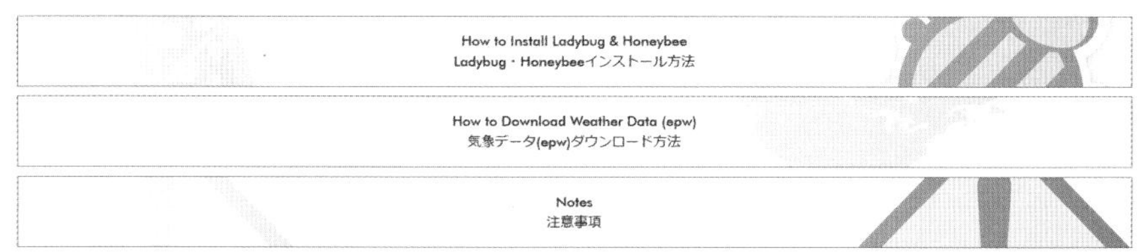

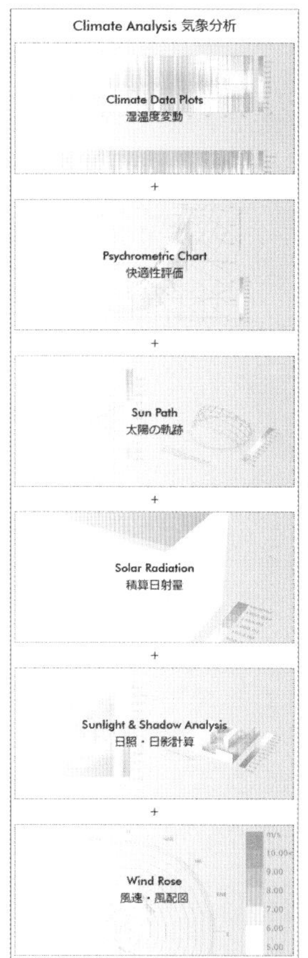

学習チャート

Learning chart

環境シミュレーションを体系化した学習フローチャートが用意され、網羅的な学習がサポートできるようにwebサイトが構築されている。

Flow chart for learning was prepared for systematized environmental simulations, and the website was organized to support comprehensive learning.

前研究室・髙木秀太事務所
共同開発 Grasshopper プラグイン
Mae Laboratory / Takagi Shuta Office
Co-developed Grasshopper plug-in

GH2FD

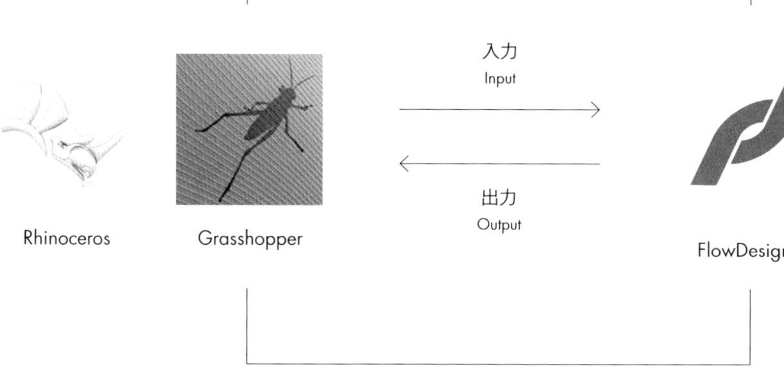

C#
開発言語
Development language

Visual Studio
開発環境
Development environment

※ GH2FD は東京大学大学院工学系研究科建築学専攻前真之研究室の大学院生・高雲氏によってプレリリース版が開発され、髙木秀太事務所が開発を引き継ぎました。

プラグイン GH2FD 開発
GH2FD plug-in development

風解析（CFD）ソフトウェアである FlowDesigner（アドバンスドナレッジ研究所）と連動したコンテンツも企画され、関連するソフトウェアもオリジナルで開発された。

Contents interconnected to a wind analysis (CFD) software FlowDesigner (Advanced Knowledge Laboratory Inc.) were planned, and related original software was also developed.

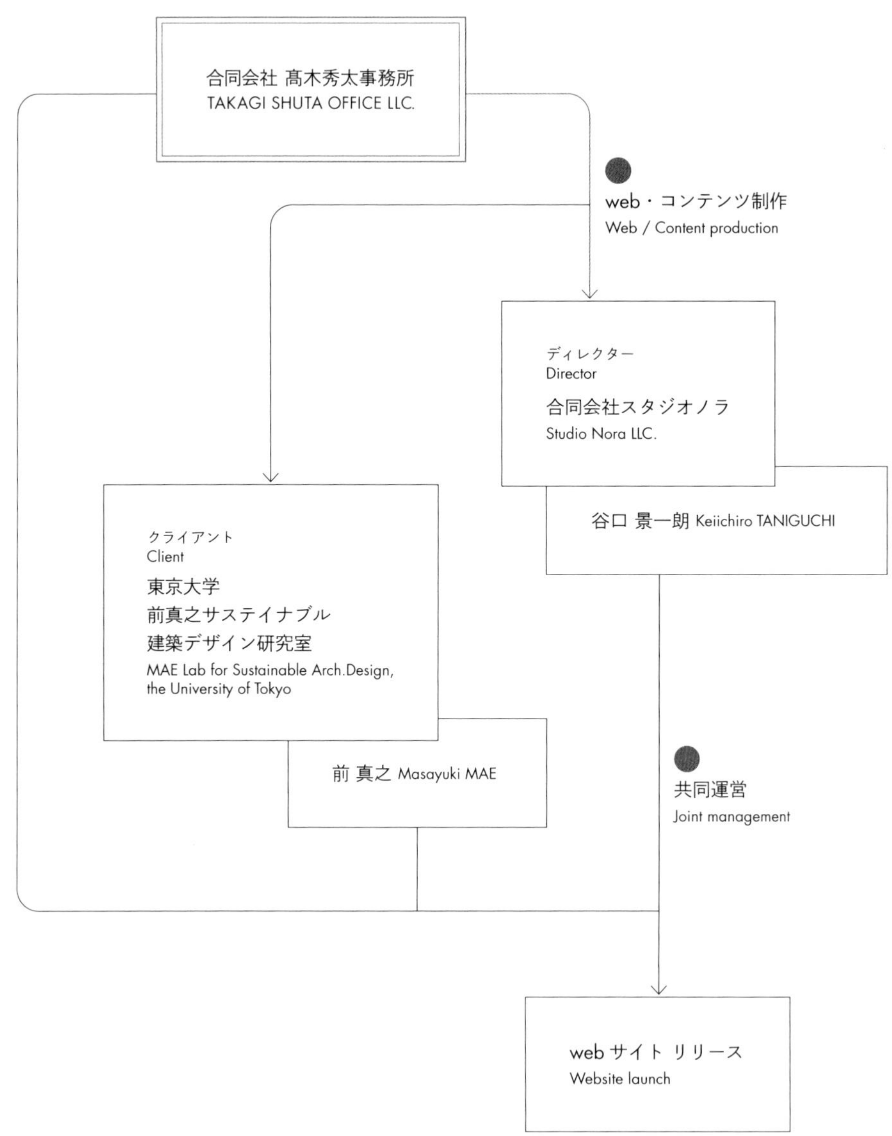

担当の谷口 景一朗氏は合同会社スタジオノラの代表であり、東京大学 前真之サステイナブル建築デザイン研究室 特任助教（当時）でもある。企画は同氏により提案され、ディレクションされた。髙木秀太事務所はweb構築や教材作成のノウハウを提供。専門分野の相乗効果が生まれたコラボレーションプロジェクトとなった。

The project was proposed and directed by Keiichiro Taniguchi, co-founder of Studio Nora and project assistant professor of Mae Laboratory at the time. Takagi Shuta Office provided expertise on website creation and production of educational materials. The collaborative efforts from specialists generated a synergistic effect.

プロジェクトID	180032
プロジェクト期間	2018.04–
クライアント	東京大学 前真之サステイナブル建築デザイン研究室
担当	前 真之
ディレクター	合同会社スタジオノラ
担当	谷口 景一朗
プロジェクトマネージメント	髙木 秀太、髙塚 悟
メインプログラマー	髙木 秀太、髙塚 悟
アシスタントプログラマー	布井 翔一郎、飛田 剛太
アシスタントスタッフ	永井 宏
ソフトウェア / 開発環境	WordPress, VisualStudio, Ladybug, Honeybee, Rhinoceros, FlowDesigner
プログラミング言語	HTML, PHP, JavaScript, CSS, C#, Grasshopper
キーワード	webサイト、教育、動画制作、環境シミュレーション、プラグイン開発

Project ID	180032
Project term	2018.04–
Client	MAE Lab for Sustainable Arch.Design, the University of Tokyo
Project leader	Masayuki MAE
Director	Studio Nora LLC.
Project leader	Keiichiro TANIGUCHI
Project management	Shuta TAKAGI, Satoru TAKATSUKA
Main programmer	Shuta TAKAGI, Satoru TAKATSUKA
Assistant programmer	Shoichiro NUNOI, Gota HIDA
Assistant staff	Hiroshi NAGAI
Software / SDE	WordPress, VisualStudio, Ladybug, Honeybee, Rhinoceros, FlowDesigner
Programming language	HTML, PHP, JavaScript, CSS, C#, Grasshopper
Keywords	Website, Education, Video production, Environmental simulation, Plug-in development

ビジュアルプログラミング言語であるGrasshopperのプラグインLadybug Toolsに関する教材がメインコンテンツ。同ツールはオープンソースの環境解析ツールと連動し、世界中で広く利用されている。

The main content was the educational material for visual programming language Grasshopper's plug-in, Ladybug tools, which has been widely used around the world in conjunction with open source environmental analysis tools.

OPEN DDL

クライアント 株式会社日建設計
Client NIKKEN SEKKEI LTD

株式会社日建設計のデジタルデザインチーム DDL（Digital Design Lab）の情報共有サイトである。同チームが蓄積したナレッジを公開・共有するハブサービスとしてリリースされた。髙木秀太事務所は株式会社アーキロイドと協働し、同サイトの改修企画から制作まで一括して担当した。

An information sharing website for DDL (Digital Design Lab), digital design team at NIKKEN SEKKEI, was released as a hub service to publicize and share the accumulated knowledge of the DDL team. Takagi Shuta Office collaborated with archiroid Inc., and was in charge from renewal plans of the website to its production.

open DL Digital Design Lab |Search Digital design...

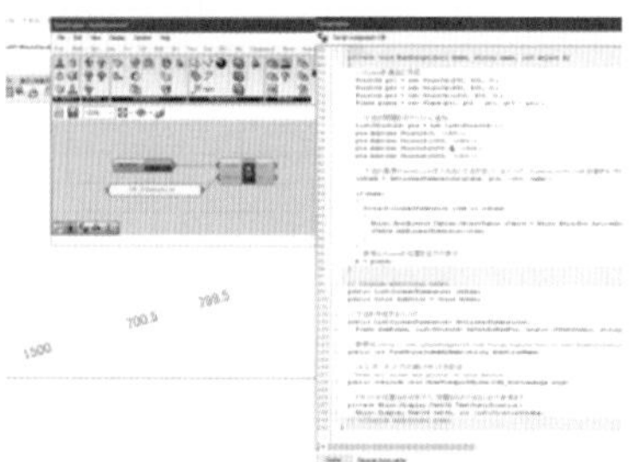

GH C#_寸法線を描いてBakeする(Rhin...

Rhino6では書き方が変わります。こちらを参照下さい。（追記：20/05/14） C#コンポーネントを使って寸法スタイルを定義し、寸法線を描いてBakeするまでの流れをざっくりで[…]

#Grasshopper #C# #bake #Dimension #Di...

Apr 16, 2018

Hiroaki Saito

Unityとkinectによるインタラクティブ...

ずいぶんと前のことになってしまいますが、昨年4月に開催されたB.Information展で展示した「BI Platform」を簡単に紹介します。B.Information展では、普段、無意識に触れ[…]

#Physical_Computing #Digital Archive #B.Infor...

Apr 13, 2018

Yoshinori Hatanaka

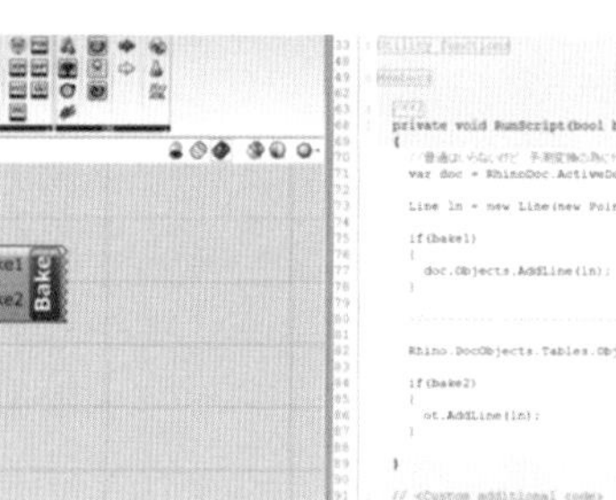

GH C#_簡単なBake Componentを作っ...

既に色んなAddonで提供されているBake Componentについて簡単に考え方を整理してみました。例えば、適当なLineをC# Component内で作ってボタンを押す事[…]

#Grasshopper #C# #bake

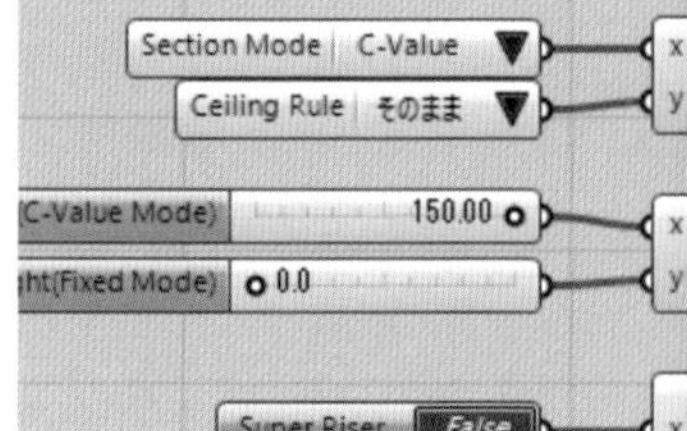

GH C#_入力コンポーネントの初期値...

Grasshopperにおいて、とあるツールを用意する際に必要な入力パラメーターの量が多くなるほどにその管理は面倒になってきます。特に初心者でも利用できるものを想定した[…]

#Grasshopper #C# #Value List #Number Slid...

webサイトは権限階層で管理されるSNSベースで構築されている。個々のスタッフアカウントによってデジタルデザインに関するナレッジを紹介する記事が投稿され、一般アカウントにはお気に入りやコメントを付ける権限が付与されている。

The website was built on SNS-based permission hierarchy management system. Each staff account allows submission of articles introducing their digital design knowledge, and the general public account can like or comment on the articles.

openDDLについて　サイトポリシー　ご利用前にお読みください　SIGN IN:　EN

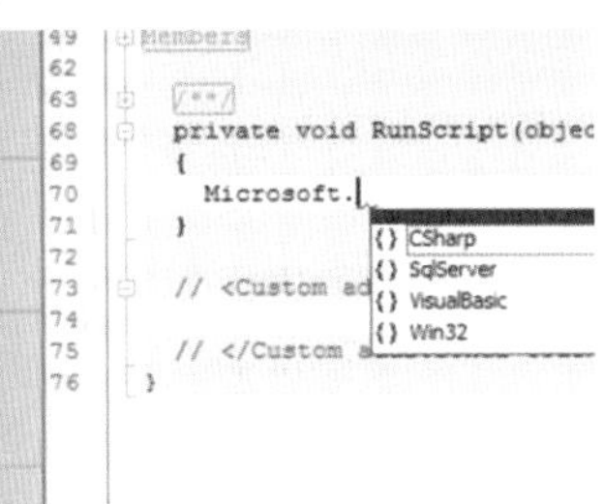

C#_Excelと連携する

言前の準備 GrasshopperのC#コンポーネン
でExcelとの読み書きを行うためには、
rosoft.Office.Interop.Excel　NameSpace
名前空間）を利用する必要がありますが[…]

asshopper　#C#　#Excel

12, 2018

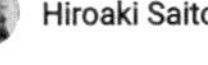

Hiroaki Saito

A Performative Table

去年四月で日建設計エントランスホールで開催されたB.Information展で展示された作品の一つ、DDLのPhysicalComputingチームメンバーでつくったPerformative Tableのシステ[…]

#Physical_Computing　#Data Driven　#B.Informa…

Apr 09, 2018

Xuhao Lin

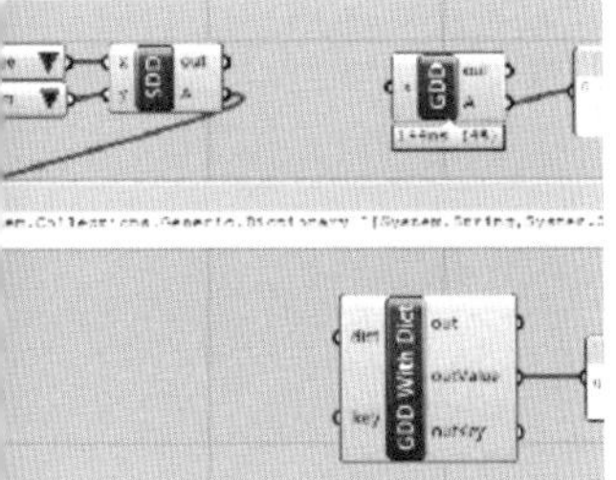

C#_データ管理にDictionaryを利用…

ータ管理にDictionaryを利用する(GitHub
tに飛びます) C# Component間でデータを
り取りする際、独自に用意したクラスで作
したオブジェクトを受け渡すことは仕様[…]

asshopper　#C#　#Dictionary

忘年会の場所決め問題を考える

はじめに こんにちは．忘年会の季節ですね．私のいる階では12月3日に忘年会が開催されるので，1年の92.3%を忘れられる計算です．冗談はこれくらいにして，パーティーの場[…]

#Optimisation　#javascript　#Google Maps API

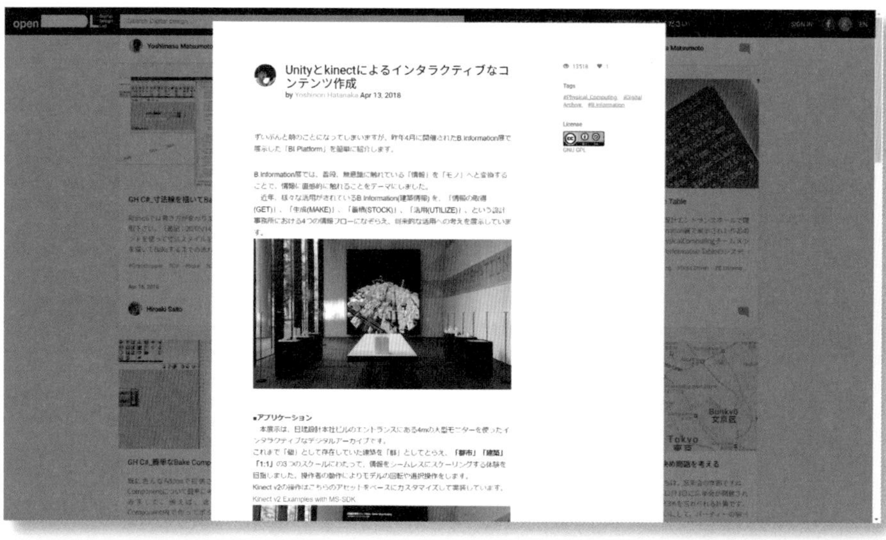

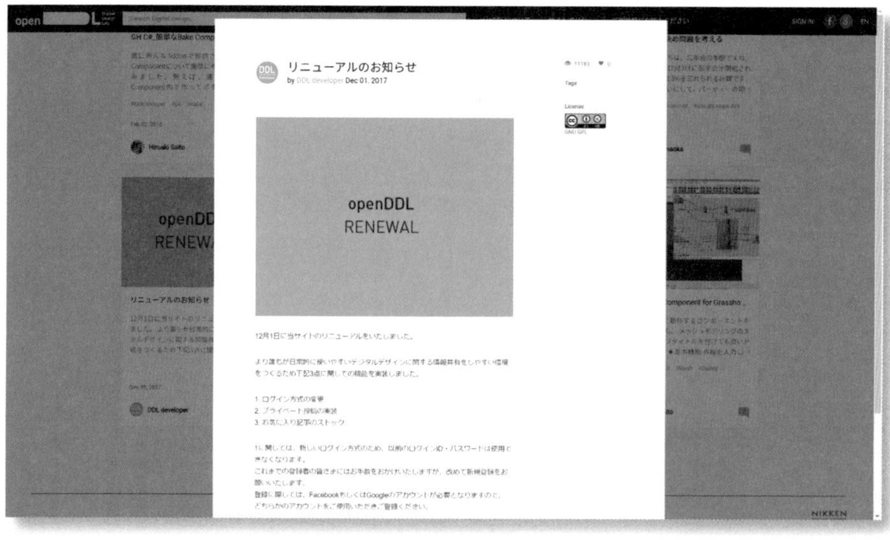

サイトのレイアウトデザインはパソコン、スマホそれぞれで最適な表示がされるように考慮された[A]-[D]。サイトのロゴデザインは株式会社日建設計 DDL ダイレクター 角田 大輔氏によるもの [E]。

The website design was considered for optimized display and compatibility on both computers and smartphones [A]-[D]. The website's logo design was created by the acting DDL Director, Daisuke Tsunoda [E].

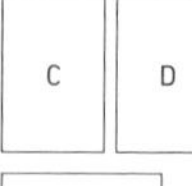

open L
Digital
Design
Lab

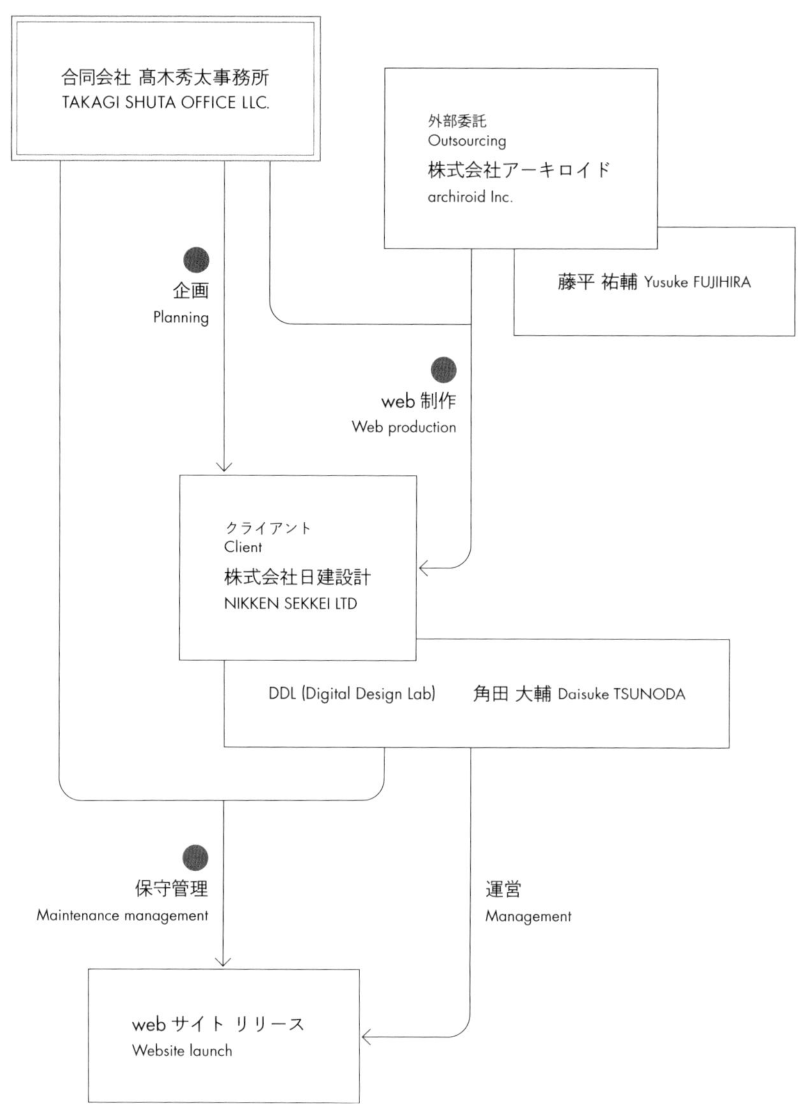

プロジェクトマスターはクライアントでもある株式会社日建設計 DDL ダイレクター 角田 大輔氏。WordPress で構築された既存の web ページをゼロベースから再構築した。開発は株式会社アーキロイドと協働。

The project master was Daisuke Tsunoda, the acting director of DDL and also the client. The preexisting website built with WordPress was rebuilt from scratch. It was developed in collaboration with archiroid Inc.

プロジェクトID	170004
プロジェクト期間	2017.08–2017.12
クライアント	株式会社日建設計
担当	角田 大輔
プロジェクトマネージメント	髙木 秀太
メインプログラマー	髙木 秀太
外部委託	web開発：株式会社アーキロイド（藤平 祐輔）
ソフトウェア / 開発環境	VisualStudio
プログラミング言語	HTML, Node.js, JavaScript, CSS, MySQL
キーワード	webサイト

Project ID	170004
Project term	2017.08–2017.12
Client	NIKKEN SEKKEI LTD
Project leader	Daisuke TSUNODA
Project management	Shuta TAKAGI
Main programmer	Shuta TAKAGI
Outsourcing	Web development : archiroid Inc. (Yusuke FUJIHIRA)
Software / SDE	VisualStudio
Programming language	HTML, Node.js, JavaScript, CSS, MySQL
Keywords	Website

サーバーサイドのプログラミング言語はNode.jsを採用。開発言語をJavaScriptに統一した。開発の主担当は株式会社アーキロイドの藤平 祐輔氏。

Server-side programming language used was Node.js., and development language was standardized with JavaScript. Yusuke Fujihira of archiroid Inc. was primarily in charge of the development.

避難所自然換気シミュレーション

NATURAL VENTILATION SIMULATION FOR EVACUATION SHELTERS

16

ディレクター 大成建設株式会社一級建築士事務所
Director TAISEI DESIGN Planners Architects & Engineers

監修 東北大学大学院工学研究科 サステナブル環境構成学分野
Supervision Sustainable Environment Creation Laboratory, Tohoku University

避難所における自然換気シミュレーションプログラムの開発・公開プロジェクトである。大成建設株式会社、東北大学大学院工学研究科 サステナブル環境構成学分野とのコラボレーション。

避難所（＝体育館）の自然換気性能を誰でも手軽に算出することをねらいとし、コロナ禍（2020年～）での災害発生時において有効なツールになることを目指し開発された。

A project to develop and publicize natural ventilation simulation programs for evacuation shelters, in collaboration with TAISEI DESIGN and the Sustainable Environment Creation Laboratory at the Graduate School of Engineering, Tohoku University.

The aim was to make natural ventilation performance at evacuation shelters (= gymnasiums) easily calculable by anyone, in order to provide an effective tool in the event of a disaster in the era of coronavirus pandemic from 2020.

Fig.A

SVE3 値カラーチャート
SVE3 level color chart

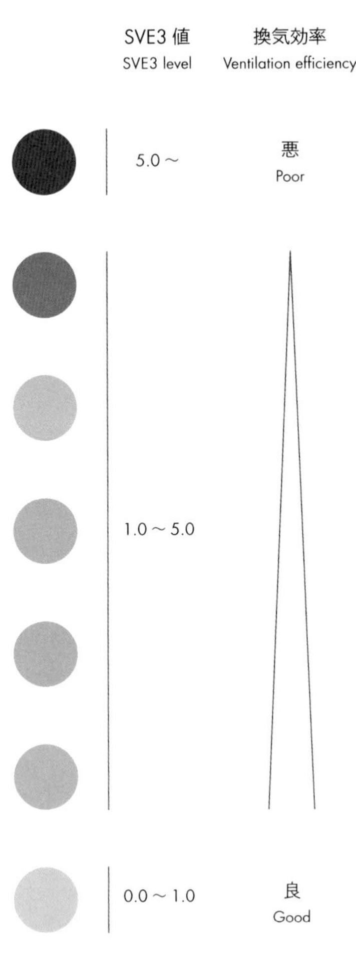

※ SVE3（Scale for Ventilation Efficiency 3）＝換気効率指標

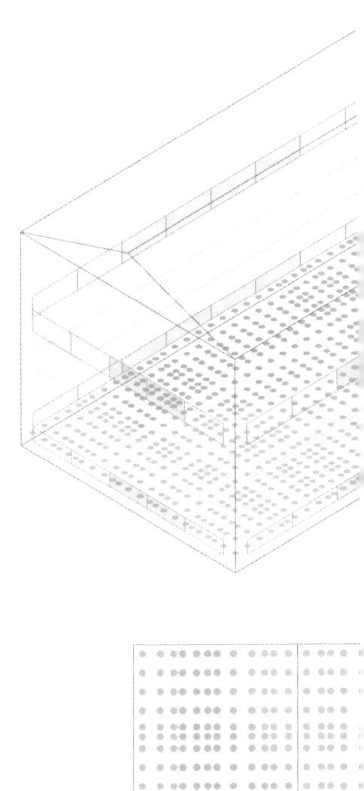

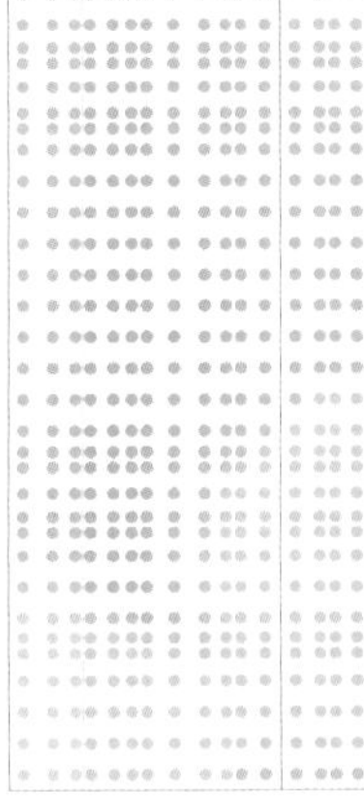

開発プログラムでは「空気齢」と呼ばれる換気効率指標を評価する SVE3 (Scale for Ventilation Efficiency 3）を採用。様々な体育館モデル、パーテーションの形状を対象に自然換気シミュレーションを試すことができる。青くカラーマッピングされているエリアは空気が滞留しやすい。

Ventilation efficiency index SVE3 (Scale for Ventilation Efficiency 3) called "age of air" was used for evaluation in the development program. Natural ventilation simulations for different gymnasium models and partition layouts can be tested. Areas mapped in blue indicate where air tend to stagnate.

Fig.B

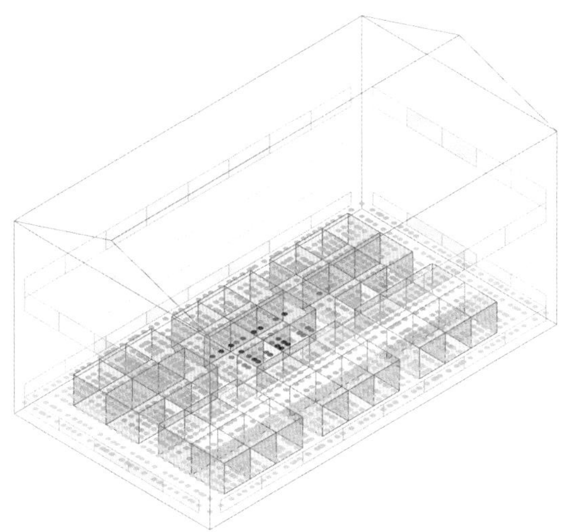

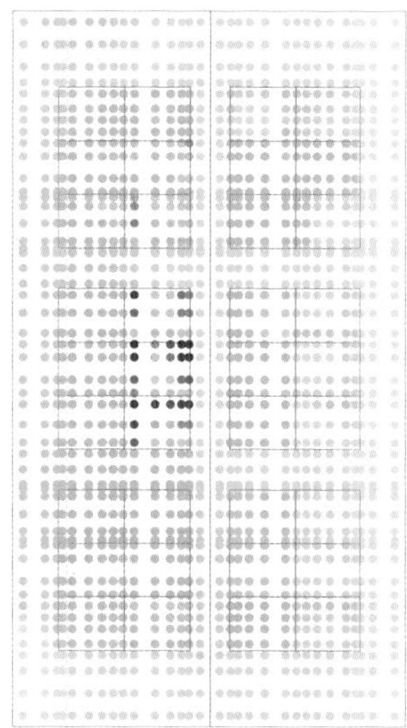

Fig.A パーテーションなし（南南東の風、窓半開）
No partitions（South-southeast wind, half-open windows）

Fig.B パーテーションあり（南南東の風、窓半開）
With partitions（South-southeast wind, half-open windows）

東北大学大学院工学研究科都市・建築学専攻
サステナブル環境構成学分野 webサイト
Tohoku University Department of civil Engineering and Architecture
Sustainable Environmental Creation Laboratory Website

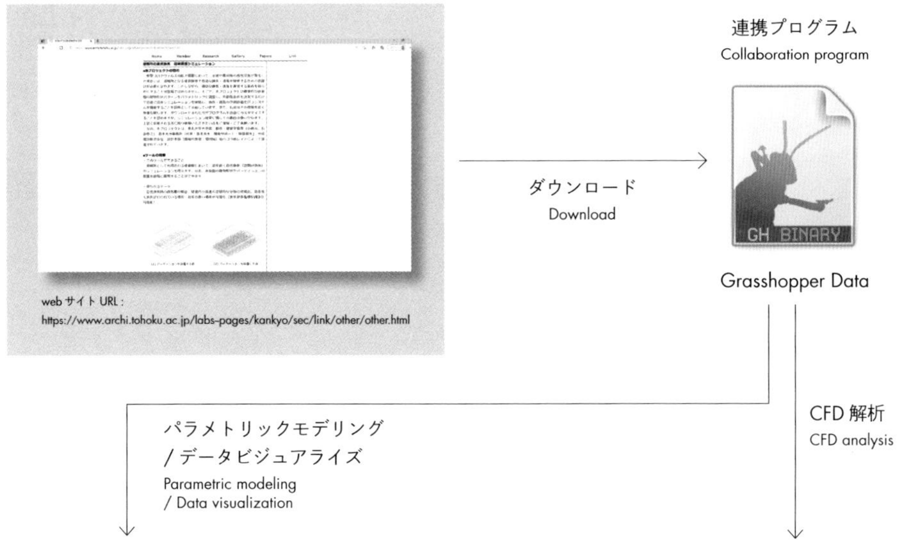

Rhinoceros / Grasshopper

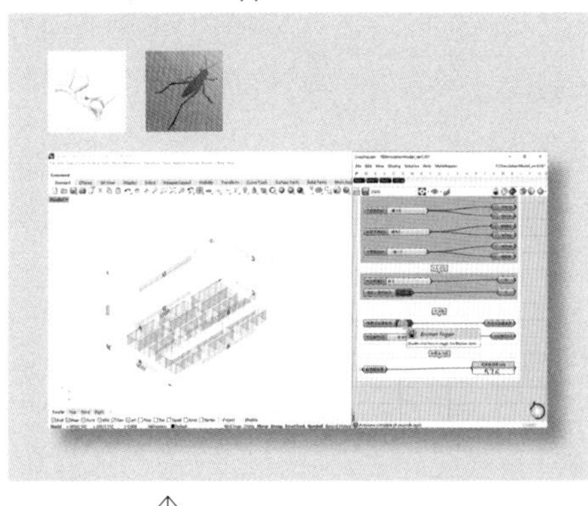

FlowDesigner

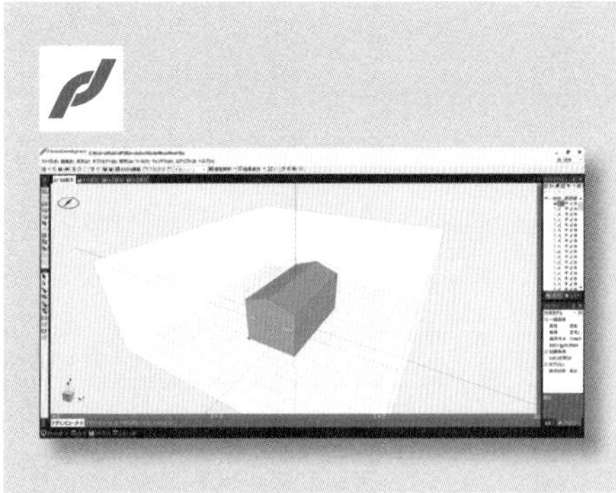

連携
Collaboration

シミュレーションプログラム システム図
Simulation program system flow chart

メインプログラムはGrasshopperで開発された。風解析（=CFD解析）のエンジンはFlowDesigner（アドバンスドナレッジ研究所）を採用。プログラムファイルはwebサイトから誰でもダウンロードできる。

The main program was developed in Grasshopper. For wind analysis (= CFD analysis) software, FlowDesigner (Advanced Knowledge Laboratory Inc.) was adopted. Anyone can download the program file from the website.

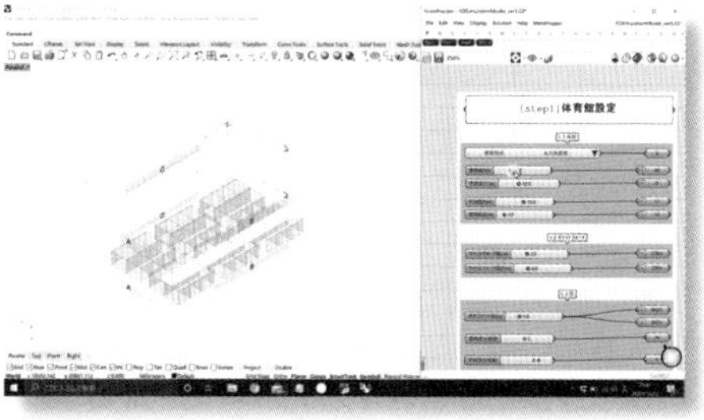

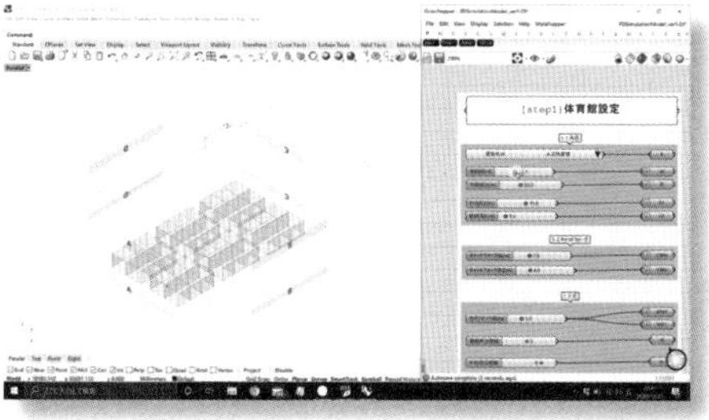

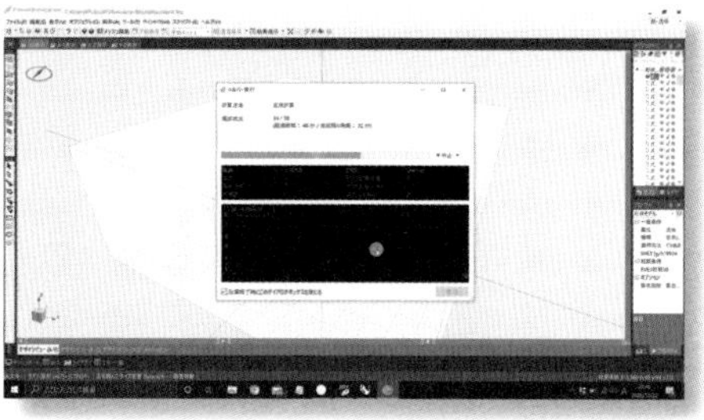

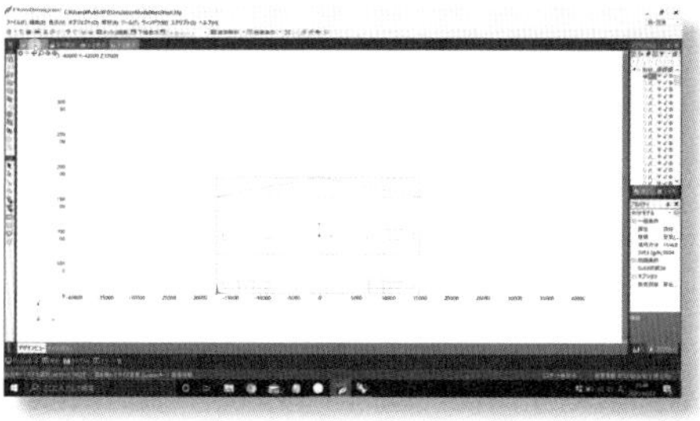

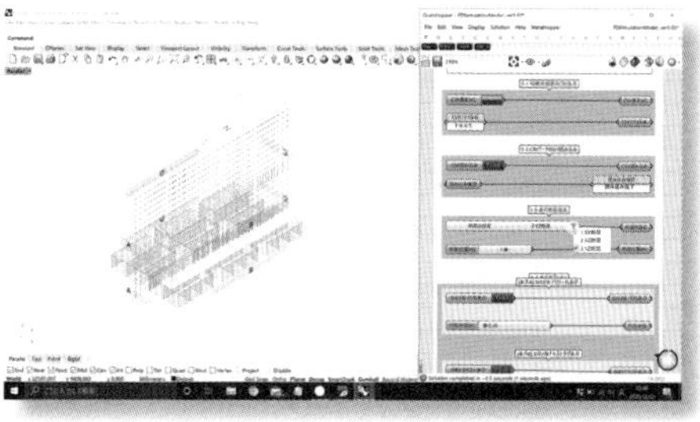

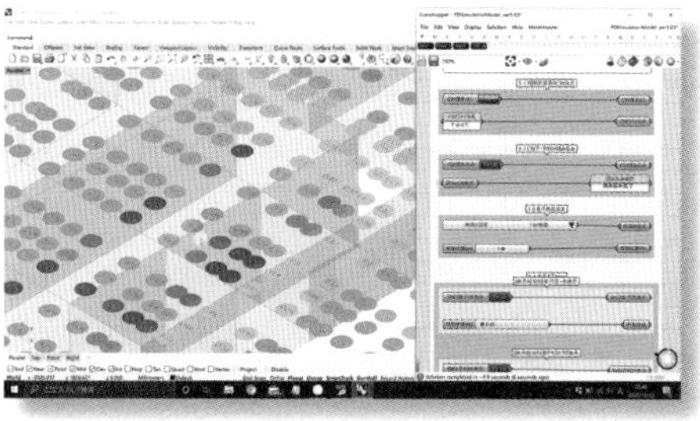

web サイト URL：
https://www.archi.tohoku.ac.jp/labs-pages/kankyo/sec/link/other/other.html

シミュレーションデモ動画
Simulation demonstration videos

プログラムを実行するデモンストレーション動画が制作された。各種パラメーターの入力方法 [A]-[C]、FlowDesigner との連携・制御 [D][E]、そして、出力結果のビジュアライズ [F][G] まで一連の流れに沿って視聴が可能。

Demonstration videos for the program were created. How various parameters can be input [A]-[C], integration and control using FlowDesigner [D][E], and visualization the output results[F][G]can be viewed sequentially.

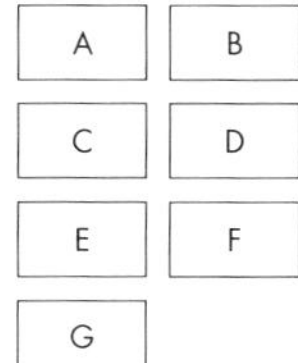

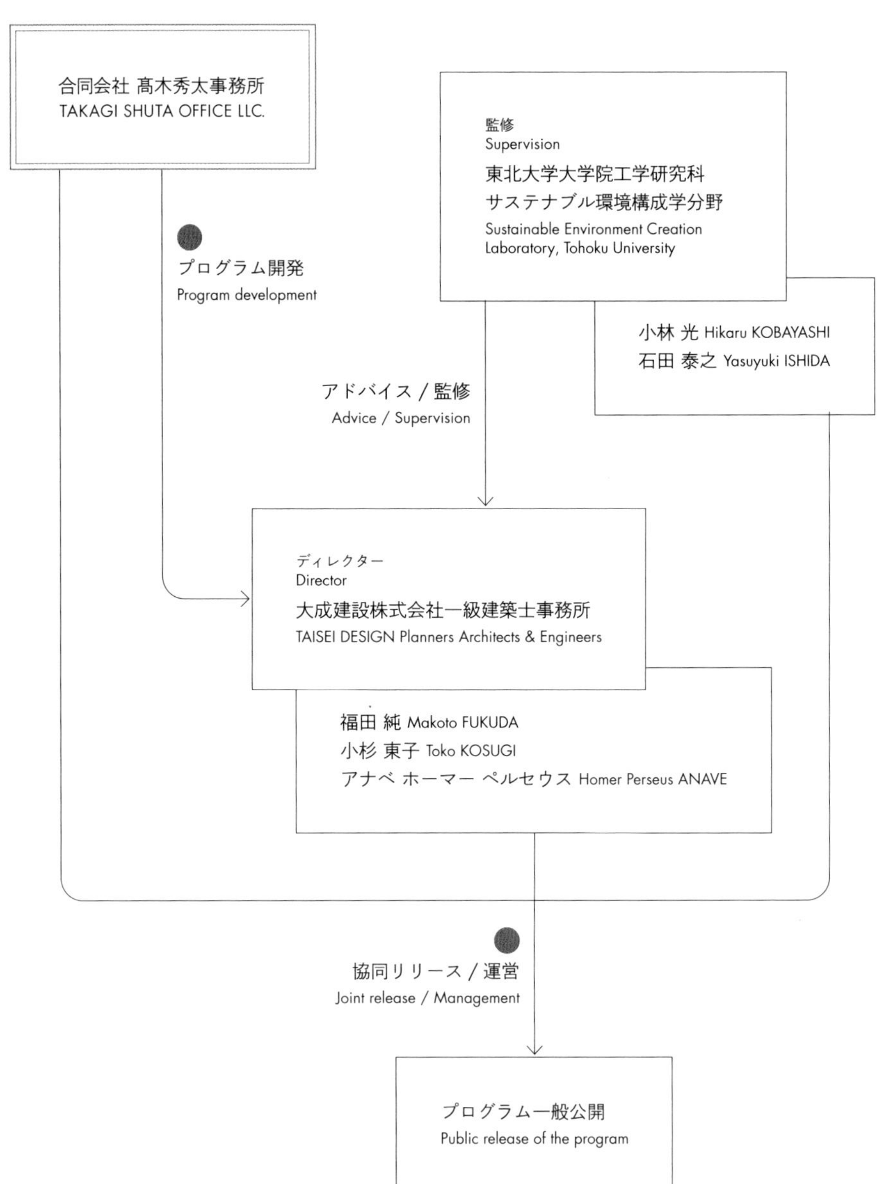

プロジェクトリーダーは大成建設株式会社 福田 純氏。東北大学大学院 准教授 小林 光氏、助教 石田 泰之氏が空気環境の専門的な知見から監修を担った。髙木秀太事務所はプログラム開発を担当。

Makoto Fukuda of TAISEI DESIGN was the project leader. Associate professor Hikaru Kobayashi and assistant Yasuyuki Ishida from Tohoku University supervised the project with their expert knowledge on air environment. Takagi Shuta Office was in charge of program development.

プロジェクト ID	200030
プロジェクト期間	2020.10–
ディレクター	大成建設株式会社一級建築士事務所
担当	福田 純、小杉 東子、アナベ ホーマー ペルセウス
監修	東北大学大学院工学研究科 サステナブル環境構成学分野
担当	小林 光、石田 泰之
プロジェクトマネージメント	髙木 秀太
メインプログラマー	髙木 秀太、飛田 剛太
アシスタントスタッフ	永井 宏、曽根 巽、川西 愛子、高見澤 勇太、野末 誠斗
ソフトウェア / 開発環境	Rhinoceros, FlowDesigner
プログラミング言語	Grasshopper, C#, Python
キーワード	環境シミュレーション、空気環境、 データビジュアライゼーション

Project ID	200030
Project term	2020.10–
Director	TAISEI DESIGN Planners Architects & Engineers
Project team	Makoto FUKUDA, Toko KOSUGI, Homer Perseus ANAVE
Supervision	Sustainable Environment Creation Laboratory, Tohoku University
Project team	Hikaru KOBAYASHI, Yasuyuki ISHIDA
Project management	Shuta TAKAGI
Main programmer	Shuta TAKAGI, Gota HIDA
Assistant staff	Hiroshi NAGAI, Tatsumi SONE, Aiko KAWANISHI, Yuta TAKAMIZAWA, Makoto NOZUE
Software / SDE	Rhinoceros, FlowDesigner
Programming language	Grasshopper, C#, Python
Keywords	Environmental simulation, Air quality analysis, Data visualization

新型コロナウイルス感染症（COVID-19）のパンデミック最中でのプロジェクトであり、日本建築学会主催の「第 30 回空気シンポジウム」でも取り組みの発表・紹介がなされた。

The project was carried out in the midst the Covid-19 coronavirus pandemic, and our efforts were presented in the "30th Air Symposium" hosted by the Architectural Institute of Japan.

LIXIL A-SPEC

クライアント/ディレクター　株式会社 LIXIL
Client / Director　LIXIL Corporation

株式会社LIXILによるパブリックトイレの自動設計補助サービスである。自動設計エンジンが搭載されたwebサービスとしてβ版が2020年にリリースされた。「A-SPEC」とは同webサービスを含めた、デジタル世代の新しいトイレ設計に関する取り組み全体を指すプロジェクトコードである。

髙木秀太事務所は3Dモデルや2D図面を出力するA-SPECの一部プログラム開発やプロモーション業務で参画している。株式会社LIXIL(企画)、株式会社AMDlab（開発）とのコラボレーション。

An automatic auxiliary design service for public toilets by LIXIL Corporation. Its beta version was released in 2020 as a web service equipped with automatic design engine. "A-SPEC" was the project code referring to the entire endeavor of new toilet design methods for the digital age, including web services.

Takagi Shuta Office was involved in A-SPEC program development for 3D model and 2D drawing output as well as promotional operations. The project was carried out in collaboration with LIXIL Corporation, which was in charge of planning, and AMDlab Inc., in charge of development.

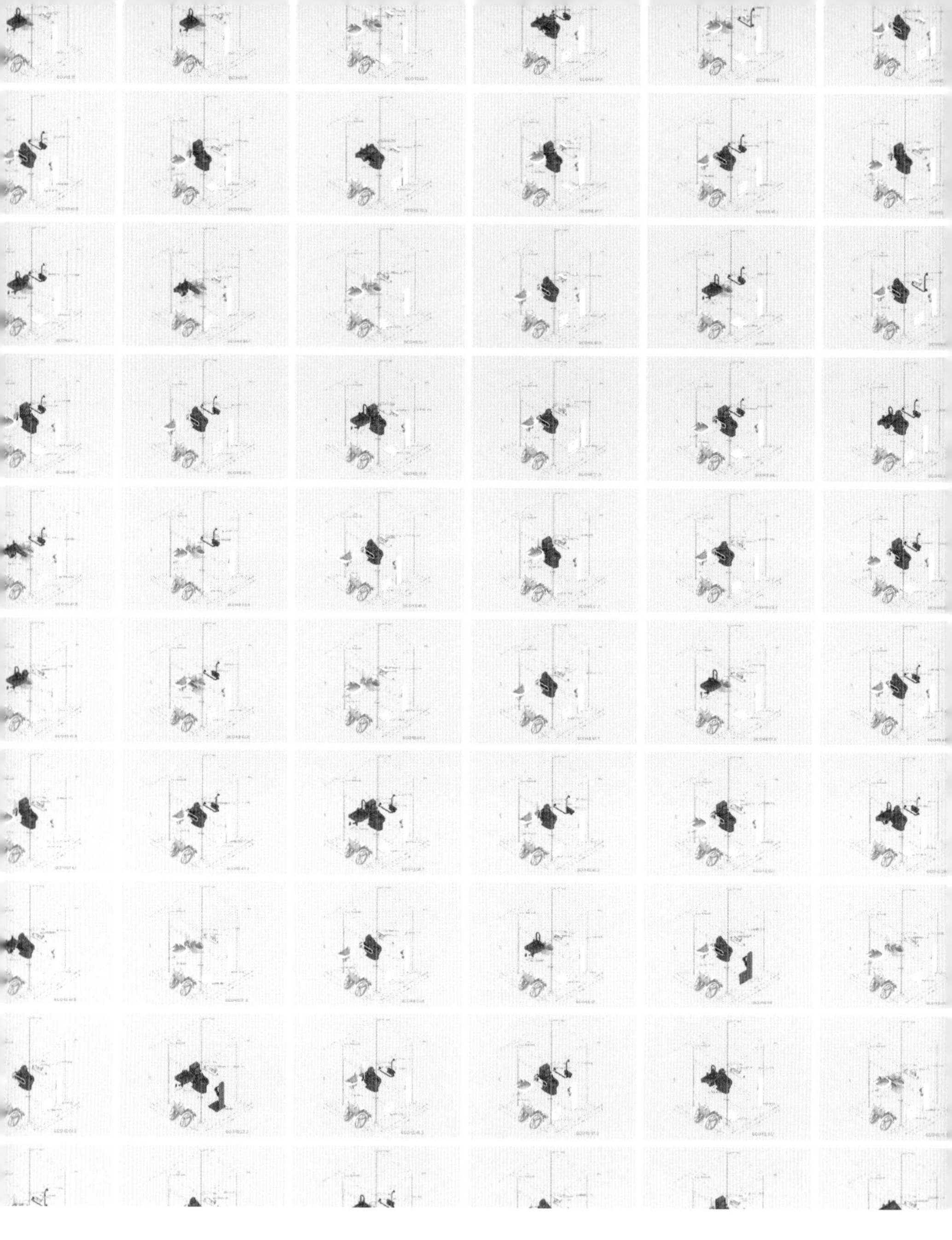

自動設計エンジンには遺伝的アルゴリズムが採用され、入力された設計要件に応じて様々な計画の出力が可能となった。同エンジンには株式会社LIXILの様々なノウハウを学習させている。主開発担当は株式会社 AMDlab。

Genetic algorithm was adopted in the automatic design engine, and a variety of plans can be produced in accordance with the input design requirements. LIXIL's wide-ranging know-how has been learned by the design engine. The main development was overseen by AMDlab.

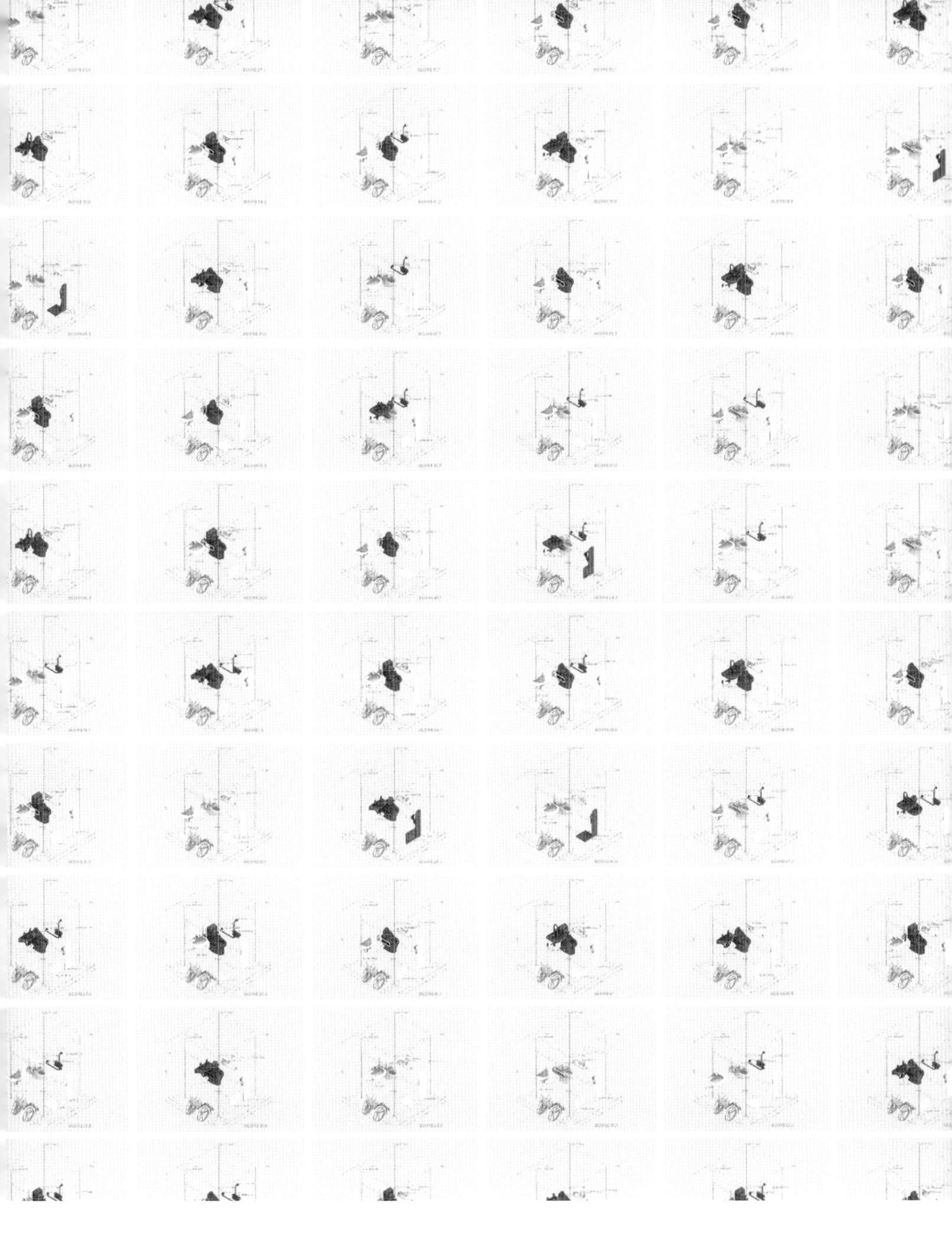

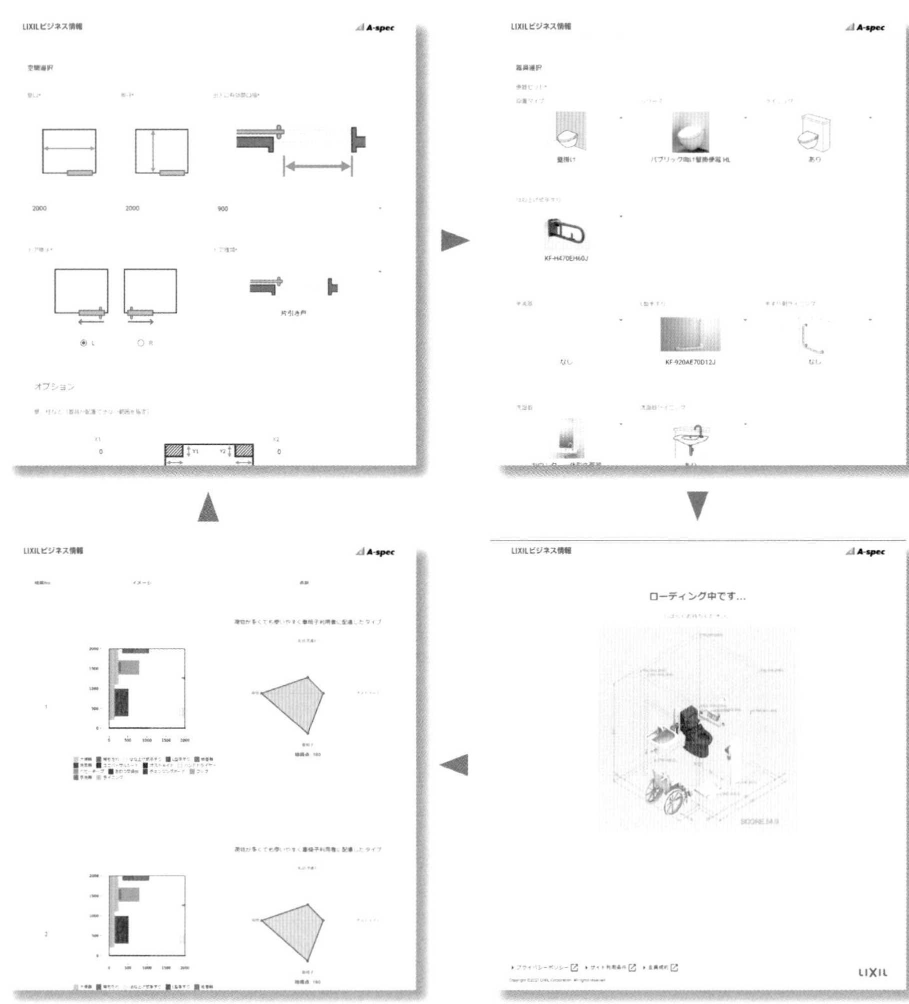

web サイト URL : a-spec.lixil.com

A-SPEC web UI / UX

建具や器具の入力 [A][B] をすることによって、自動設計エンジンがスタディを開始する [C]。スタディが完了すると、複数のトイレ設計プランとその評価値が提示される [D]。

When values for fittings and equipment are entered [A][B], automatic design engine begins a series of studies [C]. When studies are completed, multiple toilet plans and their evaluation values are shown [D].

A	B
D	C

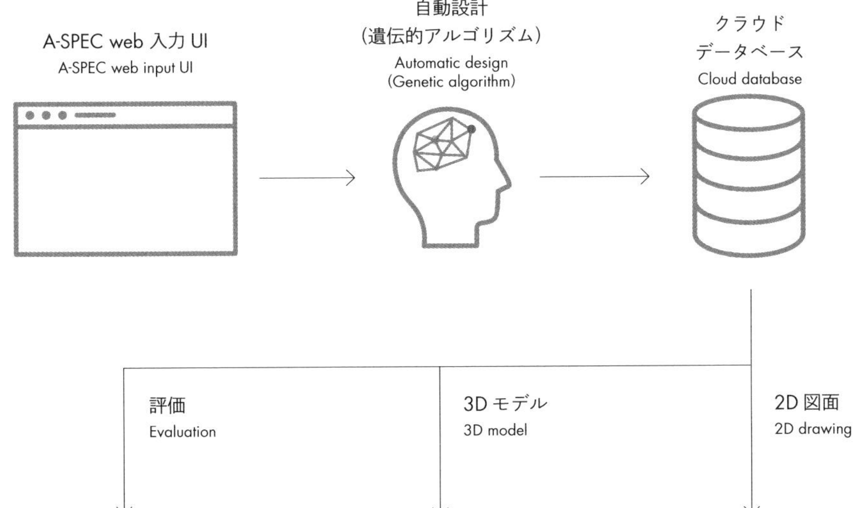

A-SPEC web 評価シート
A-SPEC web evaluation sheet

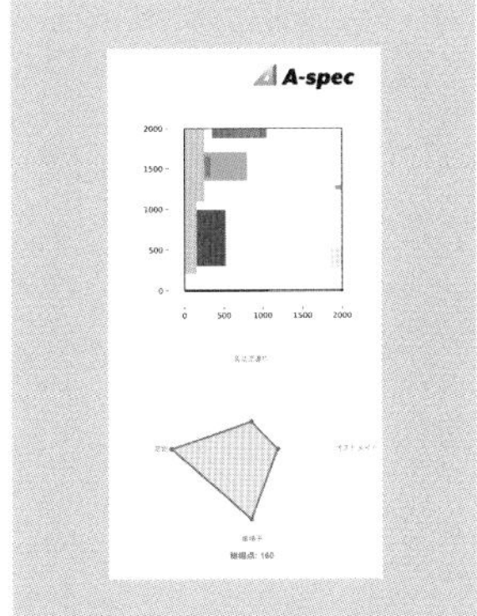

Rhinoceros / Grasshopper

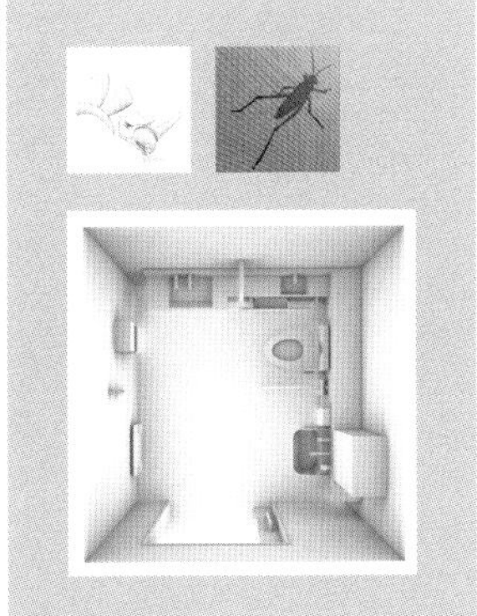

AutoCAD

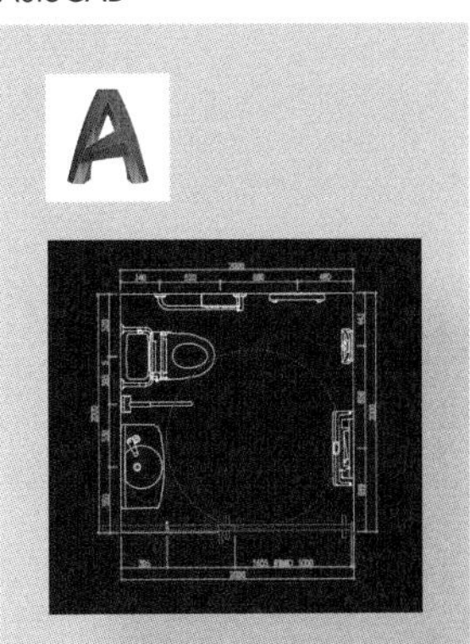

A-SPEC web システム図
A-SPEC web system diagram

webサービスはA-SPECプロジェクトのごく一部に過ぎない。作成されたトイレプランは3Dモデラーや2D CADのファイルデータとしてダウンロードが可能。

Web services constitute only a small part of the A-SPEC projects. Generated toilet designs can be downloaded as 3D model and 2D CAD file data.

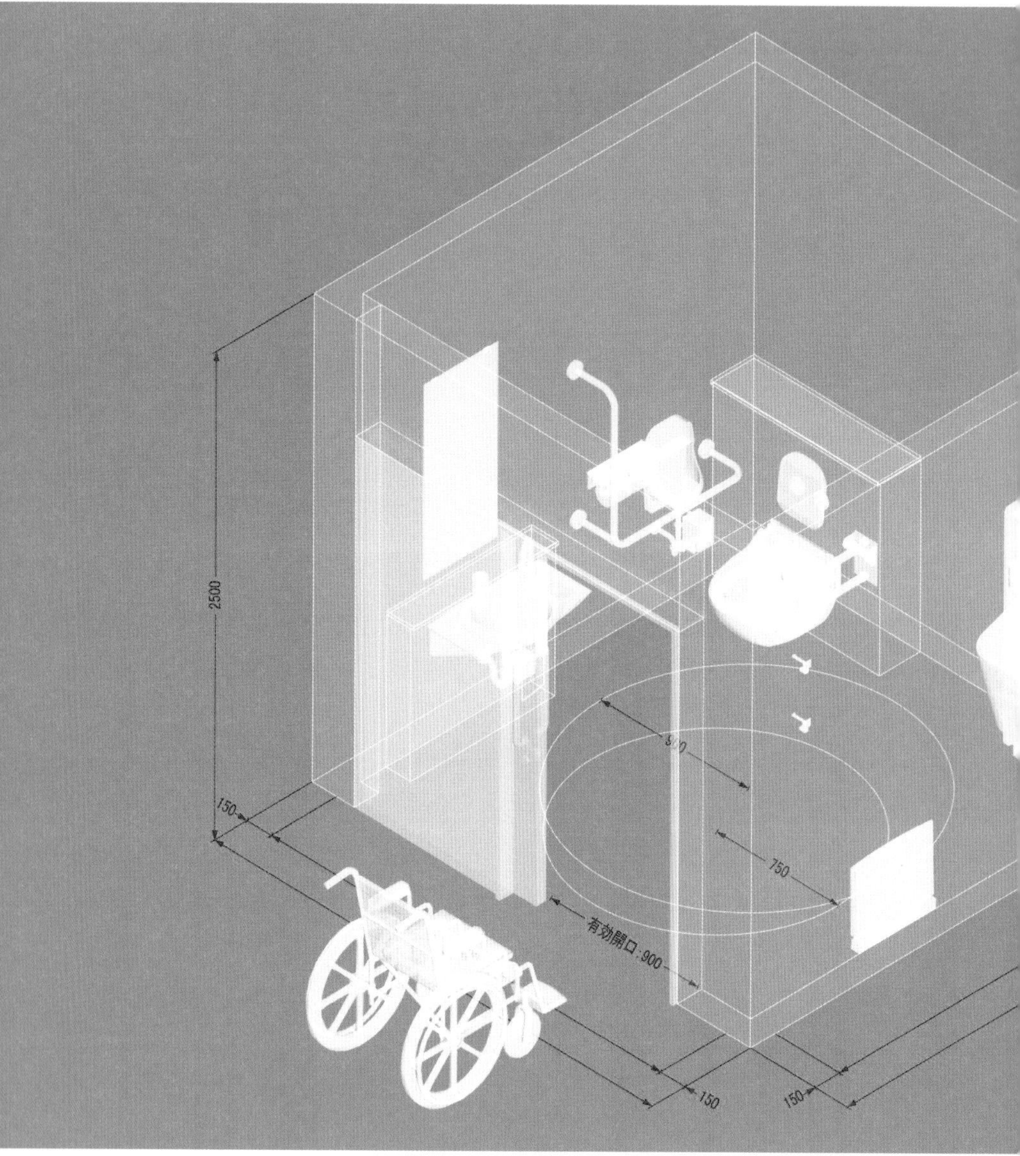

A-SPEC Grasshopper

A-SPEC と 3D モデラー Rhinoceros、プログラミングソフトウェア Grasshopper の機能連携は A-SPEC 開発の初期段階で実装された。A-SPEC で作成されたプランをパラメトリックに 3D シミュレーション可能としている。主開発担当は髙木秀太事務所。

Functional links between A-SPEC, 3D modeling software Rhinoceros, and programming software Grasshopper were implemented from an early phase of A-SPEC development. Plans produced by A-SPEC can be simulated parametrically in 3D. Takagi Shuta Office was in charge of the main development.

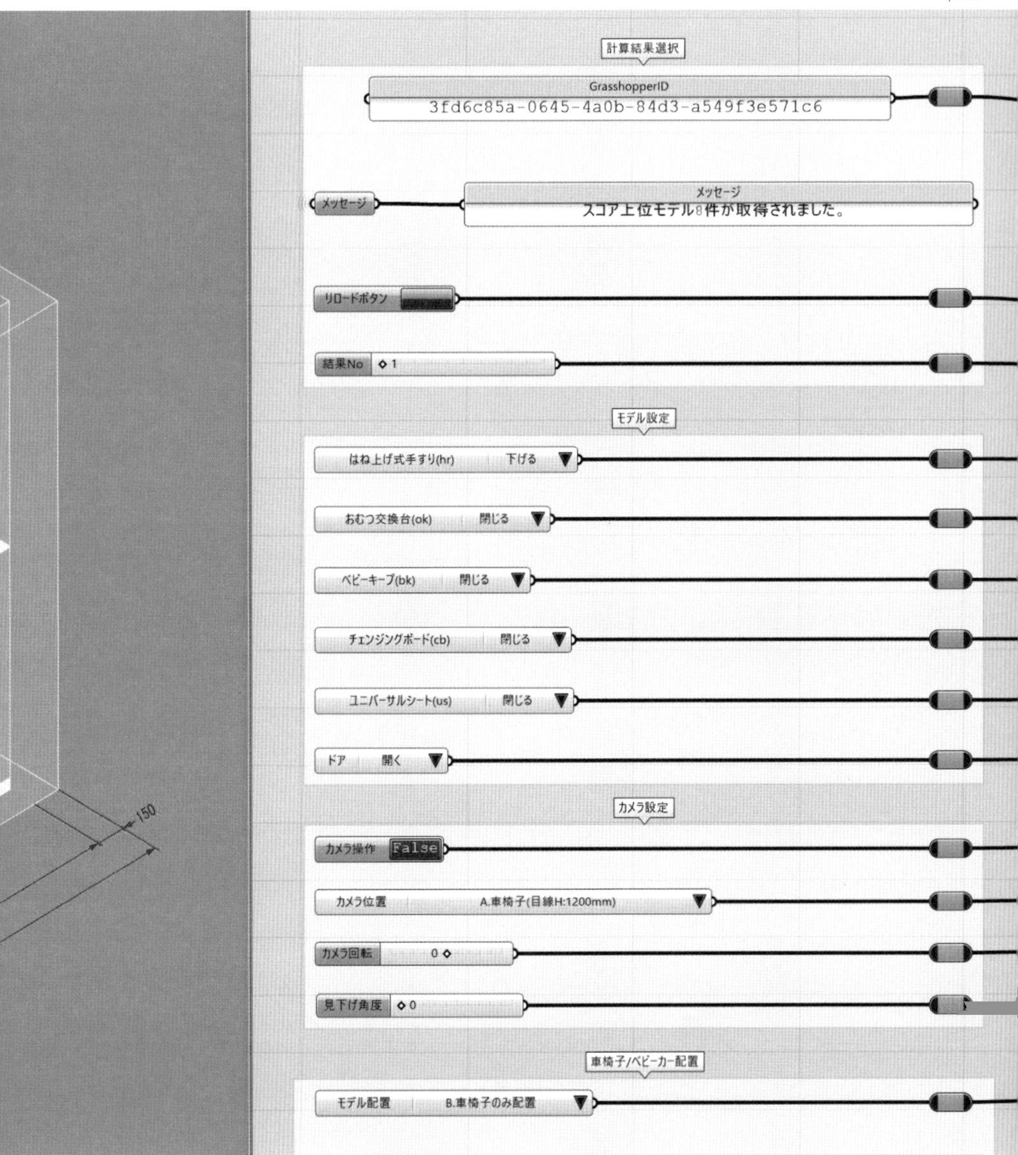

150
計算結果選択
GrasshopperID
3fd6c85a-0645-4a0b-84d3-a549f3e571c6
メッセージ
メッセージ
スコア上位モデル8件が取得されました。
リロードボタン
結果No
1
モデル設定
はね上げ式手すり(hr)
下げる
おむつ交換台(ok)
閉じる
ベビーキープ(bk)
閉じる
チェンジングボード(cb)
閉じる
ユニバーサルシート(us)
閉じる
ドア
開く
カメラ設定
カメラ操作
False
カメラ位置
A.車椅子(目線H:1200mm)
カメラ回転
0
見下げ角度
0
車椅子/ベビーカー配置
モデル配置
B.車椅子のみ配置

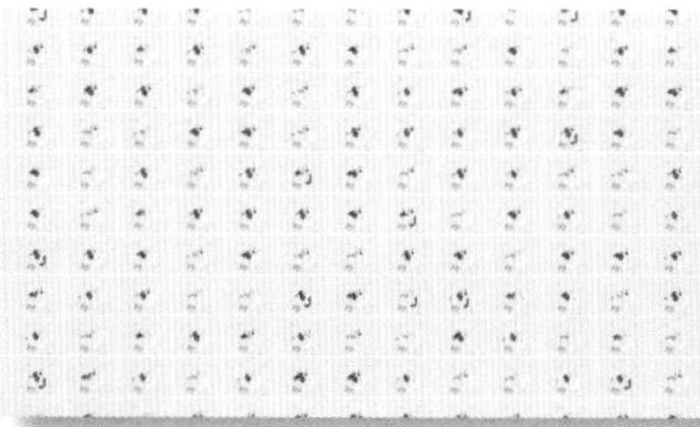

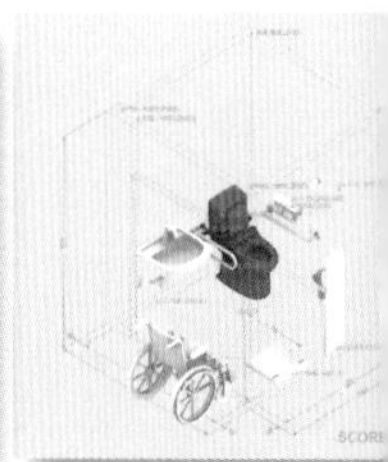

A-SPEC プロモーション動画

A-SPEC promotional video

プロジェクトリリースに際してプロモーション動画が制作された。動画作成の制作・ディレクションは髙木秀太事務所、編集は南 佑樹氏。

For the project release, a promotional video was produced. Video production and direction were undertaken by Takagi Shuta Office, and editing by Yuki Minami.

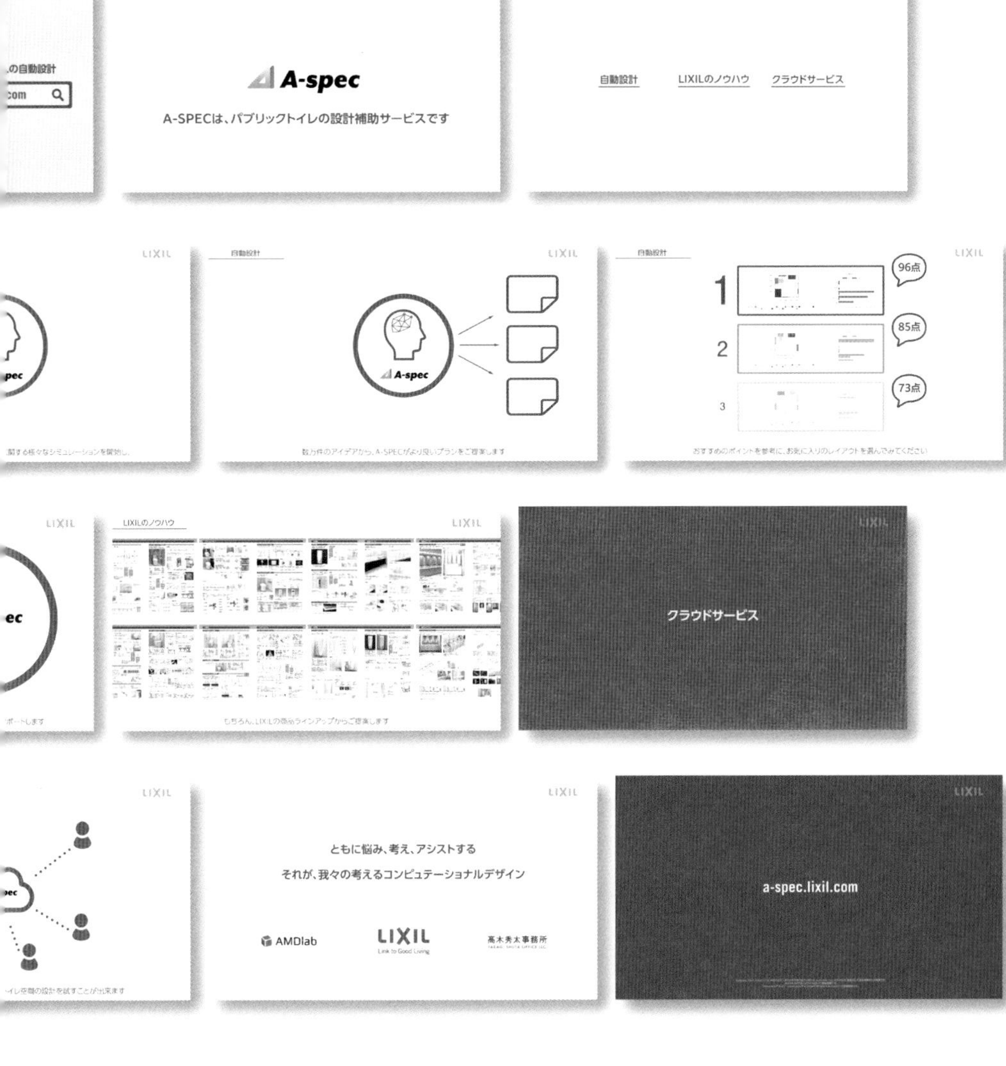

LIXIL
の自動設計
com
A-spec
A-SPECは、パブリックトイレの設計補助サービスです
自動設計
LIXILのノウハウ
クラウドサービス
自動設計
A-spec
数万件のアイデアから、A-SPECがより良いプランをご提案します
96点
85点
73点
1
2
3
おすすめのポイントを参考に、お気に入りのレイアウトを選んでみてください
LIXILのノウハウ
クラウドサービス
ともに悩み、考え、アシストする
それが、我々の考えるコンピュテーショナルデザイン
AMDlab
LIXIL
Link to Good Living
髙木秀太事務所
a-spec.lixil.com

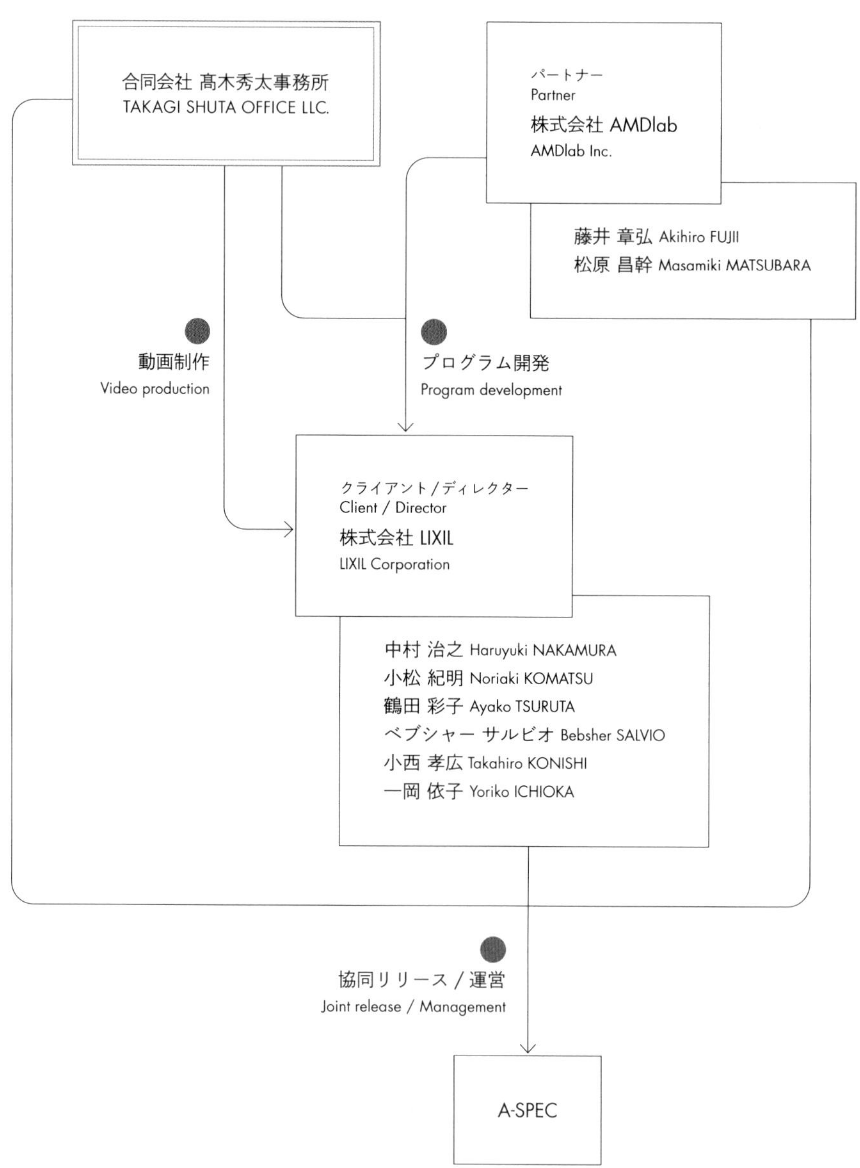

プロジェクトリーダーは株式会社 LIXIL の小松 紀明氏。同氏により複数企業による強力なコラボレーションチームが編成された。髙木秀太事務所は開発パートナーとして参画。今後も継続的な計画が予定されている。

The project leader was Noriaki Komatsu of LIXIL Corporation, who assembled a robust team of several companies for the collaboration. Takagi Shuta Office participated as a partner for development, and continuous plans are envisioned in the future.

プロジェクトID	200023
プロジェクト期間	2020.04-
クライアント / ディレクター	株式会社 LIXIL
担当	中村 治之、小松 紀明、鶴田 彩子、ベブシャー サルビオ、小西 孝広、一岡 依子
パートナー	株式会社 AMDlab
担当	藤井 章弘、松原 昌幹
プロジェクトマネージメント	髙木 秀太
メインプログラマー	髙木 秀太、槙山 武蔵、田野口 貴成、布井 翔一郎
アシスタントスタッフ	川上 朔、伊藤 世玲奈、建道 佳一郎、川西 愛子、野末 誠斗、早川 遥菜、橋口 真緒、永井 宏
外部委託	動画編集：南 佑樹
ソフトウェア / 開発環境	Rhinoceros, VisualStudio
プログラミング言語	Grasshopper, C#, Python
キーワード	自動設計、自動作図、動画制作、web サイト、プロモーション

Project ID	200023
Project term	2020.04-
Client / Director	LIXIL Corporation
Project team	Haruyuki NAKAMURA, Noriaki KOMATSU, Ayako TSURUTA, Bebsher SALVIO, Takahiro KONISHI, Yoriko ICHIOKA
Partner	AMDlab Inc.
Project team	Akihiro FUJII, Masamiki MATSUBARA
Project management	Shuta TAKAGI
Main programmer	Shuta TAKAGI, Musashi MAKIYAMA, Atsuhiro TANOKUCHI, Shoichiro NUNOI
Assistant staff	Hajime KAWAKAMI, Serena ITO, Keiichiro KONDO, Aiko KAWANISHI, Makoto NOZUE, Haruna HAYAKAWA, Mao HASHIGUCHI, Hiroshi NAGAI
Outsourcing	Video production: Yuki MINAMI
Software / SDE	Rhinoceros, VisualStudio
Programming language	Grasshopper, C#, Python
Keywords	Automatic design, Automatic drawing, Video production, Website, Promotion

開発にあたっての主言語のひとつにPythonが採用されている。自動設計エンジン、サーバーサイド処理、2D自動作図アプリケーションなど、その登場場面は多岐にわたる。

Python, one of the main languages used in the development, was widely applied from automatic design engines, server-side processing, to 2D automatic drawing applications.

おわりに
CONCLUSION

―――― 建築家のための建築家

『髙木秀太事務所白書』は弊社設立以来初の「クライアント不在のプロジェクト」です。本書の「はじめに」(p.002–003)にて「我々には『作品』はありません。」と述べましたが、実は本書そのものが作品であるというメタ構造を忍ばせています。これは、建築設計業界における髙木秀太事務所の生存戦略でもあります。心から信頼する誰かの計画のためにデジタルメソッドで精一杯尽くす――そのひとつひとつの物語たちこそがすなわち、誰にも真似ができない我々だけの設計作品になってゆくのです。本書で紹介した数々のプロジェクトの掲載をすべてのクライアントが快く許諾してくれました。掲載のためにご調整を頂いたすべてのご関係者みなさまに、ここにあらためて感謝申し上げます。

さて、本書の最後に問いかけをひとつ。こんなデジタルヒューマニスト的コンセプトを持つ不思議な設計事務所、髙木秀太事務所は果たして“建築家”と呼べるのでしょうか?「最高の便利屋になりたい」などと謳って活動をしてきた我々ですが、徐々にそのスタイルは「建築家のための建築家」と形容できるようになりつつあるのかもしれない、と思うことがあります。我々は変わらず明日も「誰か」と「建築」を計画してゆきます。どうか、これからも髙木秀太事務所をフォローしてください。そしていつかご判断して頂きたい、我々が建築家であるか否か、を。

『髙木秀太事務所白書 2』でまた、お会いしましょう。

髙木秀太事務所
代表　髙木 秀太

Architect for architects

The White Paper by Takagi Shuta Office is our first "project without a client" since its establishment. In the introduction (p.002–003) we declared that "we do not own so-called 'work'" – however, the fact that this book itself is a work embodies a meta structure. It is also a survival strategy of Takagi Shuta Office in the architectural design industry. By devoting our best efforts with digital methods to those we genuinely trust, each of these narratives subsequently turn into our own design works that cannot be imitated by anyone else. Our clients have generously allowed us to introduce the projects included in this book. We would like to express our gratitude again to everyone who have made accommodations for this publication.

Incidentally, one question remains. A peculiar design firm with the concept of being a digital humanist, can we at Takagi Shuta Office be called architects? We have been working with the aspiration of "becoming the best handyman," but over time, I feel that our approach has morphed into what might be more accurately described as "architect for architects." In any case, we will continue to plan "architecture" with "someone" tomorrow onwards. Please continue to follow what Takagi Shuta Office is up to. And one day, I would like you to judge if we are architects or not.

We look forward to seeing you again at The White Paper 2.

Shuta Takagi, CEO
Takagi Shuta Office

用語索引
KEYWORD INDEX

ソフトウェア・言語

【Adobe Illustrator】
—— Project No.02, 07, 08

Adobe 社のグラフィックデザインソフトウェア。イラストやロゴ、レイアウトの作成を行うことができる。

Adobe's graphic design software. It is used to create illustrations, logos, and layouts.

【Adobe Photoshop】
—— Project No.11

Adobe 社の画像編集ソフトウェア。写真や画像の編集、加工を行うことができる。

Adobe's image editing software. It can edit and process photos and images.

【Amazon DynamoDB】
—— Project No.09

Amazon 社の NoSQL データベースサービス。従来のデータベースよりも単純計算の処理速度が速く、容量を膨大に確保できるが、複雑な処理は従来のデータベースサービスの方が得意とする。

Amazon's NoSQL database service. It is faster than traditional databases for simple calculations and has a large capacity, but traditional database services are better at complex processing.

【Anaconda】
—— Project No.05

Anaconda 社による Python のディストリビューション。Python で用いる複数のソフトウェアを一括で管理・インストールすることができる。機械学習系の開発によく用いられる。

Anaconda Python distribution allows management and installation of multiple Python software packages at once. It is often used for machine learning development.

【Android Studio】
—— Project No.09

Google 社が提供する Android アプリケーションソフトウェア開発のための統合開発環境(IDE)。

An integrated development environment (IDE) for Android application software development provided by Google Inc.

【Archicad】
—— Project No.13

Graphisoft 社による BIM ソフトウェア。直感的な UI が特徴で、建築設計業務において有用な機能を数多く備えている。

BIM software by Graphisoft. It features an intuitive UI and has many useful functions for architectural design work.

【C#】
—— Project No.14, 16, 17

Anders Hejlsberg 氏が設計した汎用プログラミング言語。記述の難易度が高く、比較的習得が難しいが、計算処理速度が速いところに利点がある。

A general-purpose programming language designed by Anders Hejlsberg. It is difficult to write and relatively hard to learn, but its advantage is its high computation speed.

【Excel】
—— Project No.08, 10

Microsoft 社の表計算ソフトウェア。数値データの管理を得意とする。行と列によるデータ構造は他の各種ソフトウェアとの親和性も高く、連動して用いられることが多い。

Microsoft spreadsheet software. It excels at managing numerical data. The data structure of rows and columns is highly compatible with other software, and is often used in conjunction with other software.

【FlowDesigner】
—— Project No.14, 16

アドバンスドナレッジ研究所（AKL）による気体、流体シミュレーションソフトウェア。本書では、主に風環境解析で用いられている。

Air and fluid simulation software by Advanced Knowledge Laboratory (AKL). For the projects in this book, it is mainly used for wind environment analysis.

【Galapagos】

—— Project No.06

遺伝的アルゴリズムにより最適化計算を行うためのGrasshopperプラグイン。単一の評価軸（単目的）による最適化を行う。

Grasshopper plug-in for optimization calculation through genetic algorithms. Performs optimization through a single evaluation axis (single objective).

【Grasshopper】

—— Project No.01–08, 10–14, 16, 17

Rhinocerosに標準搭載されたプラグインのひとつ。ビジュアルプログラミングをベースとした形態制御、各種解析等が可能。

One of the standard plug-ins for Rhinoceros. It enables morphological control and various analyses based on visual programming.

【Java】

—— Project No.09

Oracle社による汎用プログラミング言語とソフトウェアプラットフォームの総称。webなどの各種アプリケーション開発で最も人気の高いプログラミング言語のひとつ。

A general-purpose programming language and software platform from Oracle. One of the most popular programming languages for web development and other applications.

【JavaScript】

—— Project No.08, 12–15

web開発の中核に用いられるプログラミング言語のひとつ。動きのあるwebサイトやスマホアプリの開発などによく用いられる。

One of the core programming languages used in web development. It is often used in the development of websites that have movement and smartphone applications.

【Kangaroo】

—— Project No.04

物理演算を行うためのGrasshopperプラグイン。重力、摩擦、衝突などの物理現象をシミュレーションすることができる。

Grasshopper plug-in for physical calculations. It can simulate physical phenomena such as gravity, friction, collision, etc.

【Ladybug Tools】

—— Project No.05–07, 14

気象データを分析し、視覚化するためのGrasshopperプラグイン。環境に配慮した設計に用いられる。

Grasshopper plug-in for analyzing and visualizing weather data. Used for environmentally friendly designs.

【MySQL】

—— Project No.15

Oracle社のデータベース管理システム。webサイトやネットワークでのデータ管理などによく用いられる。

A database management system from Oracle Corporation, often used for managing data on websites and networks.

【Octopus】

—— Project No.05

多目的最適化を行うためのGrasshopperプラグイン。最小化（または最大化）したい評価値が複数あるときに、それぞれの評価軸を満たすように最適化を試みることができる。

Grasshopper plug-in for multi-objective optimization. When there are multiple evaluation values to be minimized (or maximized), an optimization is used to satisfy each objective axis.

【Python】

—— Project No.01–08, 10, 11, 16, 17

Guido van Rossum氏が設計した汎用プログラミング言語。記述の容易さや、豊富なライブラリーを特徴とする。近年では、AI開発に用いられる事例が多く、存在感が増した。

A general-purpose programming language designed by Guido Van Rossum. It is characterized by its writability and an extensive library. In recent years, it has increased its presence in many cases where AI development is used.

用語索引
KEYWORD INDEX

ソフトウェア・言語

【QGIS】
—— Project No.10

Open Source Geospatial Foundation による地理情報システム（GIS）。オープンソースで提供される。地理空間データの閲覧、編集、解析を行うことができる。

Geographic Information System (GIS) by the Open Source Geospatial Foundation. Provided as an open source. It allows users to browse, edit, and analyze geospatial data.

【Rhinoceros】
—— Project No.01–08, 10–14, 16, 17

Robert McNeel & Associates による 3D モデル作成用ソフトウェア。曲面造形を得意とし、プログラミングによる機能拡張も幅広くサポートされている。

3D modeling software by Robert McNeel & Associates. The software specializes in curved surface modeling. Through programming, a wide range of functional extensions are supported.

【VisualStudio】
—— Project No.14, 15, 17

Microsoft 社による統合開発環境（IDE）。アプリケーションの開発に使用することができる。

An integrated development environment (IDE) from Microsoft. It can be used to develop applications.

【WordPress】
—— Project No.11–14

WordPress Foundation によるオープンソースのブログソフトウェア。PHP で開発されており、データベース管理システムは MySQL が利用されている。

Open source blogging software by the WordPress Foundation, developed in PHP and using MySQL database management system.

用語

【3D モデラー　3D modeling software】
—— Project No.01–08, 10–14, 16, 17

コンピューターソフトウェアの一種で、3DCAD や 3DCG のデータをデジタル空間に作図するアプリケーションのこと。

A type of computer software, an application that draws 3DCAD or 3DCG data in a digital space.

【BIM ソフトウェア　BIM software】
—— Project No.13

3D モデラーの中でも建築計画に特化したソフトウェア。モデリングされた建築部材ひとつひとつに各種情報が内包され、任意のタイミングで総括的にアクセスができる。

This software is specialized for architectural 3D modelling. Various types of information are contained in each modeled building component, and can be accessed comprehensively at any time.

【CNC 加工機　CNC router】
—— Project No.02

コンピューター数値制御（CNC：Computer Numerically Controlled）によって木材などを切削・加工する機械のこと。

A machine that cuts and processes wood and other materials by computer numerical control (CNC: Computer Numerically Controlled).

【CNN 学習　CNN deep learning】
—— Project No.05

Convolutional Neural Network = 畳み込みニューラルネットワークの略。主に画像認識で使われる技術のひとつ。

Convolutional Neural Network is one of the technologies mainly used in image recognition.

【GIS ソフトウェア　GIS software】
—— Project No.10

地理情報システム（GIS：Geographic Information System）を扱うソフトウェアのこと。地図情報の管理やデータビジュアライゼーションができる。

Software that handles Geographic Information Systems (GIS). It can manage map information and data visualization.

【webスクレイピング　Web scraping】
―― Project No.10

webサイトから必要な情報をコンピュータープログラムによって自動収集する技術のこと。

A technology that automatically collects necessary information from a website using a computer program.

【アルゴリズム　Algorithm】
―― Project No.01–17

ある特定の問題を解くまでの計算手順・手続きのこと。コンピュータープログラムもアルゴリズムの一種である。

A computational procedure or procedure to solve a particular problem. A computer program is also a type of algorithm.

【遺伝的アルゴリズム　Genetic algorithm】
―― Project No.05, 06, 17

進化論的な解法に基づいてデータを操作し、最適解探索や学習、推論を行うアルゴリズム。

An algorithm that manipulates data based on evolutionary solution methods to perform optimal solution search, learning, and inference.

【オープンソース　Open source code】
―― Project No.12–14, 16

一般公開されたプログラムのソースコードのこと。世界中の有志によって継続的な改良や再配布が行われるメリットがある。

The release of a program's source code to the public. It has the advantage of continuous improvement and redistribution by volunteers from around the world.

【カテナリー　Catenary】
―― Project No.04

両端を固定した紐を重力空間で垂らしたときに一様に描かれる放物線のこと。重力に逆らわない最適な形を示しており、ドームなどの大空間の設計に応用される。

A parabolic line that is uniquely drawn when a string with both ends fixed is hung in gravity space. It shows an optimal shape that does not go against gravity, and is applied in the design of large spaces such as domes.

【幾何学　Geometry】
―― Project No. 01–08

図形や空間の性質を研究する数学の部門のこと。古代ギリシアで成立したユークリッド幾何学をはじめに、研究対象の増加や新しい研究方法の開発などによって、多くの分野がこれに加わった。

A branch of mathematics that studies the properties of figures and space. Starting with Euclidean geometry, which was established in ancient Greece, many other fields have been added due to the increase in the number of subjects studied and the development of new research methods.

【クラウドサーバー　Cloud server】
―― Project No.09, 17

インターネットを通じて利用できるサーバーの一種。クラウド事業者が構築した仮想サーバーのこと。

A type of server available through the Internet. A virtual server built by a cloud service provider.

【クラウドデータベース　Cloud database】
―― Project No.09, 17

クラウド環境で構築、デプロイ、およびアクセスできるデータベースのこと。

A database that is built, deployed, and accessed on a cloud server.

【検算　Recalculate】
―― Project No.01–17

計算の結果が正しいかどうかを確かめる計算のこと。

The act of calculating again to eliminate errors or to verify the accuracy of the outcome of a calculation.

【最適化計算　Optimization calculations】
―― Project No.04–07

与えられた制約条件のもとで、目的の値を最大/最小となる解を求めること。代表的なものに遺伝的アルゴリズムを用いた計算方法などがある。

To find a solution that maximizes / minimizes the desired value under given constraints. Typical examples include calculation methods using genetic algorithms.

用語索引
KEYWORD INDEX

用語

【シミュレーション　Simulation】
—— Project No. 04–07, 14, 16, 17

現実に実験を行うことが難しい物事について、想定される場面を主にコンピューター上に再現し分析すること。

Analysis of things that are difficult to experiment within reality, using models that recreates situations, mainly using computers.

【主成分分析　Principal component analysis】
—— Project No.05

統計学のデータ解析において、多次元のデータを人が読み取りやすい次元にまで落とし込むこと。

In statistical data analysis, the reduction of complex multidimensional data to dimensions that are readable to humans.

【深層学習　Deep learning】
—— Project No.05

機械学習の一種で、教師データから自動で特徴を定義し学習する手法のこと。しばしば人間より高い認識精度を獲得することがある。

A method that automatically defines and learns features from instructional data. Often achieves higher recognition accuracy than humans.

【データビジュアライゼーション　Data visualization】
—— Project No.10, 16

データから読み取れる情報や発見を、第三者に分かりやすく主に視覚的に表現すること。

Visually reorganizing the primary data and findings in a way that is easy for third parties to understand.

【テキストプログラミング　Text-based programming】
—— Project No.01–17

ビジュアルプログラミングに対して、文字でコードを記述するプログラミング手法のこと。

A programming method in which code is written in text, as opposed to a visual program.

【デジタルファブリケーション　Digital fabrication】
—— Project No.02, 09

レーザーカッターや 3D プリンターに代表されるような、コンピューターによってコントロールされた制作過程のこと。

A computer-controlled production process, represented by the likes of a laser cutter or 3D printer.

【都市解析　Urban analysis】
—— Project No.10

都市の空間的要素・特性を分析し、都市計画や研究に役立てること。

Analysis of the spatial elements and characteristics of a city for urban planning and research.

【バッファ解析　Buffer analysis】
—— Project No.10

GIS において、任意の点・線・面から任意の距離内の領域を決定し、その領域と対象物を相互的に解析すること。

In GIS, an area is determined through a given point, line, or surface. The area and its target objects are then analyzed interactively.

【パラメトリックデザイン　Parametric design】
—— Project No.01–08, 17

パラメーターとアルゴリズムによって定義されるデザイン。

Designs that are defined by parameters and algorithms.

【ビジュアルプログラミング　Visual programming language】
—— Project No.01–09,11–14, 16, 17

テキストプログラミングに対して、コードが内包された図形をつなげる等の視覚的な分かりやすさを優先したプログラミング手法のこと。Grasshopper などが該当する。

A programming method that prioritizes visual clarity, such as connecting graphics that contain code, as opposed to text programming. Grasshopper is such an example.

【プラグイン　Plug-ins】

—— Project No.04–07, 14, 16

ソフトウェア等の拡張機能のこと。

Extensions to software and other functions.

【プログラミング言語
Programming language】

—— Project No.01–17

プログラムを記述するための人工言語のこと。

An artificial language for writing programs.

【β版　Beta version】

—— Project No.16, 17

正式版リリース直前のサンプルソフトウェアのこと。実際の利用者から不具合の確認などのフィードバックを得る目的がある。

A sample software program just before the official version is released. The purpose is to obtain feedback from actual users, such as confirmation of defects.

略歴
BIOGRAPHY

髙木 秀太　Shuta TAKAGI

建築家・プログラマー

略歴

1984.08	長野県長野市生まれ
2003.03	長野県長野高等学校 卒業
2009.03	東京理科大学 工学部 第一部 建築学科 卒業
2011.03	東京理科大学大学院 工学研究科建築学専攻 修士課程 修了
2011.04–2012.03	株式会社エーシーエ設計 設計部
2012.04–2016.03	000studio（ゼロスタジオ）スタッフ
2013.04–2014.03	慶應義塾大学 臨時職員
2014.04–	東京理科大学 非常勤講師 （設計基礎 2、建築都市設計、建築 IT 概論）
2015.04–2016.03	慶応義塾大学 非常勤講師（デジタルデザイン基礎）
2016.04–	合同会社髙木秀太事務所 代表
2016.08–	東京大学 T-ADS 学術支援専門職員
2016.10–2020.03	東京大学 非常勤講師 （造形第一、造形第二、造形第四）
2017.04–	工学院大学 非常勤講師（建築情報処理 I ）
2018.04–	長岡造形大学 非常勤講師 （建築・環境 CG 実習 I 、建築・環境 CG 実習 II ）
2020.10–	東京理科大学 非常勤講師 （夜間主社会人コース 建築 IT 概論（社））
2020.10–	北海道大学 非常勤講師（計画・設計特別演習 II ）
2020.10–	多摩美術大学 非常勤講師 （テキスタイルデザイン専攻 STUDIO1）
2022.04–	多摩美術大学 非常勤講師 （環境デザイン学科 CAD・CG I、CAD・CG II）

所属

2012.06–2016.03	慶應義塾大学 SFC 研究所 上席所員

著書

2019.09	『コンピュテーショナル・モデリング 入門から応用 Grasshopper × スクリプトで極める アルゴリズミック・デザイン』（中島 淳雄 氏と共著）

受賞

2018.09	SD レビュー 2018 入選 （香川 翔勲 + 佐倉 弘祐 + 髙木 秀太 + 藤井 章弘 + 筒井 伸）
2018.11	The Architecture MasterPrize Interior of the year 2018（プログラマーとして）
2021.09	SD レビュー 2021 SD 賞 （香川 翔勲 + 林 和秀 + 藤井 章弘 + 伊藤 一生 + 佐倉 弘祐 + 髙木 秀太）

写真・画像クレジット
PHOTO / IMAGE CREDITS

01_TOKYO TOWER TOP DECK

014–015 写真
Nacása & Partners Inc.

016–017 写真 A–C
Nacása & Partners Inc.

018–019 Rhinoceros UI
Robert McNeel & Associates

02_NTT DATA INFORIUM TOYOSU INNOVATION CENTER

028–029 写真
見学 友宙 Tomooki KENGAKU

030–031 写真 A, B
見学 友宙 Tomooki KENGAKU

038–039 写真 A, B
見学 友宙 Tomooki KENGAKU

03_PRISM TV STUDIO

048–049 写真
山田 薫 Kaoru YAMADA

050–051 写真 A–C
山田 薫 Kaoru YAMADA

04_FUJIHIMURO GALLERY ENTRANCE

062–063 写真
緋田 昌重 Masashige AKEDA

064–065 写真 A–C
緋田 昌重 Masashige AKEDA

070–071 写真 A–F
O.F.D.A. associates

05_OKI ELECTRIC INDUSTRY FACADE

076–077 写真
大成建設株式会社一級建築士事務所

078–079 写真 A–D
大成建設株式会社一級建築士事務所

080–081 パース、平面図、パネル詳細図
大成建設株式会社一級建築士事務所

081 Rhinoceros アイコン、Grasshopper アイコン
Robert McNeel & Associates

081 Ladybug アイコン
Ladybug Tools LLC

081 Octopus アイコン
Robert Vierlinger

087 学習写真 B
大成建設株式会社一級建築士事務所

088–089 Anaconda UI
Anaconda Inc.

06_SUNSTAR COMMUNICATION PARK FACADE

094–095 写真
株式会社エスエス 津田 裕之 Hiroyuki TSUDA

096–097 写真 A–D
株式会社エスエス 津田 裕之 Hiroyuki TSUDA

099 Galapagos UI
Robert McNeel & Associates

07_THE GARDEN WITH A GOAT

106–107 イメージパース
香川 翔勲 + 信州大学 佐倉弘祐研究室

08_KEIO UNIVERSITY SFC ORF 2017

122–123 Rhinoceros UI
Robert McNeel & Associates

09_THE UNIVERSITY OF TOKYO T-ADS STREET WALKING APPLICATION

130–131　写真A–D
東京大学 T-ADS Design Think Tank

132–133　タブレット端末
株式会社 ファーウェイ

132–133
Google マップ UI、Android Studio UI
Google LLC

136　Android アイコン
Google LLC

136　Amazon Web Service アイコン
Amazon Web Services, Inc.

137　タブレットケース構成図
株式会社ノメナ

10_CITY×PARK DATA VISUALIZATION

146　QGIS UI
QGIS Development Team (GNU GPL)

12_RHINO-GH.COM

164–165　Rhinoceros UI
Robert McNeel & Associates

13_ARCHICAD-LEARNING.COM

170–171　Archicad UI
GRAPHISOFT SE

14_BUILDING ENVIRONMENT DESIGN.COM

176–177　Rhinoceros UI
Robert McNeel & Associates

179
Rhinoceros アイコン、Grasshopper アイコン
Robert McNeel & Associates

179　FlowDesigner アイコン
株式会社アドバンスドナレッジ研究所

179
C# アイコン、Microsoft Visual Studio アイコン
マイクロソフト

16_NATURAL VENTILATION SIMULATION FOR EVACUATION SHELTERS

194
Rhinoceros UI、Rhinoceros アイコン
Grasshopper アイコン
Robert McNeel & Associates

194
FlowDesigner UI、FlowDesigner アイコン
株式会社アドバンスドナレッジ研究所

195　Rhinoceros UI
Robert McNeel & Associates

195　FlowDesigner UI
株式会社アドバンスドナレッジ研究所

17_LIXIL A-SPEC

203
Rhinoceros アイコン、Grasshopper アイコン
Robert McNeel & Associates

203　AutoCAD アイコン
Autodesk, Inc.

204–205　Grasshopper UI
Robert McNeel & Associates

※特記のない箇所は髙木秀太事務所提供

デザイン　竹内 瑠奈（髙木秀太事務所）
翻訳　高 佳音
多田 星矢（髙木秀太事務所）

Design　Runa TAKEUCHI (TAKAGI SHUTA OFFICE)
Translation　Kaon KO
Sayer TADA (TAKAGI SHUTA OFFICE)

髙木秀太事務所白書

The White Paper by TAKAGI SHUTA OFFICE

2023 年 3 月 19 日　発　行　NDC520

著　　者　合同会社髙木秀太事務所
発 行 者　小川 雄一
発 行 所　株式会社 誠文堂新光社
〒113-0033 東京都文京区本郷 3-3-11
電話 03-5800-5780
https://www.seibundo-shinkosha.net/
印刷・製本　株式会社 大熊整美堂

ISBN978-4-416-92147-0